DEAD
IN THE
WATER

Raised in Manchester, **Penny Farmer** is proud to claim herself a no-nonsense Northerner. Graduating with an English Literature degree from Lancaster University she moved to London to study for a Postgraduate Certificate in Journalism at City University.

Experiencing something of a baptism of fire as a reporter on a North London local newspaper at the time of the Broadwater Farm Estate riots in Tottenham in 1985, she learnt the trade and knew that writing was in her soul. It proved a good training ground but the appeal of attending extravagant press functions and styling photo shoots was ultimately more alluring, and she was appointed Health and Beauty Editor for *Woman* magazine in 1986. Working on the mainstream national title for five years, she developed a life-long passion for fashion and beauty. Penny is now a freelance journalist and public-relations consultant.

Living in the Oxfordshire countryside, she considers herself fortunate to share her lived-in, frenetic home with her long-suffering husband Ben, her mother Audrey, her three grown-up children who come and go, plus an eclectic menagerie of visiting partners, friends and animals.

Glued to her side, whether in the kitchen or by her desk, is her faithful companion Mungo – a sofa-loving golden Labrador who, along with Tinker the rescue Jack Russell and Rolo, the fox-red Labrador puppy, ensures that life is never dull, and that going for a walk is the best time of the day.

* * *

For further background information on the case and the author, please visit her website:

PENNY FARMER
www.pennyfarmer.co.uk

PENNY FARMER

DEAD
IN THE
WATER

BRINGING DOWN MY
BROTHER'S KILLER AFTER
HIS 38 YEARS ON THE RUN

Published by John Blake Publishing,
2.25 The Plaza,
535 Kings Road,
Chelsea Harbour,
London SW10 0SZ

www.johnblakebooks.com

www.facebook.com/johnblakebooks 🇫
twitter.com/jblakebooks 🇪

First published in paperback in 2018

ISBN: 978-1-78606-966-5

British Library Cataloguing-in-Publication Data:

A catalogue record for this book is available from the British Library.

Design by www.envydesign.co.uk

Printed and bound in Great Britain by Clays Ltd, Elcograf S.p.A

3 5 7 9 10 8 6 4 2

Papers used by John Blake Publishing are natural, recyclable products made from
wood grown in sustainable forests. The manufacturing processes conform to the
environmental regulations of the country of origin.

Every attempt has been made to contact the relevant copyright-holders, but some
were unobtainable. We would be grateful if the appropriate people could contact us.

John Blake Publishing is an imprint of Bonnier Publishing
www.bonnierpublishing.com

Dedicated to the loving memory of my brother, Dr Christopher James Burnett Farmer, 20 May 1953–4 July 1978, and Peta Ambrosine Frampton, 31 July 1953–4 July 1978.

'Those who can no longer speak for themselves.'

PREFACE

This is the true account of the tragedy that befell my family in July 1978 and its denouement, nearly four decades later. The turn of events, both then and now, has, at times, stretched credulity, but, as they say, life is stranger than fiction and the best stories are always true.

I can say with full conviction: final closure only comes when the truth is known.

ACKNOWLEDGEMENTS

This book is written with the assistance of my remarkable mother. With crystal clear clarity she has recounted to me the story's ebb and flow, its peaks and many troughs. Despite the turbulence in her own life, her optimistic outlook has remained afloat and she is my mainstay in life.

I would like to give special thanks to Russell Boston, who shared his insights with breathtaking honesty. He has lived a nightmare but his innate humanity and decency shine bright.

I owe immense gratitude to the Cold Case Review Unit of Greater Manchester Police: Martin Bottomley, Michaela Clinch and Julie Adams, but particularly Martin for his 'beyond the call of duty' guidance, delivered with humour and compassion. Without him listening and acting upon the information I brought forth in that first week of October 2015, none of this would have happened. His considerable expertise and patience steadied my sometime rolling ship.

Thank you to my dear husband Ben and my beloved

children, Alexandra, Charlie and Freya, for their unwavering, unconditional love, support and understanding. Collectively, they are my lighthouse and harbour from life's tempests.

Last, but not least, my sagacious literary agent, Robert Smith, who gave me the steer I needed.

PENNY FARMER

CONTENTS

PROLOGUE
24 APRIL 2017

I couldn't sleep. It was gone midnight and lying in bed at home in Oxfordshire, my thoughts were 5,000 miles away on the other side of the Atlantic, in a side room in UC Davis Medical Center in Sacramento, California. A room, and a city, I had never visited, but in my mind's eye was picture-perfect. I saw the two burly armed Marshals standing guard over the wizened seventy-six-year-old man, his grey beard recently shaved into a devilish goatee.

Lying prostrate in the bed in the clinical white-washed room, as a high-security prisoner, he was still shackled. Gasping for air as the death rattle began to lay claim to his body, he was *compos mentis*, remaining defiant, with a controlling, menacing glare until his very last breath.

I was one of only a handful of people permitted to know he was there.

I tossed and turned, my eyes glancing at the seconds, the minutes, the hours flashing by on my bedside alarm clock.

I constantly checked my mobile for a text or an email. It was pointless, it was on loud and vibrate. Maybe I would 'know' via some subliminal sign without even looking?

How could I want someone so evil to live? But I did.

At 02.14 the email from Detective Constable Michaela Clinch of the Greater Manchester Police Cold Case Review Unit came in: 'Sorry about the time Penny but I just got this from the US prosecution team and I know you are waiting: the U.S. Marshals Service reports that Silas Duane Boston died at 17:09 Pacific Daylight Time on 24th April 2017. Oh Penny… My heart goes out to you all, it really does. I'm devastated for you.'

That simple email represented crushing finality; an abrupt full stop to my family's thirty-eight-year quest for truth and justice. I felt physically sick. It was like hitting the buffers at 100mph.

A lot of things died with Boston that afternoon.

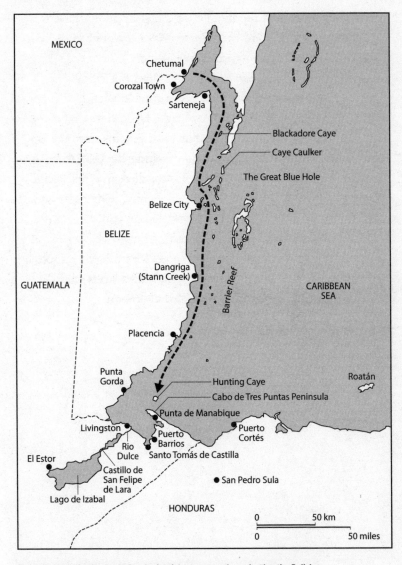

The route taken by the *Justin B* on its fateful voyage south, navigating the Belizian and Guatemalan coastline. The distance shown on the map is approximately 273.5 kilometres (170 miles).

Chapter One

ADRIFT

Why were the tortured corpses of my brother, twenty-five-year-old Christopher Farmer, a young doctor, and his twenty-four-year-old lawyer girlfriend, Peta Frampton, found floating off the Guatemalan coast in Central America in 1978? Like so many of today's young people, after years of academic grafting they had set off to see the world, with high hopes and expectations.

They had been found tortured, bound and weighted down with heavy engine parts from which they had come adrift and Peta had a plastic bag over her head. Receiving such devastating news was like a bomb exploding in our family.

Why such a ghastly fate should befall them haunted us for 38 interminable years. It was inexplicable and devastating.

Time blunts the intense searing pain of bereavement but what remains is a dull throbbing ache; a longing for what might have been and the knowledge that a life with them in it would have been so much richer for us all. You never lose that sense of loss, even decades on.

There was some talk of revenge being needed for closure and, whilst I can't deny a strong longing for justice, there is also a desire to still the mind from constantly asking the question 'why?' Your brain yearns to compute and make sense of such a tragic, senseless waste of life. Distracted for a while, one's thoughts are constantly dragged back, like some beast hauling its quarry into its lair, to the nagging question, 'why?'

There is, however, one thing worse than not knowing why a loved one has died... It is being stuck in limbo, not knowing if they are alive or dead but classed as 'missing'. It's a horrible word and one that curdles the blood and sends shivers down the spine of any parent. In our case, Chris and Peta were missing for ten months. Ten very long months in which we knew nothing of their whereabouts or what had happened to them. Ten months in which the two respective families explored every possible avenue open to them to try to find out their fate.

In amongst the pain, hope springs eternal. Whilst there is no proof of death there's always hope, but like a tidal wave, reality floods into one's consciousness and logic takes over. Your hopes are dashed on the rocks of despair with the realisation that you are deluding yourself.

Sleep did little to obliterate the debilitating daily grind of worry as a recurring, very disturbing nightmare played tricks with my head. I dreamt that Chris had returned home, alive and well, and we held a family celebration. When the party was over, I went into his bedroom to tell him how happy I was that he had returned. Sitting on his bed, I found to my horror a total stranger asleep under the bedclothes. A rubber mask of Chris's face was lying on the bedside table. It was a nightmare that was to revisit me for many years.

Daylight and awake, doubts that start as a whisper steadily

mount into a deafening crescendo, bombarding and assaulting every thought. Were they being held as prisoners, incarcerated in some Central American hellhole? Did they just want to cut off from their families and start life afresh? But, in our heart of hearts, we knew that would never be the case: their families meant too much to them.

I can remember the last time I saw them as vividly as if it were yesterday. Standing just 5 foot 8 inches in height, Chris made up in character what he lacked in stature. He was no introvert. His flamboyant dress reflected his colourful personality and that day he was wearing his much-loved, well-worn patchwork leather jacket. Peta was dark-haired, attractive and diminutive. I can still picture them in the doorway of their small rented house in the Birmingham suburb of Harborne, waving goodbye to Mum, Dad and I. It was the beginning of December 1977 and they had spent their last weekend in the UK saying their farewells to their respective families before embarking on their long-held plan to travel the world for a year. They were leaving the next morning for Heathrow to fly to Australia.

Fighting back tears, Mum gave Chris one last hug and said: 'Keep in touch,' and he replied, 'Of course I will, and remember it isn't for long. Please don't worry about me, I'm doing what I've always wanted to do.' We reminded ourselves of those last words in the months to come. They planned to return to the UK by the following Christmas.

In contrast to their excitement, which was palpable, for those of us left behind there was sorrow that they were leaving before the New Year. It was going to be a quiet, less joyful Christmas with their departure. But not wishing to dampen their spirits, we rallied and said that we would raise a glass to them and we'd speak by phone on 25 December. With their arms around each other, Chris and Peta were silhouetted in the light of the doorway against the dark night sky.

Did any of us have a premonition that something dreadful was to befall them? Certainly, there was none that we dared express to each other at the time. But during the 10 months they were missing, when we had no clue as to their fate, my eldest brother Nigel said he knew quite categorically when he said goodbye to Chris that it was for the last time.

'It was like hearing an inner voice that I had never heard before, telling me that it would be a lifetime, if ever, before I would see him again,' recalls Nigel, who, older than Chris by three years, was the more serious and sedate of my two brothers.

This experience was compounded in early July of the following year (at the same time that we were to later learn they had been murdered). Nigel was driving to an appointment in his capacity as a trading standards officer in Manchester: 'I was deep in thought as to how I was going to handle a meeting; I suddenly heard a voice. It was so physical that for a moment I actually thought there was a passenger in the car with me, but they'd have had to have been sitting beside me, it felt so close. The voice sounded as though it was either Chris or myself talking, but the message was quite clear; it said that dying was no big thing, it was a bit like the shock of diving into a cold pool on a summer's day, but it was not the end.

'It was such a surreal event that I actually had to stop and park the car to compose myself. One minute I was planning a meeting, the next my focus had taken a step-change in a totally different direction, leading to thoughts that were totally unrelated to anything happening in my life. I had never experienced anything like this before and nor have I since. I could only put it down to a very odd occurrence and after a further minute or so, I carried on driving to my meeting, but the whole event left me shaken and it became an indelible memory.

'As time passed and their disappearance became of increasing concern, I remembered my experience in the car and I was convinced that it was related and that Chris and Peta were, in fact, dead. Whilst I shared these thoughts with Frances, my wife, I felt I couldn't burden the rest of the family, so I kept my own counsel. As a consequence, although I was naturally distressed, I was not shocked to hear of the discovery of their bodies. It was only as details of the tragedy unfurled that I realised my strange experience in the car appeared to have coincided with the time of their deaths.

'To this day I don't know what to make of my experience. Whatever was the basis for my heightened emotion at the time of their departure and the incident in the car, in a strange way both events helped me cope with the eventual tragic denouement and our sense of loss in the following years. The void created by Chris's death has never been filled. He was a brother I was immensely proud of and it saddens me deeply that he has been denied the opportunity to live a life that would have enabled him to fulfil the huge potential we all know he had.'

Chapter Two

EACH OTHER'S COMPASS

As stiff twin compasses are two; Thy soul, the fixed foot,
makes no show, To move, but doth, if the other do.
John Donne: 'A Valediction: Forbidding Mourning'

Mid-1950s to 1977

Teenage sweethearts from the age of fourteen, it seemed like
Chris and Peta were always meant to be together. They were like
the two feet of a compass.

The Frampton family (of which Peta was the second youngest
of five siblings) lived in the 'big black and white house' opposite
ours in St Brannocks Road in the Manchester suburb of Chorlton
Cum Hardy. It was a fairly unremarkable place, save for the fact
that it was made famous by the four Bee Gees brothers spending
their early years there.

Peta was intelligent and of a shy disposition, but, like Chris,
also strong-willed. She was family-oriented and close to her
parents, John and Ambrosine (known to us all as Sammie) and
her three brothers, Blaise, Toby and Justin and her older sister,

Rochelle (she preferred to use the name Rocki). Chris and Peta's was an intense romance which, unlike so many that fall by the wayside, withstood the pressures and temptations of the teen years to mature into adulthood.

It was a source of great pride to Mum and Dad that at the age of eleven, Chris won the Manchester Lord Mayor's prize for achieving the highest grade in the 11 Plus examinations and the top scholarship to Manchester Grammar School (MGS), a selective academic school in the Northwest. This, of course, bolstered his innate self-confidence, although he wore it lightly and was never arrogant. From the age of ten he set his heart on becoming a doctor, overcoming his fear of blood after fainting at school whilst dissecting a frog.

A risk-taker he was not, but spirited, yes, most definitely. He had a lust for adventure and an insatiable appetite for new experiences. He exuded a sense of invincibility. His school friend, Phil Boothman, recalls how, in their first year at MGS, he and Chris went on a school trip to Chatsworth House in Derbyshire. Neither of them fancied looking round the house and grounds so they stowed away their fishing rods and tackle on the coach and, unbeknownst to the teacher, bunked off and went fishing for the day. All was well until on the way back, the fish they had caught to bring home to cook started smelling in the hot crowded coach and they were duly discovered.

Another time, Chris and his friends went fishing at nearby Lyme Park in Disley, Cheshire. The lake was frozen, but Chris in his wisdom wanted to test the thickness of the ice. Doubtless he used up one of his lives when he decided to venture out across the ice and inevitably fell in. He was saved by the quick thinking of his friend, Tom Brown, who inched across the ice on his stomach and pulled him out. Undeterred, dripping with water and very cold, Chris was determined to continue on his fishing trip with his friends.

The seeds for his love of sailing and fishing were sown annually on our family's 'bucket and spade' holidays in Trearddur Bay, on the Isle of Anglesey. My parents rented a cottage and for those two weeks of each summer the five of us would sail, swim, eat sand-filled sandwiches, climb rocks and go rockpool and sea fishing. They were happy days. It was the stuff nostalgia is made of, and, returning each year, Anglesey became the yardstick for measuring all that had happened to our family in the previous twelve months. Collectively acknowledged, Anglesey is our family's spiritual home. Now, blessed with three children of my own, they have all been initiated into its charms and enjoy nothing more than returning each year for sand, sea and invariably, rain!

Nigel recalls: 'Chris and I loved our days spent on the wind-blown beach and we were lucky that Dad built two Mirror sailing dinghies for us. Mum and Dad gave us strict guidelines as to how far we could sail. There was many an occasion when Chris and I would sail out and explore the edges of the bay to see what was around the corner. Chris found Dad curbing our explorations almost intolerable and no matter how far we ventured, it would always be a source of frustration to him when we had to turn back. He questioned boundaries.

'By the time Chris approached his mid-teens he had developed a mature, strong and colourful character. I cannot recall him ever failing to achieve a goal that he set his heart on and he set his heart on many. At the age of fourteen, he told Mum and Dad that he wanted to travel to France with two school friends on their own. They forbade him from going, saying he was too young. They were confident that he wouldn't disobey them because he didn't have enough money. However, he got a Saturday job packing Christmas cards, saved his hard-earned cash and went with two friends for three weeks, staying in youth hostels.'

Manchester was at the heart of the Swinging Sixties and Chris was a poster boy for that generation. With the city's burgeoning club scene, sportsmen, such as the Manchester United footballer, George Best, were breaking the mould and moving from a presence on the field to wider celebrity. Whilst Best had investments in Manchester nightclubs, he also had a unisex hairdressing salon and boutique in Deansgate, in the heart of the city. Here, Chris found Saturday employment, giving him an introduction to a broader and more diverse culture than previously experienced. Not afraid of embracing the trends, he wore bell-bottom trousers, cropped tops, had his ear pierced and spray-painted his cowboy boots silver. He enjoyed being outrageous but he was authentic and made things his own.

Chris and Peta's partnership crossed over into many aspects of their lives. At one stage, they turned entrepreneurs when they began producing hand-sewn unisex suede leather shoulder bags. Together they sourced the materials, sewed the bags on an old Singer sewing machine on our kitchen table and then distributed them to boutiques. They organised the negotiating, manufacturing and logistics and until school examinations became pressing, they had a lucrative cottage business.

The strength of the bond between them was demonstrated when Chris passed the entrance exam to study medicine at Cambridge University but turned it down as he and Peta had made a lovers' pact to go to the same university together. My father, Charles, was a medical student at King's College, Cambridge in the late 1930s before two years later giving up his studies and joining the Army to help the war effort. Meeting my mother, Audrey, and finding it hard to return to studying in 1945, he took up a career in the BBC. Dad would have undoubtedly liked to see Chris follow in his footsteps by taking up his place at Cambridge University but my parents knew their son was a resolute character. Chris wanted a more practical, hands-on medical course than Cambridge could offer, and, above all, he wanted to be with Peta. His mind was made up, so Mum and Dad knew there was no point in remonstrating with him.

Dad and Chris had a robust and occasionally confrontational relationship. My father was 'old school' and with his fondness for tweed jackets and sturdy brown Commando shoes, he was one of a dying breed. Emotionally, Dad was as buttoned-up as the tie he insisted on wearing, whatever the temperature. The two of them would invariably lock horns over Chris's long hair, hippy clothing and liberal views and both were equally strident, stuck in their own corners and unwilling to capitulate to the other. But scratch beneath the surface and you could see there was huge mutual love and respect. In the decades that were to follow, no father could have done more in his quest to seek justice for the unlawful killing of his son.

With their supreme intellect they were very similar. In the BBC Manchester News room, where Dad worked as a director, he was known as 'Mr Fix-it'. There was very little that he couldn't turn his hand to or fix – from making his own wireless and television set (so that he and Mum could watch the Queen's Coronation in 1953) and doing his own car mechanics (a skill he passed on to both his sons) to constructing detailed scale models of Tiger Moth planes and fishing boats and building two Mirror sailing dinghies in the garage. He taught my two brothers and me well.

But far from being one-dimensional, Chris and Dad's scientific, pragmatic exteriors belied more complex, sensitive and artistic souls and both were given to writing beautiful poetry.

They were both humanitarians. My father's donation of his body to medical research on his death in 2013 was typical of the man. Likewise, there was no surprise in learning, some 38 years after Chris had died, that his death was brought about by altruism and defending someone less able.

Blessed with a photographic memory, Chris didn't have to work very hard at bookwork to achieve outstanding scholarly success. A year ahead of his academic cohort, and finishing his A-levels at seventeen, he stayed back to work in the haematology department of Salford Royal Hospital whilst Peta finished her schooling. Working in the laboratory, he blood-matched for emergency operations. My mother recalls how, much to Chris's amusement, he would sometimes be given a police escort to the hospital in his battered old yellow Triumph Herald to get him from home to the lab quickly in an emergency. Yes, those were the days when the police force wasn't so stretched!

Peta having finished her schooling at Manchester's Whalley Range High School for Girls, the two of them enrolled at Birmingham University, she in law school and he at medical school. Shunning halls of residence, they moved into a flat together. Popular, and part of the 'cool' crowd, they were well known for their lively parties. They were certainly unconventional and had an eclectic mix of friends, drawn not just from medical and law school.

Chris loved medicine and was convinced that he'd made the right career choice. His fear of dissection long gone, his ambition was to become a surgeon.

Good friend and fellow Birmingham medical student Dr

Nigel O'Farrell recalls: 'My memories of Chris are as clear now as they were 40 years ago. When I was struggling to complete the medical course, Chris would drop round to cheer me up and encourage me, despite the fact that I was two years older than him.

'I always remember Chris defending the underdog and wanting to redress any social injustice. I clearly recall an incident in our fourth year when a lecturer made an anti-gay comment. In the middle of the lecture hall, Chris stood up from his seat and harangued him for discriminating against homosexuals, rendering everyone, but particularly the lecturer, speechless. Chris was a giant of a character, unique in many ways, and he literally breezed through medical school. Super-talented, he was one of those who really could have gone into any area of medicine he chose. He was undoubtedly the most charismatic guy in our year and had he lived, he would have been destined for great things. His memory will live on. It was a privilege to have known him.'

Another of his cohort at medical school, Dr Alan Kohn, said: 'I will never forget your lovely brother. He was a trusting sort of guy who always looked for the very best in people. In fact, I say it without reserve and without the rose-tinted spectacles of nostalgia and sentimentality, both Chris and Peta were two of the nicest people I've ever met.'

Following Chris's death and whilst sorting through the few clothes and personal belongings he had left behind in the UK, we discovered a number of cards and presents from grateful patients he had treated as a junior doctor, including a beautiful engraved pen. I think it's fair to say that had his life not been brutally cut short, he would have made a good doctor.

My own abiding memory of Chris was that he was anything

but dull; in fact, he was enormous fun. He didn't take himself seriously and he had a mischievous streak. Peta's brother-in-law, John Mills, described him as having: 'A wonderfully childlike sense of humour; he was a very special person.'

His passion was music and as he was leaving for university, Mum and Dad bought him a record player on which to play his extensive record collection. Leonard Cohen, Pink Floyd, Bob Dylan, Yes, Genesis, David Bowie, Jefferson Airplane, Supertramp, Jimi Hendrix, Journey and Santana were amongst the soundtracks of his years and listening to them transports me back to memories of him.

Aged sixteen, I remember sitting in a pink American Chevrolet belonging to one of Chris's more alternative friends. It had three seats in the front and I was sandwiched between the two of them, listening to the opening track of Pink Floyd's *Wish You Were Here* album. For me, it was the epitome of cool – I'd 'arrived'!

Maybe it was a younger sister's adulation but with him around, life always seemed that bit more exciting and edgier. Shortly before they left for their travels, I spent a weekend with Chris and Peta in Birmingham and, much to the chagrin of our Mum, Chris took me back to the train station on the back of his motorbike. I can still remember the thrill and exhilaration of being a pillion. It was the one and only time I have ridden a motorbike.

Travelling played an important part in Chris and Peta's lives; it was something they did at every opportunity. Many of their holidays were spent exploring Europe, which they funded themselves by doing menial jobs such as picking fruit, driving for hire car firms and working in factories. They spent Chris's three-month medical elective in North Africa and visited

Morocco several times, which they loved for its mysticism and different culture.

Very much children of the sixties and seventies in their desire for adventure and exploring new horizons, they lived life precariously. Best friend Rick Henshaw remembers how in 1973, he and Chris, and a couple of other friends, travelled across Europe in a battered old Morris Minor, Chris with the music of JJ Cale blaring out and on repeat. On reaching Morocco, they were involved in a road accident in which the car flipped over. Rick remembers Chris shouting to them all to get out as the petrol tank, which had ruptured, was spewing gasoline all over the road and he could see sparks coming out of the car. Shaken but unscathed, they were not thwarted and after getting the car repaired, they continued their progress to Tangier, camping in the desert before returning some weeks later to England.

With travelling in their blood, Chris and Peta lived for the day when Chris had finished his pre-registration houseman's year at Birmingham Accident Hospital and the city's Queen Elizabeth Hospital and they could take off. My mother recalls: 'They had such a love of life that wherever they went, they generated a feeling of excitement and for those of us left behind, they imbued a feeling of dissatisfaction and restlessness with one's own lot.'

It was their long-held dream to see the world together. In retrospect, it was lucky that they were so driven to live life to the full because all too soon it was to come to an end.

It was a touching reminder of just how close the two of them had become that before they set off for their year abroad, Peta wrote a will and declared her wish to leave her few worldly possessions to her 'beloved friend' Chris. It's startling that at the tender age of twenty-four she had had the foresight to make provision in the event of her death.

Chapter Three

NEW HORIZONS

Through Birmingham Medical School, Chris heard that The After Hours Medical Service in Brisbane was recruiting for British doctors to go out to Australia on a three-month contract, all airfares paid. Originally planning to leave in September 1977, he and Peta had to delay their departure to 5 December because another doctor friend they were going with was unable to get her affairs in order on time.

Chris came home for one last weekend and went shopping with Mum for cotton shirts and clothes suitable for the hot climate. Often flying by the seat of his pants, with just two days to go, he discovered that his passport was about to expire so he and Mum did a last-minute dash and spent a very long morning queueing up at the Passport Office in Liverpool to get it renewed. Eventually, with passport and visas sorted, jobs arranged and bags packed, they bade their farewells to us on a cold, overcast winter's evening. Leaving from Heathrow the next day, they embarked on their long-held dream to see the world together.

DEAD IN THE WATER

Although Chris worked long, unsociable hours in Brisbane, the flexible nature of the out-of-hours medical work and Peta's secretarial temping afforded them days off in which they could explore Australia's beautiful Sunshine Coast and for five months they took full advantage of this relaxed lifestyle. Having made friends with Chris's work colleagues, they spent their days fishing, surfing, swimming and sailing. They loved the great outdoors lifestyle, regularly eating al fresco and barbecuing, and vowed that they would one day return to Australia to live.

As on previous travels, they went to great lengths to keep in touch with their respective families. Chris regularly phoned home. A consummate letter-writer, Peta wrote long, journal-style letters to her mother, Sammie (letters which 38 years later were to provide crucial evidence in leading the police to their killer).

Globally, 1978 was a pivotal and 'happening' time. It was the year the first ever cellular mobile phone was launched and the first test-tube baby was born. In Guyana, the cult leader Jim Jones initiated the mass suicide and murder of 918 members of his church, 'People's Temple', and the serial killer David Berkowitz, 'Son of Sam', was convicted of murder after terrorising New York for twelve months. On a lighter note, it was a great year for movies with *Grease*, *Saturday Night Fever* and *Close Encounters of the Third Kind* hitting the big screen, and Argentina won the football World Cup. For Chris and Peta, life felt good and they were full of anticipation as they prepared to embark on the second leg of their adventure.

In Peta's last letter to her mother before leaving Brisbane at the end of April she wrote: 'We've bought tickets to London via New Caledonia, Fiji, Los Angeles and Miami. The plan is to start by travelling down through Mexico. We have a year to use up the remainder of the tickets. We managed to get US visas for multiple re-entry for twelve months and have got Mexican visas as well. We had yellow fever jabs and have bought travellers cheques and six months insurance so we are all set. We also got a couple of kit bags to replace the suitcases we brought and I'm now trying to get rid of more stuff so I can carry it! Chris is going to have a harder time because of all of the books and his medical bag but I think he is going to leave quite a lot of stuff here for when he comes back.'

Describing their last few days in Australia, in which Chris caught his first shark, she says: 'The last week at Surfer's Paradise was great – we spent every day out – went sailing twice – renting a catamaran on the broadwater, which was really nice. We are just about to go off to Peel Island for the night so that Chris can do some fishing before we leave.'

Before leaving the UK, Chris had recorded a lot of his favourite music onto cassettes and they listened to them on an Akai cassette recorder that he called a 'boombox', which he had bought in Australia. He intended to use the boombox to record travelogues on blank cassette tapes to post back home. He sent me a beautiful green sarong (which I still wear to this day) that quite incredibly arrived on my birthday of 1 May, probably more by good luck than good management! In with the sarong he had enclosed a chatty tape recording describing his and Peta's last days in Australia.

I was now in my penultimate year of schooling and was focused on studying for A-levels and making university applications. Being a typical teenager, I rarely spared much thought for things outside of my immediate orbit. It was, though, always a happy day when one of Chris's tapes popped through the letterbox. He liked to immerse himself in local culture and politics and was a dab hand at giving colourful descriptions. For Mum and Dad, receiving the latest communication from Chris was, above all, a reassurance that all was well on the other side of the world.

Rather than fly directly to Los Angeles, Chris and Peta took the opportunity to explore some of the stunning South Pacific islands en route. First stop was New Caledonia, with its massive barrier reef, where they went scuba diving. Next was Fiji, with its rugged landscapes, palm-lined beaches, coral reefs and clear lagoons. In a postcard home, Peta wrote that snorkelling in Nadi (a city on the western side of Fiji) was 'fantastic'. This was followed by a flying visit to Hawaii, with its diverse natural scenery, warm tropical climate, rugged landscape and active volcanoes.

Arriving in the urban sprawl of Los Angeles in mid-May, they experienced a cultural gear change and no sooner had they arrived than they wanted to get out. They rented a car and journeyed south to San Diego and down to the Mexican border. Mexico's brilliant colours, rich indigenous heritage and hot culinary traditions fascinated them and they spent many days absorbing the sights of the Mayan and Aztec ruins, swimming and their love of snorkelling.

On 13 May 1978 Peta wrote: 'We got a 24-hour train from Mexicali to Mazatlan, a thousand miles down the west coast. We are going to recuperate for three days before going to Mexico City, where Chris knows someone we can stay with. We may go to the Yucatán in East Mexico, where most of the Aztec ruins are centred.'

The last time we heard Chris's voice was in a lengthy tape recording he made on 29 May 1978, this time for our brother Nigel's twenty-eighth birthday on 9 June. He never forgot any of our birthdays. The tape was posted from the city of Oaxaca, some 300 miles south of Mexico City, along with a birthday gift of a colourful Mexican shirt. He sounded in good spirits and described how much he and Peta were enjoying life and how they were heading for the Yucatán.

Somewhat prophetically, his very last words were encouraging us all to use the possessions he had left behind in the UK, such as books, clothes, a box full of vinyl albums and a food processor.

He said: 'Don't leave them around collecting dust. There's some good music and books there, I'm sure you can find a use for them!'

He would be pleased to know that we have, and there are still reminders of him to be found in our house, some 40 years after his death. Remarkably, Chris's Kenwood food mixer is still doing sterling service in my kitchen. And, with the recent revival of vinyl records, I am thinking it might be time to bring his large library of seventies albums down from my loft. His birthday cards to me, with his distinctive writing, are amongst my most treasured possessions.

A DISASTROUS
TRIP

Chapter Four

A DISASTROUS
TACK

Peta's long, wonderfully descriptive letters to her mother tell of chance meetings with strangers and how their agenda changed daily, depending on who they met, the vagaries of public transport and even the vicissitude of the weather. They leave you with that feeling 'If only... ' I'm reminded of the poem 'Maud Muller' by John Greenleaf Whittier:

> *For of all sad words of tongue or pen, the saddest*
> *are these: 'It might have been'.*

On 6 June 1978, Peta wrote to her mother giving her an update of their travels: 'We didn't go straight to the Yucatán from Oaxaca. Instead, we caught the bus to Villahermosa and met an English couple on their way to Bolivia through Belize so we decided to go with them as Belize boasts the longest reef in the western hemisphere. As we were full up of ruins, having spent the last few days at Mitla, Yagul and Monte Alban in Oaxaca, we thought some snorkelling was in order.'

On the way to Belize they stopped in Chetumal. A city on the east coast of the Yucatán Peninsula, Chetumal is an important port for the region and operates as Mexico's main trading gateway with the neighbouring country of Belize and the rest of Central America. More than just a border town, in the 1970s there was strong evidence of an historical past inherited from Mayan ancestors, and the impressive bay was a riot of enticing turquoise and jade hues.

Peta continued: 'We stopped a night at Chetumal and drank the night away with a couple of Scottish soldiers. They said they would rather be in Northern Ireland on less pay and more danger than here! I didn't understand their attitude especially as things with the Guatemalans have quietened down so that they're unlikely to die here.' [Belize at that time was a British colony. It wasn't until some three years later in September 1981 that it gained full independence and became a nation state within the British Commonwealth. Guatemala to this day maintains a territorial claim over Belize.]

From Chetumal, Chris and Peta caught a bus south to Belize City, a journey of some seventy miles. Belize is a land of mountains, swamps and tropical jungle, bounded by Mexico to the north, Guatemala to the west and south, and the Caribbean Sea to the east. The Belizean coastline held a fascination for them because, as Peta says in her letter, it boasts a stunning coral reef and having experienced Australia's Great Barrier Reef, they wanted to draw comparisons. It is regarded as one of the world's last unspoilt destinations and of course in 1978, it was even more remote than it is today. The 386 kilometres of coastline (made a UNESCO World Heritage Site in 1996) is littered with lush jungle, beautiful coral reefs, cayes (a small sandy elevation on the surface of a coral reef) and deserted islands in the Caribbean Sea. Pocket-sized, Belize is the only Central American country where English is the official language.

Describing Belize City, Peta says in her letter: 'I was amazed – it's a town of about 40,000 people who all live in shacks. Actually, the houses are very similar to those in Queensland but just look shabbier. The people all speak English, of course, as well as Creole and Spanish, and they're really friendly. The atmosphere is very relaxed and pretty poor. They have T-shirts here with the slogan "You Better Belize It", which kinda sums the place up.'

The day after they arrived in Belize City, Peta describes in her letter how they went down to the harbour and took a '28-foot sloop owned by an English guy to Caye Caulker. He and his girlfriend (an Aussie from Darwin) have been sailing around the cayes for a couple of months having a very good time.' Peta wrote the letter to her mother from the Marin Hotel, located on a small island off the coast of Belize called Caye Caulker: 'There are several of these islands called cayes (pronounced keys) and this one [referring to the Marin Hotel] is the cheapest, the hotel room costs about £2 a night and there's a shower too!'

In 1978, Caye Caulker was, as it still largely is today, entirely white coral sand and to the north there's dense mangrove forest and diverse birdlife. The beaches and the crystal-clear, turquoise-hued waters of the Caribbean were picture-perfect, deserted and inviting.

Even to this day, Caye Caulker is described as possessing a rare rustic, laid-back charm in contrast to the hustle and bustle of the Caribbean's tourist hot spots. Its bohemian, relaxed lifestyle attracts backpackers and offers convenient anchorage and storm refuge for local fishermen working Belize's barrier reef and the coast.

Complaining about the warm, humid conditions of the tropical monsoon climate, Peta wrote: 'It is 83 per cent humidity on average throughout the year! I feel hot and sweaty all the time. Luckily there is a constant gale force wind so it's not so bad but it's terrible at night, when the wind occasionally dies, the mossies and sand flies are out in force – I'm bitten all over. Unlike on Beachcomber Island in Fiji, the reef is some way from the island so we've been out on the *Norma* (the boat we've arrived on). The coral and fish were so disappointing after the South Pacific but I enjoyed snorkelling again though I was more aware of the possibility of sharks being in deeper water.'

Caye Caulker is used as a popular launch pad for scuba diving at the Great Blue Hole. With the owner of the *Norma* and his Australian girlfriend, whose exotic beauty was defined by her wild Afro hair, Chris and Peta made the two-hour sail to the almost perfectly circular Blue Hole, located in the centre of the Belizean Lighthouse Reef and literally a large sinkhole of water, 145m deep and 305m wide. Its depth gives it a deep turquoise blue colour and makes it one of the world's most outstanding dive and snorkelling sites.

Peta describes their visit to this geographical phenomenon: 'Today we went to the Blue Hole, just by the mangroves which line part of the caye. It has a channel, which goes right under the caye, though no one knows where it comes out. Very enjoyable!'

Giving her mother some local colour, Peta writes: 'The conch shells here are unbelievable, I wish I had room to bring one with me. Also, the tortoiseshell is pretty and they have black coral here though it's very expensive. They grow sugar here. Passing a refinery is lovely – just like smelling jam roly poly. They have a really neat pie shop on Caye Caulker – coconut cream pie, orange pie, banana cake, all irresistible – consequently my middle is getting fatter all the time. There are lots of tourists here – mainly Americans, so we are not short of company.'

It was later that evening after returning from their trip to the Blue Hole that they met one such American in the bar of the Marin Hotel. The owner of the *Norma* and his girlfriend introduced Chris and Peta to an American acquaintance of theirs called Silas Duane Boston. They had spent the last couple of months sailing to different islands and often snorkelled with him and a mutual friend called Brian.

A larger-than-life character, Boston (a dislike of the name Silas meant that he called himself Duane) had become well known in Belize City and amongst the caye's handful of locals and the travellers who, like him, were drawn to Caye Caulker's bohemian lifestyle and stunning Caribbean backdrop. Making friends and acquaintances was quick and easy in the relaxed holiday setting. With days of wall-to-wall sunshine, the stunning beaches and few cares in the world, greater than where to buy a bottle of cheap rum, life was pretty idyllic. Some six months before Chris and Peta had made the journey, thirty-seven-year-old Boston had travelled down through Mexico. He had set off from his hometown of Sacramento in California with his two young sons, thirteen-year-old Vince and twelve-year-old Russell, in a pickup truck. After their truck broke down in the port of Veracruz in the Gulf of Mexico, they hired another one and headed to Chetumal, the border town to Belize that Chris and Peta had stayed in. Knowing he would be searched at the border, Boston sold his guns, which he had brought with him.

With his weather-beaten, rugged looks, experienced sea-faring skills and talent for storytelling, he was an engaging character with a devil-may-care attitude. His most prominent feature was his small, piercing blue eyes and, on his left forearm, he sported a large tattoo of a mermaid in green ink. What he lacked in conventional good looks, he made up for in megawatt charm, which he used with great success, particularly with women. A lady's man and a raconteur, he had already been married five times.

Entering Belize, Boston decided to set up temporary home with his sons so he bought a small sailing boat, but soon after it sank in a hurricane. His father Russell, with whom he was close, travelled from Sacramento to Belize in April 1978 to see him and his two grandsons and he gave him some money to buy another boat, but this time bigger. Originally called the *Marcia P*, Boston renamed it *Justin B*, after his two-year-old son Justin by his fifth wife, Kathe, from whom he was divorced in 1976.

About 32ft in length, the *Justin B* was a basic, Belizean wooden sailing boat with no bathroom or home comforts. There was a cuddy (a small cupboard-like cabin) at the front and a cramped galley kitchen to the rear, which you could look down into from small porthole windows on the deck. Very much a working fishing boat it had a large box for depositing fish.

Without a licence to trade, Boston used the six-ton fishing smack to sail tourists to one of the many Belizean cayes or ferry them back to Belize City. It wasn't long before he realised that the Robinson Crusoe way of life, making meals from the daily catch, was actually the favourite part of the trip for many vacationers. The cayes, with their lush jungle, palm-fringed, white sandy beaches, offered the opportunity to snorkel, swim and scuba dive, so Boston started to offer longer excursions. Mooring at a reef, he and his sons would hand out masks and fins to allow passengers to snorkel and they could spear the plentiful fish and lobsters for cooking.

Sometimes Boston would employ a girl Friday to help out with the cooking and he provided a big stewing pot down in the galley for making communal dishes for al fresco dining. He and his passengers would build a beach fire, gather coconuts and supplement the meal with a mixture of rice, beans, vegetables and spices, which he, or his girl Friday, would prepare in advance whilst everyone was enjoying the water sports.

For three months, Boston had operated a successful, lucrative business, but shortly before he met Chris and Peta, government officials had boarded the *Justin B* and told him that because he was American, he wasn't allowed to work in Belize without a work permit. They told him he could immigrate, but without applying to become a legal resident, he was taking business away from the local Belizeans and destroying their livelihoods. Not wishing to draw attention to himself any more than he already had, Boston decided it was time to leave the area.

Eager to keep her mother up to date with their movements, Peta added a postscript dated 13 June 1978, to the letter to her mother (as was her habit if she couldn't post it straight away):

'Sorry I forgot to post this in Belize on Saturday so I am adding a little now as all our plans have changed... We originally meant to get the bus to Merida in the Yucatán but then an American named Duane Boston, who owns a Belizean boat called the *Justin B*, offered to take us up to Chetumal by sail so we decided to do that.'

Their clothes stuffed into two duffle bags, Chris and Peta had boarded the *Justin B*. Chris also carried his black medical bag, for his next medical job in Trinidad, and his much-treasured 'boombox', upon which he played his pre-recorded cassette tapes of seventies music. Between them, they carried at least $800 dollars in Thomas Cook traveller cheques.

Accompanying them on the voyage were a Belizean called Tom and a tall blonde woman called Sharon, who was in her mid-twenties and a flight attendant from Missouri who had struck up a sexual relationship with Boston.

The short voyage from Caye Caulker to the city and port of Chetumal was perhaps Chris and Peta's way of testing the waters to see if they all got on. From there they visited Isla Mujeres, an idyllic Caribbean island about eight miles off the Yucatán Peninsula.

Returning south, they entered Corozal, where Peta wrote: 'The pier is surrounded by millions of catfish and the water boils when anything gets thrown in. It is a slightly more civilised place with a bar with easy chairs as opposed to the usual benches and sand floor of Caye Caulker. It even boasts an ice-cream parlour – one flavour only – strawberry!

'The guy who did most of the sailing for Duane, a Belizean called Tom, decided to stay at Corozal, so Duane wants to take the boat down to Costa Rica to sell it. Anyway, we thought it was an opportunity not to be missed.'

Interestingly, Peta links the reason for Boston wanting to sell the boat as Tom being no longer there to do the sailing – Boston had obviously not told Chris and Peta that he had been forbidden from trading in Belize. Did Tom decide to jump ship at short notice in the small sleepy town of Corozal because he had seen something in Boston's character that hadn't at that time been revealed to Chris and Peta?

They had sailed for about three days and it was long enough to convince Chris and Peta that they wanted to stay on board and do some more sailing. Agreeing they would pay $500 for their passage, Boston offered them the chance to sail, swim, snorkel and sample the more remote cayes in the south of Belize, after which they would disembark in Roatan, Honduras, some 220km down the coast and Boston would go on to Costa Rica to sell the boat.

From Corozal, they sailed along the coastline to Belize's North Eastern fishing port of Sarteneja and then on to Blackadore Caye, west of Ambergris Caye. Blackadore was Boston's favourite stop-off for swimming and barbecuing the day's catch and he had often taken parties of tourists there. The *Justin B* conveniently had a short keel, which meant that Boston could easily anchor close and alongside the bleached white sandy beach on the leeward side of the caye.

Such is the outstanding beauty of this 104-acre island that it was acquired in 2006 by the Hollywood actor Leonardo DiCaprio to convert into a luxury resort and protected wildlife reserve. 'It is like heaven on earth,' DiCaprio told *The New York Times*. It is set to become one of the world's most exclusive island retreats. Back in 1978, it was even more desert island existence and as near to paradise as you can possibly get so long as you were a backpacker.

Not wishing to join them in going further south, Sharon disembarked when the *Justin B* then returned to Caye Caulker, leaving Chris and Peta the only two tourists on the boat.

To two intelligent people it must have occurred to them that being on a boat with a total stranger could pose a potential danger. In fact, a boat out at sea is probably the most vulnerable place on earth. But any niggling doubts about Boston must have been pushed aside by the fact that his sons were accompanying them on the voyage. It would be natural to assume you were in safe hands with the father of two young boys.

Certainly, during their first few days on the boat all seemed well with the world. From Peta's letter, one gets a sense that she and Chris enjoyed the relaxed lifestyle: 'It's very peaceful and we can catch fish for supper. There's plenty of snapper and grunt, not to mention catfish, which is tasty. It's incredibly hot here; everyone is sitting inside suffering. There are papaya and mango to eat, but no fresh vegetables (apart from potatoes and onions), which I really miss. Still, it's a real kick being able to catch your supper. Tom, before he left the boat, made "fry-jack", a flatbread fried with baking powder to make it rise – very good indeed – he was a baker and it was a pleasure to watch him work the dough.

'This boat is not very comfortable. Originally a working boat, most of the below deck is taken up with a fish box so that it's a bit cramped for cooking and sleeping. But during the day it's super, just lying on the hatches and soaking up the sun while the boat flies along. Of course, we have been becalmed and then everyone just jumps into the water to keep cool. In spite of it being the rainy season we have only had rain a couple of times. But at night the sky is amazing – there's lightning flashing on the horizon all the time, and with no thunder it loses its frightening effect and just looks beautiful. We have had thunderstorms as well, which are quite something on a boat.'

Chapter Five

'NOTHING MUCH HAPPENS ON A BOAT'

Those are Peta's written words to her mother – words that, in retrospect, hold such poignant irony. By now, she and Chris had been in Boston's company for approaching two weeks. She wrote to her mother:

'In Belize City, we had to pay $86 BH for visas to enter into Honduras. It seems that there's nothing but hassle and money to go anywhere by boat. Chris has been doing a lot of sailing and even I have been taking the tiller a couple of times – very tiring, depending on the strength of the wind.'

Peta mentions that their schedule was seriously disrupted because Boston wanted to get ballast [heavy material, such as sand, gravel or iron, added to a boat to improve stability and control], offering perhaps the lengthy voyage in less protected waters down to Costa Rica to sell the boat as the reason.

'We had to spend nearly a week at Stann Creek (Dangriga) trying to get extra ballast. Finally, we were given about 700 lbs by a white Belizean, who is the general manager of the Belizean

Citrus Co at Pomona, about 12 miles from Stann Creek. He gave us a tour of the factory – very impressive. They make concentrated orange juice and tinned grapefruit, most of which goes to the UK under the name of Trout Hall. Have you seen any? He gave us a few tins – very good for breakfast, though you know I don't like it much. We had to get a whole load of papers stamped for customs clearance etc and paid $10 BH, which went straight into the officer's pocket, of course.'

Sailing on to the quiet Belizean fishing port of Placencia, Peta wrote:

'When we arrived, we were longing for ice-cold beer as usual (sailing makes you so thirsty) and we didn't have much water on board but there was no beer or soft drinks in town! Placencia is very pretty. It can only be reached by four-wheel drive and is built on sand with a narrow cement pathway linking the houses etc.'

Its narrow meandering sidewalk served as its main street and, like so many of the islands in this part of the world, it had a white sand, palm-fringed beach.

The beauty of their surroundings was not, however, uppermost in Boston's mind. Finding some poisonous seeds in the sand under some trees on the beach, Vince and Russell showed them to their father, who took the red and black seeds from them. Boston looked the seeds up in a book of local flora and fauna that was on the boat and said: 'I should feed these to Chris and Peta.'

Russell recalled many years later: 'It struck me as odd and it lodged in my head, both at the time and since, but I thought it was just Dad being drunk and spewing idle threats. Nonetheless, Vince and I hid the seeds from him.'

On 28 June 1978, Peta wrote to her mother: 'We have just .

set off from Placencia and it's about 7am. The sun is warm, the sky a little cloudy and the sea is emerald green and somewhat choppy so my writing may go haywire.'

Sailing south the next day, the *Justin B* reached the small island of Hunting Caye – one of the Sapodilla Cayes on the very southernmost tip of Belize's beautiful barrier reef. Halfmoon Beach, a sandy coral beach named after its crescent shape, is on the eastern shore and is an important nesting site for the Hawksbill sea turtle. The coast is paradisiacal, with reefs, white-sand beaches and crystal-clear waters teaming with life and miles of mangroves.

Impressed by what she saw, Peta wrote in a postscript on the 29 June: 'We had a perfect sail and reached Hunting Caye at about 11am. (Chris wants me to say this was due to his superb navigation with only a $5 compass.) This caye is very pretty. The only person who lives on it (it's about 500 yards by 100 yards) is the lighthouse keeper. We were surprised to see the pelicans (everywhere here, but not pretty as they're brown) roosting in the coconut palms. With the wonders of modern civilisation, this place would be an idyllic Caribbean island. We've docked only about 50 yards offshore and the water is perfectly clear. There's a reef some way off and another four cayes visible. We caught a lobster and sardines last night.

'I was very pleased yesterday when I managed to make some "fry-jack" – a flatbread fried in the pan. I'd only watched Tom, the sailor I told you about and who has now left the boat, make it once and he was a baker.

'Talking to the lighthouse keeper, this is the worst time for sailing and our next sail to Puerto Cortes in Honduras would be very hard, so it seems we may easily decide to go to Livingston in Guatemala, which is a simple sail with the wind behind us.

'If we do, I shall leave the *Justin B* and get a ferry to Puerto Cortes and a plane from Honduras to New Orleans.' [Whilst Chris had a short-term medical job in Trinidad, she was going to visit a close mutual friend – a Dr Tom Lane who lived in Louisiana, USA.]

For the first time, one senses tension and friction beginning to creep into Peta's writing. She describes the boat's cramped conditions and how tempers were starting to fray:

'I am getting a bit weary of the practical difficulties of living on this tiny boat with four other people. At least I managed to get a shower at Placencia by throwing buckets of well-water over me. I think I'm getting too old for primitive living. Like all boats, this one has cockroaches. We sleep in the galley, a space about 4 foot by 5 foot by 2½ foot. It's horrible when we turn on the kerosene lamp and they come out. We spray a repellent every day but they come out to die. I don't mind cockroaches that much, there were loads in Morocco and Australia, but I like a little space between me and them.'

Significantly, she writes: 'Another reason I wouldn't mind ending my sailing career now – I'm down as a sailor on the papers – is the two sons of Duane. They are 12 and 13 years old but behave more like 8 and 9. I find I have no patience at all with them. Of course, they squabble most of the time. I now see how irritating we must have been as children in that respect.'

With chilling prescience, she adds: 'But, on a boat there's nowhere to go. What makes it worse is that Duane curses and puts them down continually, often when things are not going quite right, like when we didn't get one of the anchors up because the motor wasn't working to give us leverage. We subsequently went back for it and managed to retrieve it – about $100 worth.

'Time seems to go so quickly here – it's nearly July already. It must be getting quite warm now in England. Did I hear there's going to be a General Election? I haven't seen a newspaper for weeks and the BBC World Service doesn't give much about the UK. I often wonder what everyone is doing and I feel very cut off, but letters are too difficult as I never know where I am going to be next.'

'I'm already a month late at Tom's in New Orleans but I'm looking forward to getting there as the music's supposed to be excellent in the pubs. Of course, it'll be about 30 degrees and very humid, but I guess I've gotten used to it a bit and it makes a lot of difference having a shower etc.'

She signs off her last-ever letter: 'Enough of the future. I don't think there's any more news – nothing much happens on a boat. Lots of love Peta.'

But an awful lot was about to happen on that boat: we were to never hear from them again.

Chapter Six

DEAD WAKE

(Dead wake: the lingering trail left behind on the surface of the water by a passing ship.)

Peta's letter dated 28 June 1978 arrived home in Manchester, England, in early August. Since the previous communication was a letter that she had written on 13 June, we were naturally worried about what had happened to them throughout July.

The letter's arrival temporarily alleviated the mounting anxiety of both families and we felt sure that it would only be a matter of days before we received a follow-up letter or a phone call explaining the silence. But as the days grew into weeks, our anxiety levels began to mount again. What really perplexed and worried us was the fact that the letter's last postscript and the date stamp on the envelope were over two weeks apart. Peta, without exception, wrote postscripts if she couldn't post her letters straight away.

In today's world of modern communications, with a mobile phone rarely out of arm's reach, it's hard to appreciate the overwhelming sense of helplessness and wretchedness that we felt back then from being unable to make contact. It was so uncharacteristic for them to be out of touch. By the end of August, both families were desperate with worry. I vividly remember Mum's perpetual angst-ridden face and how she seemed to age overnight.

My mother takes up the story: 'We went on holiday to Anglesey, and we recalled all the happy times we had enjoyed as a family. Just 12 months previous, Chris had managed to snatch a couple of days of leave from his hospital duties and he joined us at our holiday house overlooking the beach at Trearddur Bay.

'I remember how relieved I was to hear the loud roar of his Triumph motorbike announcing his arrival some ten or so seconds before he pulled up in the driveway. I was never a fan of motorbikes – Chris had recently had a high-speed tyre blow-out on a motorway and with incredible good fortune, escaped with only minor injuries. As he took off his helmet and shook his hair, I remember thinking how he exuded happiness and life. As a family, we enjoyed two brief sun-filled days with him, sailing our Mirror dinghy, visiting our familiar haunts, such as Anglesey's South Stack lighthouse and headland and the wind-swept beaches and sand dunes of Rhoscolyn and Cymyran, during which we discussed Chris's forthcoming travel plans and his ambition to become a surgeon.

'What a contrast one year on when, returning home to Cheshire, our hopes were spectacularly dashed with the bleak realisation that there was no news from them. I remember our car pulling up in the driveway. We didn't unload the luggage but went straight to the house. Pushing open the front door, we scanned the coir mat, strewn with letters; our eyes like search lights, scanning for an envelope, a postcard, perhaps a package bearing a foreign postmark containing a cassette tape recording.

We felt sure there would be a rational explanation for the news blackout... perhaps a postal strike or maybe illness but, no, there was nothing. In seconds, our disappointment and disbelief had turned to deep worry and incomprehension. There was silence and emptiness. The good of the holiday had evaporated.'

Anglesey, for so long the setting and annual benchmark for all our happiest family memories, had somehow become tainted with the angst and worry that one of our family was missing and we were now an incomplete unit. Life started to look different and uncertain. There was an air of foreboding. Anxiety and incomprehension were etched on Mum and Dad's faces.

In early September 1978, my now distraught parents met with Peta's parents, John and Sammie Frampton. Silver-haired and elegant, with red nails and lipstick, Sammie was the epitome of an RAF officer's wife – John being an ex-RAF officer who had been a World War Two prisoner of war. Peta and her mother were very close. Our two families were no longer neighbours. We had, two years before, moved to Wilmslow in Cheshire and the Framptons to Old Trafford (famous for its cricket ground), but we kept in touch through the common link of Chris and Peta.

Both sets of parents discussed a plan of action if, in the unthinkable event, we would receive no more news from them. Missing now for two months, the Framptons, like my parents, felt that the time had come to make Chris and Peta's disappearance official and enlist the help of outside agencies. Deciding a plan of action, Mum and Dad contacted the Foreign & Commonwealth Office which, using its network of contacts and offices throughout Central and South America, authorised an intensive search from the US border down as far south as Peru. Peta's parents, Sammie and John, enlisted the help of their local MP, Winston Churchill, grandson of the former prime minister Sir Winston Churchill, to bring further pressure to bear on the Foreign Office. Both sets of parents also wrote independently to all the consuls in Central and South America.

As a television director, with 30 years' experience of working in the BBC newsroom behind him, Dad was well acquainted with using news organisations such as Reuters and national newspapers, radio and television to spread the word. The *Daily Mail*, the *Express* and the *Telegraph* were just some of the national newspapers that ran Chris and Peta's story. My parents appeared on BBC and ITV's *Granada* magazine-style evening news programmes to make a personal appeal to anyone who had recently returned from Belize or Guatemala and who might possibly have seen them. I can recall thinking how surreal it was, watching them on television, talking about Chris.

On 22 September 1978, my parents had the foresight to write to the acting harbour master in Belize City, asking if he could send us the *Justin B*'s clearance records from the port of Stann Creek (Dangriga), from where Peta wrote in her last letter the boat had sailed.

My mother remembers: 'A friend of Chris's, called Dave Cox, had just returned from Central America and had phoned us to ask Chris's whereabouts, not knowing he and Peta were missing. With an unstable political situation and high crime rate, Dave thought there was an outside chance that they may have been imprisoned or kept hostage somewhere and, for a time, we began to believe and explore this theory. We desperately grasped at straws.'

That autumn was full of false leads and misinformation. Entering the realm of Chinese whispers, our hopes were raised, only for them to be thrown into unutterable despair when they

Sailor holds key in hunt for couple

By MICHAEL DUFFY

A DESPERATE search was on today among a maze of Caribbean islands for a yachtsman who holds the key to the disappearance of a couple from Manchester.

For the sailor is the last known contact of Dr Chris Farmer and civil servant Peta Frampton, both aged 25 who have vanished while on holiday in Central America.

The couple, who hitched a lift with American Duane Boston, could be stranded on a remote island miles from anywhere.

Today Peta's mother, Mrs Ambrosine Frampton, of Queens Road, Stretford, said : "We can't think of anything else but that they are on one of these paradise islands."

It is believed the couple may have asked the San Fransisco yachtsman to let them ashore on a sun-drenched beach — only to discover later that they could not get off the island.

The couple, who have known each other since childhood when they lived in the same street in Chorlton-cum-Hardy, Manchester, last contacted their parents by letter in the middle of July.

Peta said she was travelling on from Guatemala to visit a friend in New Orleans while Chris was to take a working vacation in Trinidad.

But neither of them arrived at their intended destinations.

The couple had gone to work in Australia last December and flew to Los Angeles on holiday before their planned return to Britain.

They headed south from California, through Mexico to Belize, where they hitched their lift aboard the converted fishing boat heading for Livingstone, 130 miles away.

Chris's father, former BBC newsman Mr Charles Farmer, said today: "There has been such an utter silence that anything is possible. They could have been involved in anything from a mugging to a crazy [...]

[...] that part of the [...] we can get arrested [...] king offence."
[...]ry is that they

Peta Frampton and Chris Farmer.

have been slung in jail on a false drugs charge, but the Foreign Office thinks this is unlikely, because such information would normally be conveyed to the British authorities.

A spokesman said today: "We are in touch with our consulate in Guatemala, but so far nothing has come to light."

Interpol and the FBI are now involved in the hunt for the missing couple, and the roaming yachtsman who holds the vital clues to their disappearance.

The couple's parents are in contact with both agencies.

Chris and Peta planned to get married on their return to England. After attending Manchester Grammar and Whalley Range [...] respectively, the couple [...] [Bir]mingham.
Chris's [...]
Fairbourne [...]

One of the many newspaper articles about Chris and Peta's disappearance.

resulted in a dead end. The investigation was greatly hampered by the archaic long-distance communication and, given the fact that Peta had written they might be headed for Livingston, Guatemala, we had the added complication of dealing with the Spanish language.

Word was starting to get out in the coastal towns of Belize and Guatemala that two young British tourists were missing. The Foreign & Commonwealth Office had, in the course of their investigation, alerted the British vice-consul in Guatemala, a Mr Terence Evans. My brother Nigel asked a Spanish friend to write a letter in Spanish, saying that Chris and Peta were missing. He sent a copy of the letter, along with photographs of them, to all the tourist hotels and haunts in Livingston – letters that were delayed in being received because of a postal strike in Guatemala.

We had to wait weeks to get any reply. Then we received what we thought was good news. Writing in English on behalf of the migration officer in Livingston, Sr Crisostomo Alvarez, a Mrs Jean Swanson, proprietor of the Casa Rosada Hotel in Livingston, wrote to us on 25 October. Mrs Swanson had heard that a resident of Placencia in Belize had seen Chris and Peta in the last week or two, and they were alive and well. She was even able to give us an address.

Mrs Swanson wrote: 'The Vice-Consul has already telephoned me to see if we could get any information on these two people. We looked up the records of incoming passengers and boats arriving here, but found a record only of the *Justin B* and Mr Boston and his two sons; no one else appeared on their record of entry.

'You are indebted to Sr Alvarez for the investigation that was made here. He checked all the boat repair records after a boatman from Punta Gorda told us of meeting the *Justin B*, partially disabled but on her way here for repair. He had seen no other passengers.

'Fortunately, you sent the photograph. Sr Alvarez gave me the photo to send, along with one of the cruise boats, in order to check with the officials on Hunting Caye. Late Sunday evening, a boatman came here to return the photo and to tell us that a woman there said definitely that the two young people are in Placencia. We gather from his wording of the message that she meant they are there now.'

Upon receipt of this letter, we immediately alerted the Foreign Office, responded to Mrs Swanson and wrote to the address in Placencia. With no telephone number to call, all communication was by letter and therefore painfully slow. After a couple of weeks our hopes were once more shattered when we received the news that this sighting of Chris and Peta pertained to when the *Justin B* had docked in Placencia in late June – the 'small, pretty fishing port' that Peta had described in her letter to her mother.

The Foreign & Commonwealth Office wrote to us to say that: 'An intensive investigation of all the islands and places frequented by visitors to Belize had revealed no trace of Chris and Peta and there was no confirmation on the spot of their presence in Placencia. Nor is there any customs/immigration record of their subsequent return to Belize.'

Around the same time, we received information from Peru Immigration that a passenger bearing the name of Dr Christopher James Burnett Farmer, and holder of a British passport, had boarded a Lufthansa flight from Lima in Peru bound for New York on 22 July. Our hopes once again soared, only to crash to earth with a dull thump – following extensive checks, Lufthansa drew a complete blank.

With each new lead our hopes were raised, only to be plunged into a cavern of despair when they were later disproved, each one a painful turning of the screw. My parents did their utmost to hide their crushing disappointment from Nigel and me but it was all too evident. I would often enter a room to find my mother hurriedly wiping away tears.

In early October, we received the first piece of tangible information which led to a significant breakthrough in discovering Chris and Peta's fate.

Replying to my parents' enquiry of 22 September, the acting harbour master in Belize, A.F. Mahler, wrote that he had reviewed and obtained photocopies of Belizean port records. His reply, dated 29 September, was to prove a vital piece of evidence.

'The latest information I have regarding the *Justin B* is that she sailed from the Port of Dangriga (Stann Creek) in Belize bound for Puerto Cortes, Honduras, on the 26th June. The captain of the boat was an American named Duane Boston. As you can see from the attached photocopies of the ship's clearance from Dangriga on the 26th June, your son and Miss Frampton were members of the crew for this voyage. On the 9th August 1978, the *Justin B* again entered the Port of Dangriga, Belize. Apparently, it had gone to Livingston (Guatemala) directly from Puerto Cortes [the *Justin B* actually never went to Puerto Cortes] and then came on to Dangriga from there. Your son and Miss Frampton were not a part of the crew for this voyage.'

The British Consulate in Guatemala confirmed that the *Justin B* entered Livingston on 6 July with only Boston and his two young sons on board. The commander of the Naval Base in Puerto Cortes, Honduras, reported that the *Justin B* did not enter any of the ports under his jurisdiction. Indeed, there was

CREW LIST

Name	age	Nationality	Occupation
Duane Boston	37	American	Master
Chris Farmer —	25	British	Sailor
Peter Frampton —	24	British	Sailor
Vince Boston	13	American	Sailor
Russell Boston	12	American	Sailor

Duane Boston
C A P T A I N.

The Belizean acting harbour master's report confirming that Chris and Peta had been signed on as crew in Dangriga (Stann Creek) before continuing the journey south down the Belizean coastline.

no trace of Chris and Peta's entry into Honduras at all – the country where, in Belize City, they had spent 86 BH dollars on visas to enter.

This meant that there was no official sighting of Chris and Peta being on board the boat after the *Justin B* set sail from Dangriga (Stann Creek) on 26 June and the last we had heard was in Peta's letter that they were at Hunting Caye. We constantly asked ourselves what could have happened to them. Our thoughts went through every possible scenario as we pursued each line of investigation we could think of to find them.

Exploring the theory that they might be imprisoned, Mary Gutsell, a Foreign Office official, wrote to us to say: 'Our posts in Guatemala and Tegucigalpa (the capital of Honduras) asked the police to make a search for the missing two some time ago. I feel sure, therefore, that we would have heard by now if Chris and Peta were in jail in either country.'

Ruling out any natural disaster, she added: 'I have checked on the dates of Hurricane Greta. This hurricane hit Belize on 18 September (some six weeks after Chris and Peta were known to be on board the boat) and caused considerable damage to property. However, Belize had had 24-hour notice of the advance of the hurricane and consequently there were no fatalities, either on land or at sea. The storm subsequently petered out and did not reach Guatemala or Honduras.'

Our hopes were considerably heightened when, in mid-October, we received a call from the Foreign & Commonwealth Office to say that Boston and his two sons had been traced and located. They had flown from Belize City to Miami on 14 August and from there they had taken a bus to Denver, where Boston purchased a car to drive home to California. Boston was said to be staying with his father, Russell Boston Senior, at his address in Smith's Flat in Placerville, a suburb of Sacramento in Northern California but the boys were reported as not being with him.

We felt sure that it would only be a matter of time before we heard news from Chris and Peta… or the fate that had befallen them. Missing now since the end of June, we never really articulated it, but there was a sense that we were all in our own way coming to terms with the unpalatable fact that they might no longer be alive.

Acting on our grave concerns, the British Foreign & Commonwealth Office instructed an official from the Consulate General in San Francisco to telephone Boston at his father's home on 30 October. Given that Boston was by this time a prime suspect, in hindsight it seems incredible that he should have been interviewed by a British Consulate official, untrained in criminal investigation. At the time, however, we were only too grateful that he was on the radar and that the authorities were doing something about our case. Responding to the official's questions, Boston was reported as saying:

'Yes, I remember Chris and Peta very well. I agreed to take them from Belize to Puerto Cortes in Honduras. We stopped at various islands on the way down but the *Justin B* needed some repairs, so Chris and Peta disembarked at Cabo de Tres Puntas Peninsula across the bay from Livingston in Guatemala to avoid immigration. I can't quite remember but I think they were going to hire a native boat.

'I think I may have seen those two in Livingston boarding a ferry during the second week in July, but I can't be sure it was them. I have no idea where they were heading, it could be San Andres Island or Trinidad, or that they might even have gone to Columbia or Peru.'

On hearing Boston's vague theories, we wondered how someone who had lived with Chris and Peta in the cramped conditions of a small fishing boat for two weeks could disembark them and not know where they were headed. Boston's responses raised more questions than gave answers. The phone call served to alert him to the fact that he was very much under the microscope for Chris and Peta's disappearance.

The Foreign & Commonwealth Office officials, the Framptons and our family were by now highly suspicious of Boston being, if not directly responsible, then certainly heavily implicated in their disappearance and our fears about Chris and Peta no longer being alive were increasing daily.

Convinced of foul play, on the advice of the Foreign & Commonwealth Office, on 30 October my mother and Peta's father went to Greater Manchester Police's divisional quarters in Stretford and reported the circumstances to a Detective Michael Carter. The case was put in the hands of Special Branch Detective Chief Inspector David Sacks. He and my father developed an excellent working relationship, based on mutual trust and respect. At their first meeting, Dad, who had become something of a detective himself, handed CI Sacks all the correspondence he had collated to date, including letters and research from the Foreign & Commonwealth Office, and the Belizian acting harbour master's report. The Framptons also handed over Peta's last two letters.

Over the four months that they had been missing, Dad had kept his own extensive log. In his distinctive black ink writing, he had detailed all the people and agencies he had contacted and in the margins, he had written his own personal thoughts. Sacks made a copy of the documents to keep as a 'working copy' for himself and he said that the most pertinent original documents (we retained some) were lodged with Headquarters Administration Department. Unfortunately, he says he only made one photocopy of my father's log for the Headquarters file and did not take one for himself, saying that most of the information was contained within Dad's witness statements. Sadly, that log has been lost over the years. With Dad dying in 2013, I would have loved to have read his thoughts on the case and included them in my book.

Making the whole process of communication even more protracted was the fact that all of GMP's communication with California was channelled through Interpol in Washington. Interpol is the international intergovernmental police organisation which worked, as it still does today, on an administrative level to promote mutual assistance between police authorities.

Following their telephone conversation with Boston, the British Consulate General in San Francisco was sufficiently convinced that he was implicated in Chris and Peta's disappearance that he arranged for a Consulate official to interview Boston in person. On 3 December, Boston, accompanied by his father, Russell, was interviewed for two hours.

Before the line of questioning moved on to the subject of Chris and Peta, Boston was described as appearing 'calm and relaxed'. However, when questioned about their disappearance, 'Boston sat straight up in the chair, his eyes widened and his breathing became heavy, his chest notably rising and falling. Following this, he slumped back in the chair, placing his face into his right hand, and in a softly spoken voice he said that he thought Chris and Peta would be back home by now.'

The British Consulate General was convinced of his guilt but with no concrete evidence, he said it was difficult to pursue the case. We were dismayed to learn that the investigation had reached an impasse. Chris and Peta were still missing and we had no idea what had happened to them or where they were.

With the dismal news from California, we again started to think about how we could keep their case alive and further the search for them. Following the very helpful letter from the Belizean acting harbour master reporting that Chris and Peter had been on the *Justin B* when it left Dangriga in June, but were not on the boat on its return journey in August, my parents replied, giving him the news that Boston had been traced to Sacramento and asking him for his local knowledge of the customs of the seafaring community on that coastline.

On 8 December my parents received a reply, not from the acting harbour master but this time from the harbour master himself, a Mr W.H. Longsworth, who expressed grave reservations about Boston: 'It is a pity that more definite information could not be gotten from Duane Boston, other than that "he dropped your son and his friend off the boat somewhere along the shore near Livingston" and they "might be hiring a native boat to sail to Columbia or Peru". Although not impossible, it is highly unlikely that Chris and Peta would have been able to hire a native boat to sail to Columbia or Peru from anywhere near Livingston. This gives one the impression that Mr Boston is not telling all that he knows. For my part, I really am not able to offer any further information other than that the *Justin B* has not again entered this country since August. I have been assured by the Customs Authorities in Dangriga (and Punta Gorda, which is the nearest port of entry to Livingston) that I will be contacted immediately should the *Justin B* return to this country. If, or when this happens, I intend to question Mr Boston myself.'

By now, some six months after we had last heard from them, both sets of parents were at the end of their tether. Aged eighteen and in my last year of school, I was still living at home so I witnessed, at close hand, the toll it was taking on my parents. Nigel had married Frances ('Fran') three years earlier and Chris had been his best man at their wedding. Nigel and Fran were living in the bungalow they had built themselves on a small plot of land in the market town of Glossop in Derbyshire. I am sure Mum and Dad shed many tears in private but they continued to do their utmost to hide their grief, although their anguish was etched on their faces.

We all grieve differently but my parents, in their British stiff-upper-lip fashion, felt that it was best to throw their energies into pursuing any conceivable new lines of enquiry rather than give in to the tide of anxiety that threatened to overwhelm them. Both found work was a welcome release from the business of worrying. My mother worked as a doctor's receptionist but didn't afford herself the luxury of taking any time off. Her way of dealing with grief was to take herself off on long dog walks. I stood in awe at the strength and fortitude that both my parents displayed throughout the whole harrowing period.

Everything that could be done was done. Dad employed his journalistic skills to write an article for the *Belize Times*, giving the background to Chris and Peta's disappearance and appealing for information from anyone who might have seen them. Word spread quickly. Reacting to the numerous articles in the British national press which reported them missing, many of Chris's friends got in touch to ask us what they could do to help. Amongst them was Dr Tom Lane (sadly now deceased), whom Peta had planned to stay with in Louisiana whilst Chris went to his short-term medical job in Trinidad. A tall, dark and good-looking American, he was four years older than Chris and Peta. The three of them had struck up a firm friendship when Tom was studying for a PhD at Birmingham University. Moving back to the States, he got a research job at the Louisiana State University Medical Center.

Tom proved to be the most wonderfully faithful friend to them, both in life and death, and helped enormously in our search. He was very distressed about their disappearance and, like my parents, he wrote to Boston on 19 December 1978, asking for information and saying: 'All of Peta and Chris's friends and relatives are raising money to try to find them or to find out what has happened to them.' His letter went unanswered. Tom also enlisted the help of an amateur radio ham operator to broadcast to Central America appealing for information on their whereabouts.

In December, frustrated that the investigation had seemingly stalled, Tom, the Framptons and my parents clubbed together to enlist the services of Alphonso de Peña, a Belizian friend of Tom's, to act as a private investigator. Living in Belize City, Alphonso was familiar with the territory and all the popular tourist haunts. Such was the level of our anxiety and the lack of any forthcoming information, both families felt it was the only resource open to us.

Equipped with photographs of Chris and Peta, Alphonso visited hotels and tourist haunts, jails and the ports in and around Livingston, Puerto Barrios and Santo Tomás de Castilla and the Cabo de Tres Puntas Peninsula where Boston had told the British Consulate he had set them down.

Christmas arrived and we went through the motions of celebrating but the decorations, like our spirits, were lacklustre and half-hearted. I remember sitting down to lunch with Mum, Dad, Nigel and Fran, and Chris's absence was writ large. It was unspoken, but we all knew, had they been alive and well, if ever there was an occasion when they would have been in touch, this would have been it. This was, after all, the Christmas that Chris had said he would be home for. In his last cassette recording in

June, sent from Oaxaca, Mexico, he told us he had bought an air ticket back to London that had to be used by April 1979, but he would like to be home for Christmas.

By now frustrated by the case's lack of movement and frantic with worry, Dad traced a phone number for Boston in Placerville, California. Making international phone calls was not an easy procedure for the police in 1978. Permission had to be sought, incurring a lot of red tape, so in a move that seems unbelievable nowadays, Chief Inspector David Sacks gave his permission for Dad to make the international call on his own from home. My father, being a journalist, recorded the conversation.

On 10 January 1979, my father made the call and Boston's father, Russell, answered and said his son wasn't available. His deep, gravelly voice with its slow drawl boomed down the phone, his laconic tone uncaring and nonchalant. On establishing who my father was, Russell complained about how his neighbours were talking and upsetting him because the deputy sheriff had made it known that his son, Duane, was wanted for questioning. He seemed more concerned about his standing in the neighbourhood than the fact that Chris and Peta were missing and his son might have information that could trace them. My father asked him a number of questions but he was obstructive and unhelpful and claimed to know little about the Belizean voyage despite having accompanied Boston to the interview conducted by the Consulate General in December. When asked whether his son was contactable, he replied vaguely that he was somewhere 'up north', with no phone number or address, although he let slip that he himself could get in touch with him. Dad requested that Russell ask his son to phone him in England via 'collect' (American for 'reverse charge call') with the utmost urgency.

Receiving no call from Boston, my father wrote to him at his father's address on 17 January, requesting answers to a list of questions. We were not surprised to receive no reply but every box had to be ticked. We were all shocked and taken by surprise when out of the blue, Boston rang my father via 'collect' at home on 25 January. Sounding much like his father, Boston's voice had a gravelly drawl, with an arrogant intonation and dismissive tone.

Summoning his wits, Dad tried to remain as objective in his questioning as possible. Boston replied: 'Yes, I remember them. I spoke to someone at the British Consul and told them all about Chris and Peta.'

'Where did you land them?'

'Near Puerto Barrios in Guatemala.'

'What sort of coastline?'

'Beach.'

'How were they dressed?'

'I can't just remember – jeans or something.'

'Had Chris got his medical bag?'

'His what?'

'Well, Chris was a medical doctor and as he was going on to another medical appointment he would have his medical bag.'

'No, a duffle bag.'

'Were they all right for money?'

'They seemed to be all right.'

'Had they got their air tickets to the USA?'

'I wouldn't know.'

'Any idea where they might have stayed, if not in hotels in Livingston?'

'I expect they caught a ferry.'

'Do you know who might have posted the letter on 18 July?'

'No.'

'Any mention of Chris going to Trinidad and Peta going to New Orleans?'

'Might have been mentioned in discussion. They intended to sail to Costa Rica but they were in no hurry.'

'We understand that you had some trouble with the boat, it was damaged?'

'Yes, the mast was split.'

'How? Gale damage?'

'Yes.'

'Where was this?'

'Off Puerto Barrios.'

'You were at Hunting Caye on 29 June, when did you drop them off?'

'I dropped them off somewhere between 3 to 6 July, I don't remember.'

'We have records showing you entered Livingston on the 6th.'

'Don't remember, but if you say so.'

'Whereabouts were you seen by a fisherman?'

'I don't remember any fisherman.'

'Were they clear about their next destination?'

'They were travelling to Mexico, then changed to go to Costa Rica.'

'Do you still have the boat's log or any details of the trip?'

'No.'

'How would you expect them to get into Livingston?'

'Hire a dory.' [A small, flat-bottomed lightweight boat.]

'If they had not gone through normal immigration channels in Livingston, what problems would they have arriving in Honduras?'

'Everybody does it.'

'How would they get into Guatemala if there are no entry stamps on their passports?'

'No questions are asked.'

'Had they mentioned going to Peru or Columbia?'

'Just talk and mention of San Andreas.'

'Did they pay for their time on board?'

'Yes, $500.'

(At the time, this was said to be a ridiculously high figure, considering they had signed on as crew and Chris did much of the sailing and navigation. Half this figure would have been more than sufficient, even had they been passengers. My father calculated that they could have had anything between £500 and £1,000 in currency in their joint possession at this time, so one presumes Boston stole all their money and was using this as an excuse.)

'Have you any idea what might have happened to them?'

'No.'

'There is no trace of them ever having been in Livingston, except your report of seeing them on a ferry.'

'Oh, I guess I saw them around 9 July boarding a ferry, but when I had walked round, they had gone. Let me know if you hear anything about them.'

It was a very unsatisfactory and disturbing phone call. My father was left with the strong impression that Boston was concealing the truth and was very much responsible for their disappearance. It only served to heighten our worries even more. The burning question was, who posted Peta's last letter? None of today's sophisticated DNA testing existed in 1978 and saliva tests carried out on the airmail letter/envelope for blood grouping unfortunately proved inconclusive.

At the end of January 1979, there was a major breakthrough

in the case. This time it emanated from Guatemala but it was far from being the news we had hoped for.

Our private investigator, Alphonso de Peña, in the course of conducting his enquiries, had by pure chance met a Catholic priest in Livingston called Father Gerry of the Claretian Fathers based in Santo Tomás de Castilla. He related how, when visiting Punta de Manabique, he had heard a story from the previous July that local fishermen had made the grisly discovery of two unidentified bodies, some 200m off the Guatemalan peninsula of Cabo Tres Puntas.

With its white sandy beaches, Punta de Manabique [on the peninsula's northern tip and on a direct sea route from Hunting Caye to Livingston] is one of Guatemala's least visited and most stunningly beautiful areas, and was declared a wildlife reserve in 1999. Twenty kilometres north of Puerto Barrios, it is off the beaten track and tourists are few and far between. Father Gerry told Alphonso: 'They were male and female in their mid-twenties and thought to be American or European because of their westernised clothing. Seeing their floating corpses, local fishermen alerted the deputy mayor of Punta de Manabique, who ordered the naval base in Santo Tomás to employ the services of a diver to lift their bodies out of the water as they were anchored to large motor engine parts which were at the bottom of the sea. The ropes that they had been bound and hog-tied with had come loose, allowing their decomposing bodies to float to the surface.

'The bodies were brought ashore at the dock of the Marines at Santo Tomás and from there, they were taken to the Puerto Barrios Hospital amphitheatre for a post-mortem, which was carried out on 10th July. The locals were disturbed at seeing the hideously tortured bodies lying on the dockside and felt it would bring them bad luck, so, following the post-mortem, they were quickly buried, unidentified, in two graves in Puerto Barrios Cemetery.'

Alphonso, unsure of how to break this news to us and with no conclusive proof it was Chris and Peta, decided to go through the official channels. He informed the British Consul in Guatemala City, who immediately made further inquiries and via telegram informed the British Foreign & Commonwealth Office in London. They, in turn, notified Greater Manchester Police.

Although at this time there appeared to be only circumstantial evidence to suggest it was Chris and Peta, [the corpses' American/European appearance and the tallying of Chris and Peta's last-known location with where they were found], the police felt that my parents and the Framptons should be informed immediately.

1 February 1979 remains vivid for me. Finishing school, I went to a telephone call box in Wilmslow town centre to say that I was going to a friend's house so I would be late home for supper. Mum answered in a faltering, noticeably distressed voice and said that I must come home straight away. No other words were needed, her sobbing said it all.

Reeling from the phone call and with everything and everyone I passed a blur, I walked the two-mile journey home. Alone in the dark winter night, I grappled with the fact that they were dead and I would never see them again. The world felt like it was spinning on its axis at breakneck speed and in freefall.

Wiping away my tears and taking a deep breath, I let myself in with my door key. Entering the house, I was met with a deafening hush and a palpable sense of utter desolation. As I entered the front room, my eyes caught the happy photograph of Chris at his graduation that was given pride of place on the mantelpiece and the thought flickered through my head, there will be no more photographs. My parents were sitting with Nigel, their heads bowed. Their traumatised, ashen faces said it all. I embraced each of them but there was little that any of us could say to each other; my family was diminished. The four of us knocked back a bottle of sherry (the only alcohol we had in the house) to try and anaesthetise ourselves to the searing pain of loss.

My father had taken the harrowing phone call from Greater Manchester Police that afternoon and had called Mum at work to tell her that, subject to formal examination, we should prepare ourselves for the fact that two bodies had been found and 'were most likely to be that of Chris and Peta'.

We all knew it was them. By the law of averages how many missing white Caucasian couples can there be in that area? We rationalised that the Foreign & Commonwealth Office would not have told us, had there been any doubt. Despite the fact they'd been missing since June 1978, and blunt logic told us they were most likely dead, when the news came, it was devastating. It was the full-stop finality that we had all subliminally been dreading but never dared to articulate. The question 'why?' hung in the air but there were no longer any ifs, buts or maybes. Chris and Peta were dead and we were facing the fact that they weren't ever coming home.

It was one of life's defining moments and we knew it would never be the same again. The old life of being a family of five had gone and nothing within our power could ever bring it back. That was history and the present and the future looked bleak and frightening. We prepared for the worst and withdrew into ourselves, each of us grieving in our own different way.

DEAD IN THE WATER

The Foreign & Commonwealth Office asked the Guatemalan Consul for further information and on 6 February 1979, they received a second telegram saying that the Honorary Consul in Puerto Barrios had obtained a copy of the *Bomberos'* (ambulance service) report, describing the recovery of the bodies on 8 July 1978, and the two autopsy reports. The doctor had been unable to make a detailed forensic examination because of the advanced stage of decomposition. Although the height of the bodies accorded with Chris and Peta, they could only be positively identified if the bodies were exhumed and a comparison made with dental records.

Both families immediately got down to the heart-wrenching business of arranging for their dental records from Birmingham University Dental Department to be flown out to the British Embassy in Guatemala. Each family paid the requisite sum of £442.55 for the exhumation of their child's body and the certificate that would prove unequivocally it was them.

Weeks turned into months and it was nine weeks before the exhumation of both bodies was carried out at Guatemala's Puerto Barrios Cemetery on 10 April 1979.

We had no knowledge when we would eventually receive the news and the days dragged interminably. Not hearing anything, my parents booked a break to get away from the drudgery of waiting for the phone to ring.

The *coup de grâce* was, of course, delivered when Mum, Dad and I were in Portugal. It was late afternoon on day two of our seven-day trip to the Algarve when, on returning to my parents' hotel room, we heard the phone ringing loudly. My father took the call: it was the British Consul in Lisbon. Mum and I watched as he struggled to remain composed. The colour draining from his face, he slowly sat down on the bed. His voice trembling, he tried at the same time to be matter of fact and thanked the Consul for letting him know. Putting down the receiver, no words were needed – we knew that there had been a positive identification of both bodies.

The Consul apologised for the exhumations and post-mortems taking so long but the macabre task had been made even more so by the fact that three other bodies were exhumed in error – the stakes, which marked the plots of unidentified bodies, were removed each time the grass was cut so they found it hard to locate Chris and Peta's graves. Such is the high death rate in Guatemala this was, even in the 1970s, an already over-crowded cemetery and the numbers on the graves often got mixed up. A positive identification had been made by a Guatemalan dental surgeon Dr Gustavo Berger Reyes. His report and the British and Guatemalan dental charts were then handed to Dr James Holt, a Consultant Dental Surgeon in Manchester University Dental Hospital. His own report, dated 8 June, confirmed Dr Reyes' findings.

Not only did we receive the news that the bodies were those of Chris and Peta but it was also officially confirmed that both showed signs of brutal torture. The Foreign & Commonwealth Office wanted to spare us the details but my parents insisted on knowing everything. Chris and Peta had been bound by the hands, legs and ankles and weighted down with motor engine parts. Their bodies had come loose from the ropes as they decomposed. Peta was described as having a plastic bag over her head, tied by string at the neck. The post-mortem revealed that they had both been alive when they entered the water and death occurred from drowning.

My parents discussed flying home and curtailing the so-called holiday but there was nothing further to be done. We spent the remaining days trying to make sense of the shocking details that were now our reality. Why would anyone want to kill them and for goodness' sake, torture them? Our hotel rooms looked out on the great expanse of the Atlantic Ocean, serving as a constant reminder, as if any were needed, that they had died by drowning in the sea.

To reinforce the ghastly news, waiting for us on our return to the UK was a copy of the *Bomberos'* report bearing a graphic description of the recovery of their bodies the previous July:

'At the request of the Justice of the Peace of this port, we were transported by a unit of the Marines to Punta de Manabique. On arrival at the place mentioned we became aware that approximately 200m from the beach two corpses were floating in the sea. We had to go into the water, since we had already attempted to lift them from the deck of a small boat supplied by local commissioners. When we were in the water we became aware that one of them, the male, was wearing a blue canvas jacket and blue shorts, the body was decomposed and we could not obtain major details of complexion, hair, face, etc. This corpse had its hands bound behind the back and legs and ankles were also bound; round the neck it had a yellow nylon string 15m long tied to a "shock-block" [part of the engine of an automobile]. It has signs of torture. The other corpse, the female, was wearing a green T-shirt, no brassière, green shorts, and was also decomposed. Her hands were bound in the back as were her legs and ankles and from the string in the bottom of the sea hung part of the engine of an automobile commonly called *Espejo con toda y su corona*. She had a plastic bag covering her head, as a hood, tied around her neck, and it was observed that her hair was blonde, her approximate age was between 15 and 18 years, 1.65m high. After picking up the bodies, they were taken from Punta de Manabique to the dock of the Marines at Santo Tomás and from there to the Puerto Barrios National Amphitheatre in unit 78 of this company.'

Opening the next official-looking envelope, my parents discovered the two autopsy reports by Dr Angel María Vásquez Cuéllar who said that his examination on 10 July was made particularly difficult due to the severe decomposition of the bodies which had actually worsened since the bodies were taken from the water. It would seem that they were not refrigerated whilst awaiting post mortem and in fact we did hear later that their bodies were left on the dockside for a period of time, awaiting collection:

'Unidentified female corpse, young adult whose age isn't calculated due to the advanced state of decomposition, wearing no dress and covered with only a white nylon panty. [It would seem that at some point between recovery of the bodies and the autopsy, some of Peta's clothes had been removed.] Her height was approximately 1.65m and weight approximately 50–55 kilos. She had fish bites over her body and the aspect of the corpse was monstrous. The examination of the visceras shows congestion of the lungs, and upon cutting, dropped fetid foamy blood serum. The efficient cause of death was recorded as asphyxia by submersion.

'Unidentified male corpse of approximately 65 kilos of weight and 1.67m tall; young adult whose age cannot be calculated by the advanced stage of decomposition; his aspect is monstrous and has fish bites over his body. From the examination of the visceras is reported a lung congestion with intra-lung blood material. The efficient cause of death was recorded as asphyxia by submersion.'

I think the true enormity of their deaths hit me personally

when, a couple of weeks after receiving the news, I entered the kitchen, where Mum was going through the motions of preparing supper. She turned to me and wiping away the burning tears that were coursing down her face, she said: 'I don't feel that I will ever be able to feel true happiness again. The best part of my life is over.' As an eighteen-year-old, hearing such despair from a parent was heart-wrenching. What possible words of comfort could I offer?

My dear, optimistic mum, who always tries to find some positivity in any situation, no matter how grim, did her best to recover her composure and said: 'At least I now know what happened to them and I can stop thinking that one day Chris will walk back in.' For a while I know that she had kidded herself that he was working abroad but one day there would be a knock at the door and he would once more be a part of our lives. Endlessly wishing and hoping can be soul-destroying so now that all hope was gone, we could at least begin the process of moving forward.

Both sets of parents requested that they should be reburied in the British cemetery in Guatemala City, where the graves would be tended and cared for, but we were denied even this small crumb of comfort. Under a bizarre Guatemalan law, no corpse was allowed to be removed for reburial elsewhere until four years after the first burial. Working tirelessly on our behalf, the British Consul sought special dispensation but it was refused.

Chris and Peta were interred within close proximity to each other in plots 58 and 59 of Puerto Barrios Cemetery in Guatemala. Dr Reyes had kindly made a rough sketch of the cemetery for the Framptons and us which he sent with his dental report confirming identification. The simple but very poignant sketch shows the two graves 'he' and 'she'. In the absence of any photographs or any contact in Guatemala, this simple line drawing helped both families visualise Chris and Peta's last resting place.

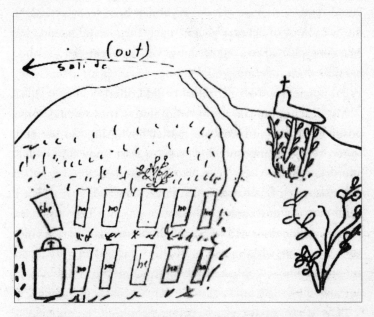

Sketch map of the graveyard in Puerto Barrios, with 'He' and 'She' highlighting Chris and Peta's graves.

We asked for two crosses to be made, bearing their names (the mason unfortunately misspelt Peta's surname) and their birth and death dates. The crude, locally made crosses marked two pitifully small mounds in a bleak, desolate cemetery in a distant country, many thousands of miles away from home. Together since the age of fourteen, it was fitting that Chris and Peta should lie close to each other in death.

Just as their bodies had been buried, so too had any evidence, including the motor engine parts and ropes that had been lashed around their bodies. As far as we know, after the naval diver cut their bodies free from the heavy engine parts, no attempt was made to recover the weights from the seabed. Incredibly, the crime was never investigated by the local police and the story never made the papers. Had their bodies been recovered in the British colony of Belize, it is more likely their deaths would have been investigated and reported, but Guatemala at that time had no diplomatic relations with Britain.

Writing a report on 30 August 1979 for the Sacramento Police Department to aid their investigation into Boston, Greater Manchester Police's Detective Chief Inspector David Sacks said: 'Little or no investigation of what was a cruel and brutal double murder appears to have taken place and our own efforts to obtain the assistance of the Guatemalan Police have only met with the minimum response. Indeed, a large amount of cash was requested by the Guatemalan authorities from the bereaved parents in order to finance the commencement of this investigation. Of course, no money was sent. Most of the information has been obtained through the British Embassy in Guatemala City at our request.

'The death of these two young people is undoubtedly a tragic waste of life and we find ourselves in a helpless position without the effective co-operation of the police in Guatemala. The political situation between Belize and Guatemala lends no support to this situation. It can only inhibit the trained investigator where interviews have already taken place by untrained interrogators. Despite these handicaps and the shortfall in detail, it will be greatly appreciated if Boston could be interviewed in greater depth about the deaths.

'Boston is highly suspected because of the circumstances. It would also seem apparent that Boston's two young sons will be able to give vital information for, or against Boston, and it is highly desirable that they too are interviewed.'

Sacks asked permission to go over to California to assist the police in their enquiries but this was refused by his boss.

On 15 September 1979, Peta's family held a small memorial service for her in the picturesque East Woodlands Church in Frome, Somerset. It's a special family church where her parents were married and where she and her siblings were christened. Her Mum and Dad had arranged for the unveiling of a commemorative brass wall plaque in her name.

Gathering in the rural eighteenth-century churchyard under a leaden autumn sky, the small melancholic party constituted her parents, Sammie and John, her three brothers (Blaise, Toby and Justin) and her older sister, Rocki, and her husband, John Mills, plus a scattering of friends and my family. Celebrating the life of a much-loved twenty-four-year-old woman who had so much to live for but had died so tragically was never going to be anything other than sombre and heart-wrenching. We all struggled to hold back the tears and feebly, we went through the motions of singing Peta's favourite hymns. Reading the dates of her birth and approximate death on the commemorative brass plaque was a stark reminder that she and Chris had lived brief lives and were now gone from us for ever.

The poignant ceremony over, our heads bowed, we trailed silently out of the pews and towards the door of the dimly lit church. As the old oak door creaked open, the daylight streamed in. We gathered in a huddle in the churchyard, with its centuries-old crumbling gravestones. The graves lay in the shadow of a line of ancient oak trees that stood like sentinels, watching the enactment of life's milestones and final acts.

During the service there had been a brief rain shower and the air was now heavy with the scent of late flowering Old English roses, interspersed with phlox, woodbine and Michaelmas daisies, which spilled out of the flowerbeds. The clouds had parted and the dappled autumn sun shone down. The quintessentially English rustic setting served to emphasise the distance between us and Chris and Peta, who were now lying in some distant, very foreign land that none of us, until the recent tragic events, had barely even heard of.

Conversation was muted and difficult – there was so very little to say. Chris and Peta had left England with such excitement and high hopes but their journey had ended in the most horrific and inexplicable of circumstances and 14 months on, we still had no answers.

Any religious beliefs that my parents might once have held were now well and truly expunged by the senseless tragedy that had befallen Chris and they decided against holding any kind of church ceremony: religion was well and truly dead in our family and had no place. Instead, my parents arranged for a carved wooden chair, with a small plaque bearing Chris's name and dates on the back, to be placed in the Queen Elizabeth post-graduate Medical School in Birmingham.

My family received many letters of condolence but friends and acquaintances were often at a loss for words and found it too awkward to talk. Some avoided meeting my parents entirely. Mum said that if she had learnt one thing from losing Chris, it was that when someone dies, it is best to acknowledge that death rather than ignore it, no matter how difficult or awkward it is to face. The most meaningful card she received was from a friend who wrote: 'I'm so very sorry.' To Mum, those four simple words meant more than any outpouring of fancy prose and platitudes.

Chapter Seven

HEADWINDS

In the unlawful killing of a loved one, there's an inclination to go one of two ways – either sink into inertia and despondency, or put all of one's energy and waking hours into finding answers. My family fell very much into the last category. Far from accepting the shocking news of Chris and Peta's murders as a fait accompli, their response was to redouble their efforts to seek justice and so they threw themselves into the task, body and soul.

With the advent of the internet and the widespread use of mobile phones, it's hard to appreciate just how difficult that was. Back in the 1970s, most international communication was painstakingly carried out by letter with the occasional, poorly connected, very expensive long-distance telephone call. Communications with America were difficult enough, but with Central America they proved nigh on impossible.

There was now a firm conviction, shared by us, the Framptons, the Foreign Office and the Greater Manchester Police, that Boston was wholly responsible for their deaths.

DEAD IN THE WATER

The harbour master had confirmed that Chris and Peta were signed on as crew for the *Justin B*'s voyage on 26 June 1978 from Dangriga (Stann Creek) but they were not on board when the boat put into Livingston, Guatemala, on 6 July.

A Punta Gorda fisherman reported that he had seen the *Justin B* disabled on 5 July, heading for Livingston, and only Boston was sighted as being on board. Presumably, his sons had been ordered to stay below in the galley.

The location of the bodies tallied exactly with where the *Justin B* was known to be sailing at that time. Peta's last letter to her mother referred to the tensions onboard the boat, with the two boys constantly squabbling and Boston losing his temper with them. In her letter she said that they were at Hunting Caye on 29 June but the letter was postmarked 18 July from Livingston, Guatemala. It had always been her custom to add a postscript to her letters if she had been unable to post them at the time, even if it were one or two days' gap. It is unthinkable that she would not have done so after 19 days.

Boston did not carry out his plan to go down to Costa Rica and sell the *Justin B* as Peta, in her letter to her mother, had claimed was the stated aim in travelling south. Instead, he docked in Livingston on 6 July. On 19 July, he then turned around and sailed back up north again along the Belizean coastline, returning to the port of Dangriga (Stann Creek) on 9 August. This is where Chris and Peta had last been sighted in June and were recorded by the harbour master as being on board as crew and from where they had picked up the ballast that Peta refers to in her letter.

We learnt from the Foreign & Commonwealth Office that Boston and his two sons then sailed on further north to Belize City. Very suspiciously, he changed the *Justin B*'s name and sold the boat on 14 August before flying to Miami and returning overland to California in late August.

Discrepancies had begun to creep into the two interviews that Boston gave to the British Consul and my father. To the Consul, he maintained that he had put them ashore on the Cabo de Tres Puntas Peninsula and to my father, near Puerto Barrios. Either way, the story didn't stack up because the coastline is largely jungle down to the beach and at that time there were no access roads down to the coast.

Their tortured bodies were weighted down with heavy engine gears and they were located 200m offshore, suggesting they were killed aboard a boat. Death was by drowning. It is inconceivable that, had they been put ashore, as Boston maintained, someone would have bothered to take them out to sea to kill them.

Like scenes from a silent thriller on repeat, various scenarios played out in our minds of how Chris and Peta could have been apprehended, tied up and killed at the hands of one man. Was the motive financial, sexual or a moment of hot headed anger, metered out under the relentless burning Caribbean sun, or maybe a combination of all three? And where were the boys when it happened? Were they ashore or did it happen under the cloak of darkness?

Our belief that Boston was responsible was confirmed when Interpol informed us of some staggering news. Boston's third wife, Mary Lou (mother of the two boys on the boat) had disappeared in September 1968 in Sacramento some ten years before Chris and Peta were killed, and was untraceable. We were incredulous to hear this latest news and it took some time to assimilate.

Many years later, Boston's younger son Russell was to describe to me what he remembered about events during this period on his side of the Atlantic. On his arrival back in his hometown of Sacramento in Northern California in late August, Boston became paranoid that the authorities would interview his sons about the events in Belize so he moved them between the care of his mother at her home in Roseville, a suburb in the northeast of Sacramento, and his father who lived with his second wife, Carmen, about 37 miles away to the east in Placerville.

It wasn't long before Boston started to come under scrutiny for Chris and Peta's murders. Following our contact with the Foreign & Commonwealth Office, the British Consulate in San Francisco traced him and started the process of interviewing him in October (as previously described), but by spring of 1979, convinced of his guilt, they placed the case in the hands of the police and Interpol. Such was their interest in him that Boston's lawyer accused them of harassment.

Russell recalls: 'My dad told me that an officer working on behalf of Interpol had informed him that Chris and Peta's bound bodies had been washed up with weights attached to them. The locals found them and were scared, so they buried the bodies in haste but then word got out and made it to the authorities, who dug up the bodies. At that time there was a missing persons report for them so they found out who they were. They found out that my dad was the last person to see them on his boat. They came to my grandfather's house in Placerville where we were living at the time, and took dad to lunch a couple of times. It was a police officer from Scotland Yard or Interpol, or maybe both, I am not sure. (No one, as far as we were made aware, flew from England to interview Boston.)They asked my dad what he knew about Chris and Peta.

'The officers who were questioning him were being really nice to him and asked him if he would be interested in showing them the last place that he saw them alive. They offered to fly him down to Guatemala so he could show them himself. My dad said no, he didn't want to go back down there. My dad assumed that the police knew he was responsible but that there wasn't enough evidence to extradite him. As long as he didn't go down there, he believed he was fine. He showed them on a map where he had last seen them, so for them to say they would fly him down there to show them, there would be nothing to be gained. I believe they were trying to get Dad down there to be further interrogated or do something to make him confess.'

In May 1979, 10 months after killing Chris and Peta, I learnt from Russell that Boston fled Sacramento to get away from the mounting police interest in him. He took with him not just Vince and Russell, but also his four-year-old son, Justin, from his marriage to his previous wife, Kathe. She had divorced him three years before in a very acrimonious split. Filled with jealousy and wanting to spite her, he abducted Justin. He took the three children all over including Shasta Trinity Alps National Forest, to the north of Sacramento, Colorado, Bishop in Inyo County, Los Angeles, and then Lake Tahoe National Forest in the Sierra Nevada Mountains. Since the 1800s the Boston family had a claim to an old goldmine called Last Chance, located in the desolate Lake Tahoe Wilderness, where there was some property and old cabins and he was familiar with this territory.

Russell recalls that summer of 1979 well and described to me what happened next: 'We were at Last Chance, in the middle of nowhere, with no phones, no communication and the only contact we had with the outside world was through our grandfather, who would drive out to bring us food. Without our welfare cheques coming in, he was our only source of income.

My grandfather realised that it was a hopeless situation and that he needed to take control. He negotiated a deal with Kathe, whereby she agreed to drop all charges against my dad for the safe return of her son Justin.'

With the winter approaching, Boston slowly began to accept that it wasn't a well-conceived plan to have three young kids in tow and his father's offer sounded a good one. After six months of hiding out, in October 1979 he finally returned Justin to Kathe in return for the piece of paper that she had signed absolving him of all charges for the abduction of their child. Boston thought the case was done and dusted and that would be the last he heard of it, but it wasn't.

Some sixteen months on, Boston and Russell were living with his now sixth wife, an Irish woman called Angela and her two children, Mia and Kevin, in Shingle Springs, Placerville. Boston had already shown her his dark, evil side by drunkenly damaging her previous home, vandalising it and spray-painting the walls with profanities. He had driven to Los Angeles and slandered her in front of her ex-husband to try to convince him to take the children away from her, simply as a way to cause her pain and distress.

Russell recalls one memorable night in February 1981: 'I was watching TV with Mia and Kevin. The phone rang and I answered it. The voice demanded to talk to Dad. I said he was busy, because he had already gone to bed. They said it was the police, the house was surrounded and they wanted Dad to come out with his hands in the air. I thought it was a prank call, so I opened the front door and looked outside. Even though it was dark, I could see dozens of police officers hiding behind pretty much every tree, building and car. It was several police departments and possibly SWAT [Special Weapons and Tactics team, in the US, a group of highly trained police officers who specialise in high-risk tasks]. It was a huge production!

'I shouted to Dad, who came out of his bedroom wearing only a pair of jeans, and he took the phone off me. They instructed him to come to the front door with his hands up. Then, with the loudspeaker, they told him to slowly back out onto the porch, turn around and make his way to the middle of the front yard. They tackled him and he fell into a bunch of poison oak and was yelling at them to stop as they put the handcuffs on him.'

That night in February 1981, the San Rafael Police Department in Marin County arrested Boston for a warrant that had been issued for abducting Justin in 1979. It wasn't for the murders of Chris and Peta. Even though he had safely returned Justin to Kathe, the police warrant was still active. He was then released on bail and the case was subsequently dismissed after his lawyer contacted Kathe's lawyer and the piece of paper (in the deal made between his father and Kathe) was duly produced. This exonerated him from all abduction charges. Spending two weeks in jail he was questioned about what had happened in Belize but they were unable to extract a confession or even progress the case. So, after his brief flirtation with the law in 1981 he was once again a free man!

* * *

Back in England, we were grateful for any scraps of information we could source but news was thin on the ground. Following the British Consulate in San Francisco interviewing Boston on his return to California in autumn 1978, we were told that he was interviewed by the police but we were given no details, and by the spring he had disappeared off the radar and couldn't be found.

September 1979, I left to go to Lancaster University to study

English Literature but I frequently returned home at weekends and holidays. One year on from their deaths, we had begun to pick up the pieces of everyday life, although there was always a tangible sense of melancholy. Mum and Dad made sure that Nigel and I didn't wallow in the sadness of it all, but of course the question of what had happened to Chris and Peta and the unanswered question of why, was never far from our minds. We all wrestled in our own individual ways in coming to terms with how to get our lives back when there was no closure or justice.

My father, an intensely private person, threw himself into working even longer hours than normal. Having left the BBC, he was head hunted to work for a government quango called the Distributive Industrial Training Board. He was responsible for designing and then running a television studio and establishing the professional technical standards for the use of videos in government training. Mum still worked tirelessly as a doctor's receptionist but for her, solace came from going on long walks with the family dog. Both my parents continued to devise ways of keeping the case alive, writing letters to anyone and everyone they could think of who had links with it.

Totally frustrated by the case's lack of progress, in January 1980 my mother wrote very pointedly to Boston at his father's address in Placerville, asking if he had any 'theories' about Chris and Peta's fate:

'It is perhaps useless to go over old ground, but Peta's family and ours have suffered enormously as a consequence of some callous and cold-blooded killer. We can only hope that whoever is responsible suffers in a similar manner, and if he has children, it is to be wondered what he would feel if such a monstrous fate should befall his own son or daughter. I am sure you will be as appalled as we are and will join us in wishing that whoever is responsible receives the torment of the damned. We hope most fervently that he may never have a moment of peace from his conscience, until he too comes to as violent and cruel a death as his victims.'

There was no reply and in fact we received no more news about Boston from either Greater Manchester Police or California throughout the whole of 1980.

That summer, I spent my university vacation island hopping around Greece. After such a tragedy had befallen our family, the expected response from my parents might have been to lower the portcullis, but instead they displayed an enormous amount of self-control in not clipping my wings.

So having received no news from California for almost two years, out of the blue on 26 February 1981 our spirits were raised. My parents received a letter from San Rafael PD saying that Boston was in custody for child abduction. The letter didn't mention Justin by name, only that it was for the kidnapping of 'one of his children that wasn't on the boat'. We were nonetheless jubilant... with Boston in custody we had every expectation that our case would now receive a proper and in-depth investigation.

Little over one year after the murders, CI David Sacks had been moved off the case and assigned to take temporary charge of the Special Branch Unit at Manchester Airport. Such was the depth of trust and confidence he had in my father and wanting to push the case forward with as much urgency as possible, in the light of this unexpected communication from America, he wrote a letter to the San Rafael Police Department saying:

Mr Farmer, an ex-journalist and medical student is a highly intelligent, well-educated and well-balanced individual with a pleasant personality... I found that I was able to take Mr Farmer into my confidence almost completely – far more than would normally be the case with a bereaved parent in such an unpleasant matter. I found him completely trustworthy. Whether you enter into any direct communication with him is a matter for yourselves, of course, but I would urge you to certainly take note of the points he will undoubtedly raise in any letters he sends to your department. He in fact asked me if I, or anyone would be likely to object to his writing. Frankly, if it could assist to detect this brutal double killing, I could see no logical objection, and gave him your details and address as requested.

On Sacks's recommendation, in his absence, Mum and Dad became the main point of contact. It seemed that just as my parents had made all the enquiries during the first four months of them missing, once again they were the ones now actively involved in trying to keep the case alive. After Sacks moved onto other duties in early 1980 dad and he still kept in tentative touch but no one person at Greater Manchester Police or Interpol took the case over that my parents were aware of. They were told, however, that the case would never be closed until the murderer had been apprehended.

My father immediately sat down to reply to San Rafael Police Department saying: 'We do not know whether during your questioning of Boston, you have reached a consideration as to whether to raise the issue of Dr Farmer and Miss Frampton. If you believe any further information we might have, even if circumstantial, rather than proven fact, could be of use in your questioning, we would be glad to co-operate fully. If there is a question of a further charge, both my wife and I will travel to the

USA and assist you in any way we can. Is it possible under US law for you to question the two children, supposedly his, that were on board the boat over the crucial days?'

The next piece of news we received was in a letter from San Rafael Police Department in March, from Detective Sergeant James Kelly, who was tasked by Interpol to interview Boston about the events in Belize whilst they had him in custody. It would appear they received very little help from Interpol in Washington – their only contact was conducted through teletype and Kelly says he never actually spoke with anyone. He says he received copies of Peta's letters but never received the originals which he believed were held by Interpol. Vince and Russell, who were now aged 16 and 15 were never interviewed.

It was during this interview that Boston gave another version of events: 'Leaving Hunting Caye, the weather was bad so we tied the *Justin B* up whilst we waited for the weather to clear. A boat came past with two natives on board, heading for Puerto Barrios. Chris and Peta disembarked and went on this other boat as it was going to be quicker to reach their destinations.'

Boston said that he had no idea who could have committed the murders, and making light of it, he added that this type of violent crime is very common in Central America. He said that during his time down there, he had seen numerous acts of violence which seemed to be a way of life for Guatemalans.

It was with little surprise that we read: 'Boston has an extensive record dating back to 1961. He's been arrested for disturbing the peace, assault, burglary (several counts), possession of stolen property, carrying a concealed firearm and rape. It is also my understanding that Mr Boston was a main suspect in a homicide investigation in Sacramento approximately 13 years ago. This investigation extended from the disappearance of his second wife [an error, this was in fact his third wife and the boys' mother, Mary Lou] who has never been found.'

At the end of the letter, our hearts sank to read: 'Boston is presently out on bail pending charges.'

Sergeant Kelly asked my father what questions he would like them to ask on our behalf. He sat down that night and wrote an extensive report and a series of questions for Sergeant Kelly to present to Boston. Dad added: 'Due to the long-distance investigations in Belize and Guatemala, and the non-existence of sophisticated forensic evidence being available, we realise that it is extremely doubtful whether a successful case could be brought against a suspect, unless there is some sort of admission.'

Dad requested a further update to the case and again asked whether Boston's sons could be interviewed to see if they could corroborate any of his version of events. Poignantly, he concluded: 'I am writing to you in this detail as you are most likely the only law enforcement officer in the world who is in a position to progress any enquiries regarding this case.'

Mum describes the endless waiting for further news: 'We felt like we were operating in a vacuum. California, seemed so remote and every communication took so long that by the time we received any answers, they were out of date.'

Indeed, it was six months before we heard from the police in Sacramento again when, in mid-August 1981, we received a letter dated 29 July from Sergeant Kelly: 'I would like to bring you up to date in regards to my involvement with Silas Duane Boston. The warrant I had obtained for Boston charged him with abducting one of his own children.'

Then came the bombshell... 'After spending a short time in jail, Boston's case was dismissed due to a legal technicality.'

Reading that word 'dismissed' took some comprehending.

How on earth could that be? There was a massive consensus of opinion on both sides of the Atlantic that Boston was guilty of murdering Chris and Peta, yet it was obvious that their murders were not top of the police's agenda, indeed they had seemingly been pushed aside. Boston was now once again free and there was little prospect that he would ever have to answer for what had happened to them. Despite repeatedly asking, we were never told what exactly that 'legal technicality' was at the time. We only learnt, some 38 years later, that Boston was released because his lawyer showed the police the piece of paper from his ex-wife Kathe, stating that in exchange for the safe return of Justin, she would not support the abduction charge. Although the police strongly suspected him of murdering Chris and Peta, they could not prove it and so they had no option but to release him. The only punishment Boston received was the denial of visitation rights to Justin up to the age of eighteen.

Sergeant Kelly brought us up to date on what had happened re our case: 'Since that time [his release], Boston has moved, and his present whereabouts are unknown. Boston has had numerous brushes with the law. With his type of background, he is an extremely elusive and conniving person.

'During my investigation of Boston, he managed to elude law enforcement officers throughout Northern California. This was an extremely intensive search as Boston had possession of the child [Justin] and it was feared he would leave the country.'

Sergeant Kelly's letter then turned to Boston's sons, Russell and Vince – the two people we were desperate for the police to interview. 'Interpol has forwarded the information from Inspector Sacks to Inspector Michael Mergen of the El Dorado County Sheriff's department. He has made several unsuccessful attempts to locate and interview Boston's children. This was due to the fact that the children are moved around quite a bit and their whereabouts are often concealed by both of Boston's parents. Inspector Mergen then forwarded the Interpol information to me on the premise that I would have contact with Boston first.

'Boston became visibly upset when I informed him of the deaths of Dr Farmer and Miss Frampton. Prior to this he had been very calm and was freely discussing the child abduction case with me. Boston was confused about exact dates except for the telephone call he made to his former wife, Kathe, from Livingston, Guatemala, on July 16th or 17th 1978. He remembered this date because July 16th is his daughter, Vicki's, birthday and that was the reason he made the call. He called his mother first because Vicki was staying with her but they were on holiday in Utah.

'In an interview with Kathe, she confirmed receiving a telephone call from Boston on July 16th. She stated that Boston was in Livingston, Guatemala, at that time. It is interesting to note that Kathe states Boston did not advise her of any major repairs to his boat. She was quite certain that Boston would have related any such information to her.

'About one week ago, I contacted Kathe by telephone for additional information. I advised Kathe of your letter and asked if she could advise me of Boston's whereabouts. She stated that she had received a telephone call from Boston approximately two weeks ago. He indicated that his children were with him during that time. Additionally, he refused to tell Kathe where he was. Kathe also stated that Boston is quite capable of committing such a crime. She further stated that whenever she makes mention of this investigation to Boston, he becomes extremely defensive.

'Since that telephone conversation, Kathe has furnished

me with three letters she had received from Boston and his children during the time of his trip. The letters are postmarked Livingston, Guatemala, July 15th and July 18th (the same as Miss Frampton's last letter) and Placencia, Belize, July 31st. The letters do not contain anything of significance. However, I am forwarding them to Inspector Sacks via Interpol. Kathe is also looking up a tape recording which she had received from Boston during the same time. I will forward that if I receive it. I will also be forwarding photographs of Boston to Inspector Sacks at Greater Manchester Police.'

The date 18 July was, of course, hugely pertinent to our case because that was the date of the Livingston postmark on Peta's last letter (posted some two weeks after they were known to have died). The reference to the tape recording was also significant because in Chris's belongings was the portable cassette recorder he used to record tapes to send back home and play his music on.

My father, in one of his letters, had raised the question of extraditing Boston to the UK, to which Sergeant Kelly replied: 'I contacted our local District Attorney, who felt that treaties between the US and Great Britain would allow Boston to be extradited. He stated that the Greater Manchester Police would be responsible for initiating the process. Please be advised that I am deeply sympathetic to your situation and will assist in any way I can. I hope that one day we will achieve more than a circumstantial conclusion to this case.'

To our knowledge, the promised tape recording and Kathe's letters never surfaced at GMP. It was another example of the hopelessness of long distance communication with Interpol as the intermediary after Sacks moved on to other duties.

In his reply to Sergeant Kelly, penned that same day, my

father wrote: 'Your information regarding the possible existence of a tape recording with Kathe has aroused our interest. One of the pieces of property that we know my son had with him was an Akai multi-band radio/cassette recorder; among the cassettes that he sent to us were some ex-medical advertising tapes over which he had recorded his news. On two occasions the machine had not completely wiped the previous recording, which was faintly audible in the background. The radio/recorder was one of the things that I mentioned to Boston on the only occasion I have spoken to him. He claimed at that time he knew nothing of its existence. Strange object to hide on a small boat!

'I still have at least one original cassette containing a recording made on this machine. It would be interesting if Kathe can provide another one, especially if it is dated after the murder period.

'A recent case proved that an electronic tape print can be associated with an individual machine. Microscopic markings made on the plastic cassette case can, on entry to the machine, leave a print. It is also possible to reveal microscopic linear marks along the tape made by a particular machine. Even if Kathe's tape confirmed an identical machine recording, Boston could claim it was a present prior to their "departure" but it would be one more facet.'

We never received a reply to my father's letter and in fact we heard nothing more from the Sacramento Police after the letter of 29 July 1981.

When he was let out of jail in spring 1981, we were to learn, almost four decades later, that Boston flew like a bird released from its cage, first to Los Angeles, then to a desolate stretch of beach in Westport, Mendocino County in Northern California. Boston, often with his young son Russell in tow, made several trips down to Baja, Mexico, and then moved there semi-permanently in 1983. It was easy for him to hide out in Baja, especially as he was fluent in Spanish. Just half an hour's drive from San Diego, it's ideal for those wishing to escape responsibility – whether criminal, financial, or familial. It offers a life of cheap food, virtually no tax and no questions are asked. You can drink your sorrows away with cheap alcohol under a hot sun and with crime a facet of everyday life, Boston must have felt right at home. He still made regular trips to Los Angeles and San Diego for supplies but lived for the most part in Mexico until around 2012.

We felt that Interpol, the Foreign & Commonwealth Office and the police were no longer interested, and indeed after 1981 we never heard from either Sacks or anyone at GMP at all, presumably because they felt there was nothing else they could do.

Slowly, as a family, we resigned ourselves to the fact that after Boston had got off on a 'legal technicality' for a crime other than Chris and Peta's murders, he had disappeared. Too slippery, the police had given up pursuing him and the case had gone cold. It seemed that Boston and his two children constantly moved around and even though several Californian jurisdictions were now involved in trying to track him down, he was a master in eluding capture. As if that in itself wasn't difficult enough, the case involved three very disparate countries and, with no scene of crime evidence, forensics or apparent witnesses, no one country was willing to pick up jurisdiction and pursue the case. All this, despite police forces in America and the UK having more than a very strong suspicion who the likely perpetrator was. It was beginning to feel like Boston had committed the perfect murder.

DEAD IN THE WATER

Although they never entirely gave up in pursuing their enquiries, my parents felt they were banging their heads against a brick wall. They had gone down so many avenues only to meet a dead end. Both my family and the Framptons came to a reluctant, very sad acceptance that this extremely tangled international case was too complex for anyone to solve. But the case haunted us and Chris's absence was the wreckage that we had to come to live with.

Chapter Eight

TIME AND TIDE WAIT FOR NO MAN

Naturally, we often wondered what Chris and Peta's final resting place was like. With Dad retiring, my parents discussed at some length the possibility of flying over to Guatemala, but not only was the journey going to be expensive, the officials at the Foreign & Commonwealth Office discouraged them from making such a trip. It was felt that the cemetery and their crude, basic graves would be a disheartening and distressing experience.

They were right! In spring 1984 (some six years after they had died), a work colleague of my mother asked a clergyman friend, Pastor Garry McClure, who was living in Guatemala, to take some photographs of Chris and Peta's graves in Puerto Barrios Cemetery to post back to us. When the internet is so intertwined in all our lives today and photos from the remotest parts of the earth can be sent to the other side of the world in seconds, it is hard to appreciate that we hadn't seen any photographs. Like every facet of the case, it was another waiting game.

DEAD IN THE WATER

The first time the pastor visited the cemetery, the man who was in charge and had worked there for 17 years was on holiday and no one else knew where Chris and Peta's plot numbers 58 and 59 were.

Pastor McClure wrote to us: 'There is no plan or map of the cemetery. The head man has it all in his head.'

The second time he visited the cemetery, the man in charge was expecting his visit.

Pastor McClure wrote: 'He remembered the graves because he had made crosses to put on them. He said he "always remembered important people and where they were buried. All foreigners are important!" He said "foreigners" means anyone not from Puerto Barrios. Well, he took me to the far corner of the cemetery – uphill and down dale, through high grass and into sunken holes until we found the crosses. That day it was 98 degrees in the shade. At 4pm, when I was there, not even a slight breeze was blowing. The sun was tremendous. It was on getting home, however, that I realised there was no film in my camera!

'The third time was a charm. I went to the graveyard for another funeral and I accomplished my mission. The graves are in a sorry condition. Cleaning them would help but not much. They are in a part of the cemetery that the graves are irregular, placed helter skelter. One cross faces one way, the other cross another way. They are located in a hollow, which looks like it is close to water (swamp) during the rainy season. There is no path to this part of the cemetery... the last 60m one has to walk through high grasses, trying to avoid graves and bushes. The last part before arriving at the gravesite is steeply sloped. An older person would need a lot of help to get to these graves. Also, the names seem to be misspelt.'

The Guatemalan law stating that the bodies should remain

in their original burial place for four years had now lapsed, so both families once again discussed moving Chris and Peta to the British Cemetery in Guatemala City, where the graves would be better looked after. They also discussed flying their remains back to the UK. However, after a lot of joint consultation, they decided against both of those ideas. Their bodies had already been exhumed once and it was felt that they should remain together where they were.

Life moves on, as indeed it should. After graduating with an English Literature degree from Lancaster University, I moved to London in 1982 to study for a Postgraduate Diploma in Journalism at City University and after a couple of years on local newspapers and a trade magazine, I became health and beauty editor at IPC's *Woman* magazine.

Ten years on from the murders, through my second cousin Vivienne, I met my husband to-be, Ben, in 1987. At our wedding the following year in Wilmslow, Cheshire, Chris's absence was very keenly felt by us all and we raised a toast to him and Peta at the wedding breakfast. Shortly after the arrival in 1990 of our first child, Alexandra, Ben and I moved out of London to live in Oxford. I commuted to London for six months, but losing someone close to you makes you appreciate life is brief and I wanted to spend as much time as possible with my newborn. It was only on becoming a mother myself that I fully appreciated just how devastating the loss of a dearly loved child is.

I gave up working in London and worked for our local newspaper, *The Oxford Times* before becoming a freelance journalist and PR consultant so I could work from home. We were fortunate to have two more children, Charlie in 1993 and Freya in 1996, whose presence brought great comfort not only to Ben and me but also Mum and Dad, and we made monthly trips up north so that they would feel fully involved as grandparents. It was always my dream to have three children – maybe subliminally, I was trying to replicate the family unit of five that I had had and lost. Our family felt full again but our loss of Chris was only ever a split second away from all our thoughts and despite the passing of the years, we never gave up hope of one day finding their killer.

In 1991, my mother again wrote to the Sacramento Police Department enquiring if there had been any further developments in the case and asking: 'Has Boston been traced? Have Vince and Russell ever been questioned as to what happened on the boat? You will appreciate that, in spite of the passage of time, the extreme pain of such an inexplicable tragedy does not lessen and the desire to know what has happened is forever present.'

With the arrival of the internet, my father emailed Sacramento Police Department on 22 August 2001, outlining the details of the case and adding: 'One big question that we had and still have is the whereabouts of Boston's two children, aged in 1978 Vince (13) and Russell (12), who were known to be on the boat with my son and his girlfriend. We have received no news from you or Greater Manchester Police since 1981 when we learnt that Boston was arrested but subsequently released on a legal technicality for the abduction of one of his other children. We are enquiring as to whether there have been any developments in the case and whether you managed to take any further action? Trusting that this enquiry does not give you too much trouble to update but we would be very grateful for any news. Audrey and Charles Farmer.'

I still find it amazing that there is no trace of anger or bitterness in my father's email. It is measured and almost apologetic in tone for causing the police extra work. Again, our enquiry was met with total silence.

Each birthday, Christmas, anniversary and family milestone brought back memories of Chris. The year 2004 was memorable because by then Chris had been dead longer than he had lived but still there was 'a hole' in our family, which nothing or no one could fill.

So, we came to live with the knowledge that Chris and Peta had been tortured and murdered and the strong conviction that Boston was responsible but with police forces on both sides of the Atlantic unwilling or unable to investigate further, we were powerless. It seemed the world had forgotten them but their families hadn't and the question that continued to haunt us and the Framptons was: 'Why... why did it happen?' As if, of course, there can ever be a reason or excuse for such a heinous act.

Chapter Nine

A VOYAGE TO MY BROTHER

L ike a shaft of bright sunlight streaming through the crack of an open curtain in a darkened room, the thought came to me some thirty-seven years on from their deaths that the internet could hold the key to unlocking the mystery and give us the answers we had been searching for, for what now seemed like a lifetime.

It was a random thought that literally came from out of the blue but it was pivotal in ultimately solving Chris and Peta's murders.

It was 2 October 2015 and savouring autumn's last hurrah, I was sitting on the edge of a magnificent cornfield, within a stone's throw of our Oxfordshire home. The tall, majestic trees, surrounding the field's perimeter displayed every artist's hue of russet, red, gold, orange and copper. A warm mellow sun was beating down from the sapphire blue, gin-clear sky, interrupted only by the crisscross of contrails from planes taking off and landing from the nearby RAF Brize Norton airfield.

Accompanying me was my ninety-year-old mother. Despite her advancing years, she is blessed with a razor-sharp intelligence and an encyclopaedic knowledge of current affairs borne out of a daily diet of Radio 4 and BBC News 24, a habit inherited from her sixty-seven-year marriage to Dad. They had met at the end of World War II in September 1945, at the BBC in Manchester, and got engaged five months later on Mum's twenty-first birthday. Mum was a producer's personal assistant and Dad a news reporter before later going on to direct a ground-breaking medical programme called *Life In Their Hands*, a subject complementing his previous medical studies.

Mum embodies the truism that in order to be interesting, you need to be interested and her enquiring mind extends well beyond the life she leads and the people she meets. A great conversationalist, with a mischievous sense of humour, she likes nothing more than engaging in a robust, contentious argument and invariably wins hands down. But, for me, what defines her is her strong denial of self and staunch stoicism, doubtless wrought from her days spent as a Wren (Women's Royal Naval Service) in the Second World War. Intensely private at all times, to meet her you would never guess that she had lost a son in very tragic circumstances.

Making no concession to her age, she's fiercely determined to remain independent. She still drives her own car, would not be seen without make-up, walks her dog daily, visits the hairdresser weekly and much to mine and my two daughters' delight, she returned from her manicurist with green nails for Christmas. With her penchant for staying abreast of the times, she must be one of Zara's oldest customers!

19 November 2013, with my three children returning home from work and studies we held a small family gathering to

celebrate Dad's 91st birthday at a restaurant in the neighbouring village of Woodstock. It was a great evening and Dad was in jovial spirits.

He was a great lover of his own home so after a brief stay they returned to Cheshire. As my father got in the car, we waved them off and I shouted:

'See you back here for Christmas, Dad.'

To which he replied: 'You will have a job! Christmas is for spending with Kara [the dog] by my own fire and hearth and the comfort of my own bed.'

The following morning he was in John Lewis, Cheadle, returning a 'wireless' (as he referred to his radio, which blasted out either the BBC World Service or Radio 4 pretty much all day) because 'it was disappointingly not loud enough'. Some 36 hours later he was dead of pneumonia – just the way he would probably have chosen to exit this world. Some eight months later, Mum moved down to live with my family in Oxfordshire. Not one for sitting around, idling away the hours, she has voluntarily morphed into our housekeeper and gardener.

No longer Dad by her side, it was her sixteen-year-old Golden Labrador, Kara, who slowly ambled alongside her that stunning autumn day. Mum, with her trusty wooden walking stick, and Kara, with her arthritic gait and swaying hips, the two of them cut an endearing picture of life in the twilight years.

There was a tangible, melancholic sense of resignation that summer was over and days as stunning as this would now be numbered. The hush of the tranquil setting was broken only by the soothing buzz of a bumblebee, the distant hum of an aircraft and the heavy panting of Kara and my own seven-year old Golden Labrador, Mungo, who were both basking in the late autumn sunshine. It was probably that subliminal sense of joi de vivre that made Mum say wistfully: 'I wonder what Chris would have looked like. He'd have been sixty-two now. He's forever young in our eyes, isn't he?'

It was this light-bulb moment on that enchanting autumn day when, on returning home from the walk, I began to scour the internet and Facebook for their suspected killer and possible witnesses to their murder. The thought grew into a conviction and was like a sapling taking root in the soil, growing leaves and bearing blossom. Aware that I had some deeply buried resentment that the case had lain unsolved for so long, I was driven by emotion, a strong sense of injustice and an unwavering self-belief that I could, if I just looked hard enough, get to the truth.

I was barely in the house five minutes before I had found the old file containing copies and some original documents that my parents had collated back in the late 1970s when they were so actively involved in trying to solve Chris and Peta's disappearance and once their bodies were discovered, their horrific murder. The file was kept in the bottom drawer of Mum's walnut bureau that had moved with her when she came to live with us. The large dossier tucked under my arm, I raced up to my office with a sense of anticipation and excitement. I started sifting through the papers, which must have numbered well over a hundred pages.

Never convinced about the relevance or value in divulging one's thoughts and laying bare one's life for potentially all and sundry to see, I hadn't at that time got a Facebook account in my own name. However, as a mother of three, I had, some twelve years before, rightly or wrongly, made an anonymous Facebook account, using the pseudonym of Alex Fortnum, in order to keep a watchful eye on my children's activities.

A VOYAGE TO MY BROTHER

Knowing that Boston was more than strongly suspected of Chris and Peta's murders, I started searching for him and his two sons that we knew had been on the boat at the same time. The only information I had to work on was their names and the likelihood that they were living in California, which was the last-known location for Boston and his parents in the early 1980s. I berated myself as to why I had never done this before – it seemed so obvious!

I was amazed to find that I didn't have to dig too far to find the eldest son, Vince (then aged fifty-two). From looking at his relatively public Facebook account, his age, timeline, list of connections, friends and his posts, I could deduce that I was looking at Boston's eldest son.

I could see that Vince was an aviation electrician and engineer, living in Tucson, Arizona, and he has a son. I was desperate to build a mental picture of his character.

I was heartened to read that Vince was anti-gun crime and opposed to the current gun laws in America. Recalling that the police had told us in 1981 that Boston's third wife (Mary Lou Boston, the mother of Russell and Vince) had disappeared 10 years before Chris and Peta were murdered, my eyes were out on stalks when I read the following: 'My mother was killed at 23 with a gun'. The Facebook entry read:

Vince Boston The point he [President Obama] made is we make it too easy in our country to get weapons designed to kill lots of humans quickly and efficiently.
We can change the laws by educating ourselves, using common sense, and voting.
The right to buy assault rifles and 6000 rounds or more of ammo is a right I'm willing to give up.

DEAD IN THE WATER

My mother was killed at 23 with a gun. My son lives about
half an hour from where the Aurora tragedy took place.
I believe we can make a change.
If enough of us want it, the politicians and lawmakers will
listen. That's the point he was making.

I did a double take. It seemed a peculiarly nonchalant way to
announce to the world that his mother had been killed, or was
it already common knowledge in his circles? It certainly seemed
to imply that Vince had some knowledge of the circumstances
surrounding her death. I presumed that in the intervening years
there had been some confirmation that she was dead or, more
specifically, in his words, 'killed'.

I looked for Boston's younger son, Russell, in Vince's
friend contacts but couldn't see him, which, being brothers, I
thought was strange but I was nonetheless, soon able to track
him down. From Russell's Facebook, I could see he was aged
forty-nine, living near Laguna Beach, California, an artist and
illustrator and the co-owner of a vehicle-renovation business.
I got as far as tracing a phone number for him, rang it on a
withheld number, but put the phone down when a male voice
answered. I'm not sure why I didn't speak, probably because
I didn't know how to open what would have been a mind-
blowing conversation, and at that point I hadn't formulated
in my head what I was going to do with the information I had
gleaned. My head was spinning.

The two people who all along we suspected of possessing
valuable information regarding the horrific events on that small
boat in 1978 were there before my eyes in glorious Technicolor!
As my father and mother had said from the beginning, Vince
and Russell were the two people we desperately needed to talk

to and now, for the first time in 37 years, we had a way of contacting them.

We had never seen photographs of them as boys on the boat so I was fascinated to see their faces as grown men. I studied their profile pictures long and very hard, as if their faces would throw up information on their characters.

I gleaned that they were both leading busy and fulfilling lives. I surmised that whatever trauma Vince and Russell might have experienced with their father as young boys, they had, on the surface at least, got over it, but of course appearances and social media can deceive. I couldn't help but feel a mixture of anger and envy that they were alive and Chris and Peta were dead.

By now, I had a sense that I was on the trail and I was like a dog with a bone. I was convinced that if I just drilled down far enough, I would be able to unlock Chris and Peta's case and maybe, just maybe, get the answers we had been searching for.

The greatest revelation was, of course, tracking down and seeing Boston for the first time on his Facebook.

The picture staring back at me was of an old man. Aged seventy-four, with a white, greying beard, Boston was wearing a T-shirt under a denim shirt, a baseball cap and sunglasses and he looked like an American trucker and the sort of serial murderer you see in a horror movie. The words 'trailer trash' instantly came to mind. I was doubtless pre-conditioned to detest the sight of him and I, of course, did. His Facebook account was opened on 14 March 2012 (just six days before his birthday on 20 March) and gave his location as being Sacramento, California. I could see he had 32 friends, including his son Russell and his daughter Vicki, but interestingly, not Vince. My overwhelming feeling in seeing Boston's Facebook was relief in knowing that he was still alive and thus presumably able to face justice. It would have been so painful to discover that he had just recently died. I had a strong sense though that time was of the essence and we needed to move fast.

I searched for any piece of information I could find on him, no matter how small. Tellingly, on Boston's Facebook page in April 2012 he had added a link and commented on a NBC video report of a woman whose car had accidentally gone into a lake. She was about to drown but was 'miraculously' saved. The report said that all the windows were shut when the car was retrieved from the river and yet she had got out of the car and escaped alive. A religious website, GodVine, claimed it was the 'Hand of God' that had saved her.

I pondered over the obvious parallel with the drowning of Chris and Peta and whether the story's presence on Boston's Facebook page was a reflection of the inner turmoil in his psyche and an obsession with drowning. Did he perhaps wonder if Chris and Peta were still alive? But how could they be? They never stood a chance of surviving. With their legs, ankles and hands tightly bound behind their backs and heavy engine parts connected to their bindings, he had made sure of that. In that state, they would have drowned even in one foot of water.

I then started to look for Boston's fifth wife, Kathe – the mother of Justin, who Boston had abducted in 1979 to spite her for seeking a divorce.

I also found the Facebook account of Vicki Boston, the daughter of Boston and Mary Lou and the older sister of Vince and Russell. I spent most of that weekend researching all of their Facebook posts, trying to construct a picture of their characters and the lives they now led. I then tried to reconcile this information with my preconceived ideas that I had developed over the many years that we had spent coming to terms with Chris and Peta's deaths.

Extending my research outside of Facebook, I found this:

MARY LOU BOSTON

ABOVE: Boston, circa 1968

Vital Statistics at Time of Disappearance

MISSING SINCE: September 1, 1968 from Sacramento, California

CLASSIFICATION: Missing

DATE OF BIRTH: December 4, 1944

AGE: 23 years old

HEIGHT AND WEIGHT: 5'4, 120 pounds

DISTINGUISHING CHARACTERISTICS: Caucasian female. Brown hair, brown eyes.

DETAILS OF DISAPPEARANCE: Mary Lou Boston was last seen in Sacramento, California on September 1, 1968. She has never been heard from again. Few details are available in her case. Investigating Agency. If you have any information concerning this case, please contact: Sacramento Police Department 916-808-0621I.

In 2012, I could see that Vince had lodged a missing person enquiry requesting information about his mother, Mary Lou Boston (née Venn), and the circumstances surrounding her disappearance. This puzzled me – why would he be seeking information about his mother when he had made a categorical public statement on Facebook pronouncing she had been 'killed at 23 with a gun'?

The mystery was deepening. These people all seemed alien to me, like characters from a novel, and yet here they were living real lives on the other side of the Atlantic. The burning question was how much could Vince and Russell remember about Chris and Peta and the events surrounding their murders?

It was literally as if the fog that had surrounded the case for almost four decades was beginning to clear and the pieces of the jigsaw were all beginning to come together in slow motion. By now I was starting to draw a clear mental picture of the characters of Boston, Russell and Vince. Sensing the significance of what I had stumbled across, I talked to Mum about what I should do with the information. Never, in the 37 years since the deaths of Chris and Peta, had she seen photos of Boston or his two sons and she was eager to see what they looked like. Not surprisingly, she was still highly sceptical that the information that I had found would help re-open and solve the case because nearly four decades of police inertia had elapsed. I called my brother, Nigel, and emailed him my research but he too was dubious that it would lead to anything.

In my overwhelming desire to make contact with Russell and Vince, over the course of that weekend I sent them messages on the private Facebook inbox messaging service, asking what they remembered about events on the *Justin B*. I sent Russell a Facebook friend request but heard nothing. With no reply, my messages became more demanding and insistent. Although she had never been on the *Justin B*, I messaged Boston's daughter, Vicki, asking for her father's contact details and confirmation that he had sailed off Central America in 1978, but again, no reply.

Having waited 37 years to make contact with Boston's sons, and now seeing them on the internet, I was desperate to make contact, as my pseudonymous Facebook messages show:

October 2, 2015
Alex Fortnum
Please can you tell me if you were off the coast of Central America in a boat with your brother and father in 1978. Thank you.
[this message was repeated twice]

Alex Fortnum
Please reply then I will tell you why I am writing to you.

October 3, 2015
Alex Fortnum
Why won't you reply? Because you already know why I am writing to you? Do you know or remember the truth? I will not leave this matter alone.

I neither would nor could let it go. I literally 'sat' on Facebook waiting for a reply, but much to my dismay, I didn't get one from Vince, Russell or Vicki. Or rather, I didn't immediately.

I counted down the minutes till on Monday morning, at 9am on the dot, I called Greater Manchester Police (GMP), who had handled the case in 1978. There had recently been a spate of television programmes about decades-old cold cases being solved so it seemed that the Cold Case Review Unit would be a good starting point. Even though I was fully confident in the information that I had found, I had a low expectation of the police taking it further, simply because the case was nearly four decades old and all interest had fizzled out in 1981. I reasoned if they weren't interested in pursuing it further, why would they now take up the cudgels?

'I know this is a very long time ago,' I said hesitantly to Detective Constable Michaela Clinch at Greater Manchester Police, 'but my brother, Dr Christopher Farmer, and his girlfriend, Peta Frampton, were found murdered off the coast of Guatemala in 1978 and I believe that I have some information that might lead to the solving of their case. Please can I make an appointment with you to discuss it?'

Chapter Ten

EDGING FORWARD

(Edging forward – a small advance by repeated small tacking movements.)

I n readiness for our meeting with the Greater Manchester Police (GMP) on the morning of 12 October 2015, Mum and I drove the 160-mile journey north from Oxfordshire the night before. The subject matter of Chris, Peta, Boston, Vince and Russell monopolised our conversation for the duration of the three-hour journey. On the back seat, was the file containing our documentation of the case from 1978.

Earlier that morning, we had met my older brother Nigel and together the three of us drove to GMP's Nexus House in Ashton under Lyne – a vast, imposing, red brick building with a large glass atrium in the centre. Located on the outskirts of Manchester, it looks like any other impressive office building, with the majority of its personnel wearing plain clothes. There is little to denote that it is home to many of the Force's specialist criminal investigation units. Even so, approaching the high-security compound, bristling with surveillance cameras, the environment seemed alien and slightly foreboding.

We checked in at the gated security entrance, parked up and then went through further security in the building's cavernous glass-fronted foyer. Bathed in the mellow rays of the autumn sun that streamed through the long glass windows into the reception area, the three of us sat and waited patiently. Grateful to be there and filled with anticipation, we passed the time with inconsequential chatter and commented on the news stories that flickered across the lobby's big wall-mounted television monitor. We felt cautiously hopeful about the outcome of the meeting. After all, we now knew the whereabouts of the last three people that Chris and Peta had been with on the boat and to the best of our knowledge they were the last people to see them alive. Surely, the police couldn't ignore that? But our hopes were tempered by the age of the case and we didn't want to set our expectations too high.

After five minutes or so, Detective Constable Michaela Clinch swept through the high-security double doors of the building's inner sanctum and warmly greeted us. Dark-haired, slim, smart, attractive and in her late forties, she introduced herself with an air of gentle, calm authority.

We felt in competent hands. Invited in 2004 to work in GMP's newly established Cold Case Review Unit, Michaela has vast experience in investigating undetected homicides and serious sexual assaults, and it shows. She exudes efficiency, attention to detail and dedication to the job, coupled with her ability to extend great empathy.

Introductions over, she took us up in the lift and guided us through the impressive open-plan offices that were a hive of activity. With an air of expectancy and excitement, we entered a spacious airy boardroom with a long conference table, big wall-mounted television monitor and large picture windows offering stunning views of the Pennines.

Welcomed with coffee and biscuits, we were joined by the Force Review Officer, Martin Bottomley. With responsibility for the Cold Case Review Unit, it is Martin's job to investigate historic undetected cases of rape and murder, and also review current investigations, both in GMP and for other law enforcement agencies. His impressive 40 year career in the police force includes leading reviews for the Royal Military Police into allegations of abuse by British soldiers in Iraq and Afghanistan and reviews of terrorist murders on behalf of the Police Service in Northern Ireland. He has served at all ranks, in uniform and CID, including detective superintendent in charge of the Major Incident Team, with responsibility for investigating all murders in the Greater Manchester area. A more outstanding team leader we could not have hoped for.

With a good dose of British reserve, Martin, on first meeting, possesses a measured, slow-to-trust demeanour which conveys a razor-sharp ability to size up a person's character from 20 yards. There's a touch of the inscrutable about him. He is as enigmatic and unreadable as the amount of information he is so obviously processing in his head. I can imagine if he was trying to extract a confession, his presence would be unnerving but for us, he was a very reassuring authoritative presence. In this, and subsequent meetings, we were to find that beneath the reserved exterior lies a compassionate, warm-hearted humanitarian. It was heartening to learn that he, like Chris, had been a pupil of Manchester Grammar School, albeit a couple of years after him, but it felt like a connection.

When, at this first meeting, we got down to the business of discussing what I had found on the internet, I felt I was being assessed, both on the veracity of my information but also me as a person. As I had given Michaela a brief background to the case over the phone, she had, in the interim, tried to locate the original case files from 1978. However, nothing turned up in her search of the archives – the hard paper copy of the file had seemingly been lost and it was before computerisation.

I was therefore delighted to be able to produce from my bag our own personal file.Tatty and dog-eared, after surviving in the bottom drawer of Mum's bureau, the big green file was brimming with the faded, yellowing photocopies plus some of the original documents for example, Chris's death certificate, the communication with the Foreign & Commonwealth Office and the last letters from San Rafael PD in 1981. We brought every scrap of evidence relating to the case that we could muster, including the last two cassette tapes that Chris had sent to us, describing his time in Australia and travels in Mexico. We also gave them the old reel recording that Dad had made of his phone conversation with Boston's father, Russell on 10 January 1979.

Martin and Michaela, whilst expressing caution in being too optimistic, assured us that they would contact Interpol to request that they reach out to Sacramento Police Department to see if there had been any further update on Boston after the case went cold in the early 1980s. After we had given them a full resume of the case, Martin and Michaela promised they would be in touch as soon as they had any news.

Ninety minutes later, we left the building, grateful for their time and for the fact that they hadn't dismissed our case simply on the grounds of its age. Indeed, Martin had assured us: 'If new information comes to light which could lead to a prosecution, then no case is too old.' But our expectations of them re-opening the case were incredibly low.

What we hadn't banked on, however, was the most extraordinary set of coincidences and stroke of good fortune that came into play that autumn of 2015, and in some cases within days of each other.

The first was one week after our initial meeting with GMP. Returning from a late afternoon dog walk, I received the call that I had been hoping for from Michaela. She had been in touch with GMP's former Chief Inspector David Sacks, who was put in charge of the case in November 1978. Their conversation, as related by David, ran as follows:

'Hello, this is Detective Constable Michaela Clinch. Please can you confirm that you were the officer who investigated the murders of Dr Christopher Farmer and Peta Frampton in 1978.'

'Yes, I remember the case well.'

'The Farmer family were left feeling very dissatisfied and want the case re-opened,' continued Michaela. 'What can you tell me about it?'

'I can tell you a lot. It wasn't a run-of-the-mill case but the file should be at headquarters.'

'That's the problem, David, we can't locate it.'

'Well, not only can I tell you about the case, I can give you a complete copy of the file.'

'What's in it?'

'Everything you're looking for!'

'Really?'

David was moved off the case after about a year to take up

other duties but on his return to police headquarters in 1981, he says he looked in the main file in the administration office and found and photocopied the communication that had taken place between my father and the Sacramento Police. Although we were not made aware of anyone taking over the case when David left, Dad, nonetheless was meticulous in sending copies of all communications to GMP to keep them in the loop.

David explains how he came to have a copy of the case file at home: 'On my retirement from the police, six years later, I was clearing out my desk in my office in Leigh [in Greater Manchester] when I came across the file in a cabinet. I have no recollection of how it got there. I looked at the wastepaper basket, which was overflowing with papers, and then thought about shredding it, but I didn't have time. So, I put it in the box to take home with me with the intention of burning it, but fortuitously, it lay in the box in my garden shed.

'After I put the phone down to Michaela, I then began to think to myself, "Exactly where did I put that file?" I hadn't seen it for fourteen or fifteen years. It wasn't where I thought it was so I had to rack my brains hard. Eventually, I located it at the bottom of a box in my garden shed. Some of the sheets of paper were stuck together from being damp so I carefully peeled them apart and placed them in my conservatory to dry out.

'I was delighted, and very much relieved to find that everything on all the documents was still entirely legible. I realised though, that once I had parted with these copy documents, I would most probably never see them again so I went up to my study and spent some considerable time, and a lot of paper, copying everything all over again! Also, being an amateur photographer, I photographed every sheet so that the whole copy file of documents was additionally secured on my digital camera's SD card!'

As a detective, David said he made a habit of taking copies of all the cases he worked on so that he didn't have to handle the originals, which may have been needed as exhibits when the case came to trial. Although Mum and Dad's file had some of the originals, it's my belief that the file containing Peta's original letters was sent to Interpol in Washington. We know that they sent San Rafael Police Department copies of Peta's letters when they interviewed Boston about our case when he was in custody on the child abduction charge. Although David's file contained nothing that we didn't already have in ours, it nonetheless helped support our case, as did his recollections and testimony.

From that phone call with Michaela onwards, Chris and Peta's case was uppermost in my mind and the task of securing justice for them became an abiding passion. I could think of little else.

Michaela reached out to Interpol in October but it took five whole months for Interpol to put GMP in direct touch with Sacramento Police Department. It wasn't until 29 February 2016 that Michaela spoke directly to Detective Amy Crosby of the Missing Persons Unit at Sacramento Police Department. From that conversation, they learnt that they had both instigated enquiries with Interpol at almost the same time.

It transpired that in the autumn of 2015, Amy was working on the disappearance in 1968 of Vince and Russell's mother, Mary Lou Boston. Her very poorly investigated missing persons file was on her desk for Amy to review. However, the case was going nowhere because there was no body, no eyewitness and no confession. Boston's eldest son, Vince, had given Amy a statement on 13 October, just 11 days after I had sent the anonymous Facebook message and one day after we ourselves had been to GMP. In that conversation, he told her that it was an open family secret that his father had killed his mother in 1968 but no one knew where he had buried her. Vince then told Amy how he had witnessed the cold-blooded and unprovoked murders of Chris and Peta in broad daylight on the boat.

Going to the police with my Facebook and internet research was thus a massive game changer because it put Chris and Peta's case back on the radar and reconnected GMP with Sacramento Police Department. Like GMP, it appears that Sacramento PD could not locate the original files from 1978 to 1981, detailing the murder enquiry into Chris and Peta's deaths. It probably didn't help that there were several jurisdictions in California looking for Boston in the 1980s, so records may have been scattered.

We were then asked to attend another meeting with the Cold Case Review Unit, where Martin Bottomley was able to give us the unbelievably good news that the case was no longer cold but now very much active. If someone had suggested six months before, that Chris and Peta's case would be reopened, I would have politely said they had taken leave of their senses. For the first time in 38 years, we dared to believe we might just possibly see justice. The seed for writing this book was sown when chatting to Michaela over a cup of coffee about my background in journalism, she said: 'You should write a book about Chris and Peta. It is your story to tell, after all.'

The case started to gain momentum when we learnt that Boston's youngest son, Russell, had willingly given his eyewitness statement to Amy Crosby on 19 January and it had corroborated Vince's account of events on the boat. In addition, on 27 January, Russell handed to the police photographs and evidence dating back to 1978, proving that Chris and Peta had been present on the boat – all vital material for the prosecution team.

At this point, I was told to attempt no further Facebook contact with either Vince or Russell for fear of prejudicing any future trial. But I didn't need to be told not to contact them – for me, Facebook had done its work and it had taken us further than I could have ever dreamt of.

I was therefore stunned when, on 24 February 2016, I received in my Facebook inbox a reply from Russell relating to my messages in October of the previous year in which I requested information about events on the boat in 1978. I wanted so much to reply but I knew that it wouldn't be wise as the defence could claim that we had corroborated on our testimonies. Russell's response, to the same questions that I had sent to Vince (see page 105), also as 'Alex Fortnum', read:

02/24/2016
Hello Alex,
I just saw your messages for the first time. Because we are not friends on Facebook, your messages were automatically filtered and were sent to filtered messages. Please send me an email at [his address] and let me know who you are and what this pertains to. Thank you, Russell Boston

I immediately emailed Martin Bottomley with the above and he replied: 'Thank you for letting us have sight of this e-mail and also thank you for not responding to Russell, as it is now more important than ever that you don't. I say this because only in the last two days, we have been put in touch via Interpol with the investigator in the US who is dealing with the queries we have. This contact has only been by e-mail and so far, routed through Interpol and therefore it's difficult to judge precisely what progress has been made. However, DC Michaela Clinch is arranging a telephone conference to speak directly with the US. case officer early next week to clarify a number of questions which arise from this indirect communication.

'I realise that this e-mail in itself will be equally tantalizing, but my firm impression (put it no higher yet) is that we will have some meaningful information and an update to provide to you within the next week or so. In view of that, I would really like to meet with the three of you again, rather than speak formally via e-mail or impersonally over the phone.'

At a further meeting at GMP, we learnt that GMP were in consultation with the Crown Prosecution Service to establish whether the UK had jurisdiction and Boston could be extradited to stand trial in this country. We were introduced to Detective Sergeant Julie Adams. With 23 years' police service behind her, Julie was put on stand-by to accompany DC Michaela Clinch to California to conduct an interview with Boston.

It was a defining moment when, in March, Nigel, Mum and I gathered once again in GMP's large meeting room. Martin was sitting at the head of the boardroom table and in front of him were Vince and Russell's witness statements containing the damning and shocking facts about their father and their incriminating accounts of the events in Belize. Martin solicitously enquired: 'You have waited long enough to know what happened. How much would you like to know?'

Nigel and I turned to Mum to answer and, without hesitation, she replied: 'I would like to know everything, I don't want to be spared any details.' Martin, with great tact, began to summarise the events on the boat in early July 1978, as told by Vince and Russell. It seemed as if Chris and Peta's ghosts were talking beyond the grave. What we heard was spine chilling and the sheer terror that Chris and Peta must have felt was palpable.

As the story unfolded, we realised just how unlucky they had been. In a chance meeting on a remote island off Central America, they happened upon one of life's total psychopaths, who, like them, was a stranger to the area. Holding a police record since the age of twenty, Boston was a man with an extensive serious criminal history. It was known within the immediate and extended Boston family that he had shot dead his third wife, Mary Lou, at the age of twenty-three when Vince and Russell were aged just three and two. Her disappearance was very poorly investigated and dismissed by Sacramento police at the time as they believed Boston's story that she had cleared their joint bank account and run off with another man. Whilst Boston often bragged to his family about how he killed her, her body has to this day never been found.

One wonders whether Chris and Peta ever wondered or thought to ask what an American was doing down in Belize with two young boys who were obviously missing a lot of schooling. If they did, they obviously didn't get the truth.

The reason Boston was in Belize in early 1978 was because he was escaping law enforcement in Sacramento. Police had first arrested him in 1977 for shooting the lock off a storage unit but had subsequently released him. The police had then issued a warrant for Boston's arrest on a statutory rape charge with a minor, a girl he had met in a bar. His sons recall what happened: living in 57th Street off Folsom Blvd, Sacramento, Russell and Vince, who shared a bedroom next door to their dad, in the middle of the night heard a young girl yelling at him to stop and he didn't. Vince says: 'I woke Russ up and I asked if he too had heard the noise, which lasted for quite a while. The next morning, we were with Dad and a friend of his. Russell and I were in the back seat of his car and they were in the front and his friend mentioned something about the night before and we said: "We heard some weird noises last night," and my dad just played it off like: "Oh, I don't know what you're talking about." Then when he got us alone, he said: "You better shut the fuck up about that – I don't ever want to hear about that again. Don't talk about what happened last night."'

Knowing the police were onto him, Boston escaped the area, and his aunt Grace came to look after Russell and Vince before they then went to live with Boston's mother. The police quickly caught up with him and Boston was, in autumn 1977, arrested again. His mother and father stood bail but Boston jumped bail. Knowing that he needed to leave Sacramento, he left his fifteen-year-old daughter, Vicki, who has Turner syndrome (a chromosomal condition that affects female development), with his mother. He kept Vince and Russell with him to claim the children's welfare money and give himself an air of legitimacy and respectability. The three of them went to get passports and buy snorkelling gear at the Big 5 Sporting Goods store in Sacramento. They then journeyed down through Mexico in Boston's truck and reached Belize, which Boston deemed remote enough to escape the prying eyes of Californian law enforcement.

In Belize they purchased the *Justin B*. The boys described how drinking excessive amounts of cheap rum became a common pastime for their father, after which he would become very violent. It was on one such occasion when Chris and Peta were on the boat that Boston started beating up Russell. When Chris intervened and pulled Boston off him, he tried to swing out at Chris but missed and fell in a humiliating splash into the sea. After telling him to behave, Chris then helped him back on board. According to Vince it was that very night when Boston began plotting Chris and Peta's murders.

The following evening, at dusk, Boston told Chris to pull up the anchor. As Chris obliged, he crept up behind him and repeatedly bludgeoned him over the head with a billy club until it broke. He then attempted to stab Chris in the chest with a fillet knife until that also broke. Chris cried out: 'I give up, give up!' and eventually, Boston stopped. That night, although Chris was himself very badly injured with a fractured skull and multiple wounds from the beating, he quite astonishingly gave Boston a muscle relaxant as he complained that he was in agony, having hurt his back whilst beating Chris up.

The next morning, Boston told Chris and Peta that he was going to drop them on the Cabo de Tres Peninsula near Livingston in Guatemala, but to stop them reporting him to the police before he had made good his escape by boat, he said he would need to tie their hands loosely and strip them naked so they couldn't escape.

Martin then described to us how over the next 36 hours Boston manipulated Chris and Peta through his wicked, sadistic mind games to the point where they were rendered totally defenceless, incapacitated and, in Chris's case, badly injured. The following day, when Boston had had his fill of torturing them, as daylight broke and the boat was out at sea, he callously pushed them both overboard fully conscious. Trussed up with ropes, plastic bags over their heads and heavy motor engine parts weighing them down, they never stood the remotest chance of surviving. His two sons, aged twelve and thirteen, witnessed it all.

When Martin had finished narrating the shocking events to us, a hush descended on the room. The fog that had enveloped Chris and Peta's case since 1978 had cleared and the full grotesque extent of Boston's evil crimes was revealed in its most vivid glory. We were filled with many emotions but probably incredulity was the abiding one; we were speechless. Over the years, we had all wondered and envisaged how Chris and Peta may have met their end but the events related to us entered the realms of a horror movie script. It took us some time to assimilate and process the full horror of it.

We felt immensely proud that Chris had come to Russell's defence and had died honourably but were appalled and horrified by the extent of Boston's evil and the pain and abject fear that Chris and Peta must have endured over the 36 hours or so prior to being killed. Even though it was 38 years on, and they had long been dead, the details of their excruciatingly distressing deaths were hard to bear.

One can only guess at the unimaginable fear that they must have experienced in their last hours and the feeling of utter helplessness when they were so callously pushed into the ocean and pulled underwater by the weight of the engine parts. There must have been a point when it dawned on them that they weren't going to get out of it alive; we can only hope that that realisation was near the end.

Martin told us that Boston was suspected of killing many others. Our hearts went out to Russell and Vince – losing their mom, Mary Lou, at the hands of their father. There was only one fitting word for Boston: monster. Not only was his twisted, disturbed mind and breathtaking lack of humanity staggering but so too was the fact that he had got away with his vile crimes for so long.

We were incredulous, both because of what had happened to Chris and Peta but also incredulous that 38 years on we now knew. Some two hours later, we exited the room, shell-shocked but grateful for finally knowing the truth.

Chapter Eleven

'ON A BOAT THERE IS NOWHERE TO GO'

Peta's prophetic words in her postscript to her mother dated 29 June 1978. She was right – there *was* nowhere to go to escape the murderous monster that was Silas Duane Boston.

Just how much Chris and Peta fell prey to Boston was revealed to me 39 years after their murders. In a private visit to California, I met with his son Russell in what was an emotionally charged but cathartic meeting. He gave me the following, shockingly honest, eyewitness account of their horrific murders, and described in detail the days leading up to the event and the aftermath.

THURSDAY, 29 JUNE 1978

Journeying to the southern tip of the Belizean Sapodilla Cayes, the boats and tourists became few in number. Most visitors tend to frequent the cayes around Belize City to the north but those who head for the more off-the-beaten track in the south are rewarded with the most spectacular unspoilt Caribbean scenery.

As Peta mentioned in her last letter home, the *Justin B*

anchored at Hunting Caye at 11am. A remote island, in 1978 its sole resident was the lighthouse keeper. It is everyone's dream of a desert island existence.

Russell Boston describes their arrival: 'We took the boat in very slowly and gingerly as the caye is surrounded by a dense coral reef. The boat's motor had broken, so I sat in the bow, barking directions to Dad on which way to steer. The lighthouse keeper was amazed we made it without running aground as boats don't usually approach from that side of the caye.

'The lighthouse keeper told us there would be a big party that weekend. We actually thought he was delusional, because he described it as big, with hundreds of people. Then, a couple of hours later, as if from out of nowhere, these excursion boats started arriving. The beaches started to fill up with young people enjoying the party atmosphere. They set up hammocks, pitched tents, played music, and made campfires for cooking. With the sun beating down on the sea, making the turquoise shadings of the shallow reefs sparkle, the blinding white sandy beaches looked idyllic.'

The event was sponsored by the Canadian nickel mining company, Inco, to celebrate Canada Day on 1 July. It was similar in style to a present-day Full Moon party in Thailand or a rave in Ibiza, but smaller in size. Belize in the late 1970s was fast becoming a popular hangout on the hippy trail. Its laid-back, relaxed culture with the 'No shirt, no shoes, no problem' philosophy of the locals and expats, coupled with breathtaking beauty and isolation, suited the hippy culture. Alcohol and Quaaludes (a recreational drug popular in the 1970s) were in wide use.

As the boats arrived and started to spill out their passengers onto the caye's beaches, Vince and Russell took themselves off for the afternoon in the *Justin B*'s dug-out boat to visit Lime Caye, just a stone's throw from Hunting Caye – an island that Russell recalls was populated by very large rats!

FRIDAY, 30 JUNE 1978

The party got into full swing that afternoon and evening and Boston was in his element. As the swashbuckling hero of a fishing boat, his arrogant air of bohemian nonchalance and two young children, and a young British doctor and girlfriend in tow, he played to the gallery and quickly became the centre of attention. With his love of adventure and storytelling and his blustering loud character and his booming deep American drawl, he went down a storm with the revellers and the owners of the nickel mine. He was the life and soul of the party.

Russell recalls Chris got into the party spirit too: 'Chris had a wonderful, extrovert personality; he had a real lust for life. He often spoke about the time he and Peta had spent in Australia and his love of sailing and surfing. He was an accomplished sailor. Peta was quieter and more reserved and the thing I most remember about her was her writing long letters home.

'In amongst all the merriment, the organiser and manager of the party (who was "something important" at the Canadian nickel mine) was running around and getting increasingly intoxicated. Dad lent him his sharp diver's knife, which he normally kept strapped to his leg, as a tool. The manager used the knife to help himself to the roast pig on the spit, which was being rotated by a guy who cut off pieces as it was cooked. Because the manager helped himself, he cut off strips of raw pork. It wasn't long before he was violently sick from eating the uncooked pork and in the course of him being taken ill, Dad's knife was lost'.

He was so ill, the party had to be stopped and on the Saturday morning, everyone began to disperse, packing up and then boarding the boats they had arrived on. On board the *Justin B*, a discussion broke out as to where their next destination should be.

Writing the day before in her last letter home to her mother, Peta wrote: 'Talking to the lighthouse keeper, this is the worst time for sailing and our next sail to Puerto Cortes in Honduras would be very hard so it seems we may easily decide to go to Livingston in Guatemala, which is a simple sail with the wind behind us.'

The party had also given Boston another reason to change the course of their next destination. Before the manager of the nickel mine had fallen ill, he had invited him to be their guest at the nickel mining company in El Estor in Guatemala. Boston was keen to accept this invite from his new, well-connected friend and told Chris and Peta that he was going to take a seven- to ten-day detour, going first to Livingston, and from there sailing the *Justin B* up the Rio Dulce to Lake Izabal, where the El Estor nickel mine is located. Chris and Peta said they didn't want to go as they were already late reaching their respective destinations and added that he was reneging on the original plan. Having bought visas for entry to Honduras when they were in Dangriga (Stann Creek), in order that Boston could take them to Puerto Cortes on the mainland or Roatan, an island off Honduras, they naturally wanted to use them.

Russell says: 'Dad started talking about dropping them in or near Livingston in Guatemala. That was a problem for Chris and Peta because at that time Guatemala and Belize weren't on friendly terms – you couldn't just cross over the border and they didn't issue visas.'

Chris said that if Boston was intending to drop them short

of Honduras, for which they had previously agreed to pay a sum of $500 at the outset, then the agreement needed to be re-negotiated. Boston replied that the original arrangement didn't work for him and that as he was taking them most of the way, they should pay the previously agreed sum of $500.

'Dad and Chris made their positions clear then nothing more was said but I did notice that after that, Dad started drinking even more heavily than usual. He became very quiet and moody and there wasn't a lot of talking.'

SATURDAY, 1 JULY 1978

Along with a flotilla of other boats, the *Justin B* set sail later that morning, bound for Cabo de Tres Puntas Peninsula, a richly forested sand spit which separates the Bay of Amatique and its port of Puerto Barrios and Livingston from the Gulf of Honduras. It wasn't long before the other boats had disappeared over the horizon and the *Justin B* was alone at sea. Making landfall in the afternoon at a small remote fishing village (a collection of huts), at the end of the peninsula, Chris and Peta went ashore with the boys to buy eggs but they could only find turtles' eggs.

Russell recalls: 'Peta and Chris made the best scrambled eggs in the world. I'm not sure if it was the butter or the stirring, but it was phenomenal. When we made them, they were like rubber.'

When they returned to the boat, Boston was showing signs of inebriation. Rum was cheap in Belize, and when intoxicated, it was his habit to start cussing and yelling at his sons and particularly Russell, who was very much his physical and metaphorical punch bag. It fell to Russell to do much of the cooking on the boat and to keep Boston supplied with his favourite drink called the 'Justin B' – a combination of rum, honey and lime juice.

Russell says: 'By dusk, Dad was drunk from drinking all day and he was slurring his words and chanting a silly rhyme to wind me up: "Make me some rice, Russ, make me some Russ rice." I was perpetually scared of Dad so I ran with lightning speed down to the galley to prepare the rice, which he liked me to mix with curry powder. In the middle of making it, he then ordered me to come back up to the deck and jump overboard.'

Boston: Russ, Get your ass overboard now.
Russell: What?
Boston: Get your fucking ass overboard NOW!

'Frightened of what would happen if I didn't, I jumped off the boat, unsure why or what I was supposed to do. From the side of the boat he shouted that the anchor was stuck and told me to unhook it. I tried to swim down to the bottom but the water was dark and murky and I couldn't see but I was perplexed because I knew the anchor wasn't stuck. I got back on board and went to the front of the boat and started to pull up the anchor.

'Without any warning, Dad came up behind me and punched me hard in the small of my back and started beating and pummelling me. I collapsed on the deck but he kept raining fists down. Because he was a sailor, he was a stocky guy. Dad hitting me wasn't unusual but this attack was particularly vicious.

'Chris and Peta were screaming at him to stop and Chris rushed up to him to pull him off me and shouted: "Stop it! Stop it, Duane – leave him alone!"

'Dad yelled back: "Don't you fucking dare tell me how to raise my kids!"

'He kept on pounding me, at which point Chris grabbed him and pulled him off me. He tried to take a swing at Chris but missed and Dad ended up going overboard into the sea. As he fell, he tried to grab the empty water containers that were lashed to the side of the boat, in case of a storm, and these made his entry into the water even more spectacular.

'Vince says that Chris and Peta laughed at him but I don't remember that. I was at the front of the boat and maybe didn't see it. Dad's humiliation was made worse by the fact that the locals were standing onshore at the fishing village and witnessed the whole noisy commotion. It was a very tense situation. The sea wasn't very deep at this point and Dad stayed in for a while, treading water and just glaring at us as if he was thinking of what to do next. He was fuming. From the deck of the boat, Chris asked Dad why he had done it and told him to behave. He then lent him a hand to pull him out of the water and help him back on board.

'That evening, Dad told them that on the following day he was going to drop them off on the peninsula so they could get a ferry from Livingston. That night we anchored somewhere off the peninsula. An uneasy peace settled on the boat but there was a tangible sense of foreboding.'

Later that evening, with venom in his voice, Boston muttered to Vince that he wanted to kill Chris and Peta and was plotting their murders.

'I remember feeling very sore, not just physically, but mentally,' recalls Russell. 'It was a severe beating and I was stunned and sad, because I hadn't done anything to deserve it – Dad just lashed out at me. Dad didn't do much in the way of talking that night, and Vince and I went to bed on the deck of the boat when it got dark (we always slept there unless there was a storm). Dad usually slept in the front small cabin area of the boat and Chris and Peta in the back of the galley.

DEAD IN THE WATER

'In the morning, Dad said to Chris and Peta: "I am going to drop you both off on the peninsula but under the cover of darkness." Chris and Peta agreed but it was very quiet and no one talked and, unusually, Dad didn't drink at all that day.

'At dusk, Dad told Chris to go up to the front of the boat and pull up the anchor. I thought to myself, that's odd because as a guest on the boat he wouldn't normally be asked to do that, but by this time he was a member of the crew and he did as he was told – Chris was a good sailor and would sail the boat, pull up sails, etc. At this time, we were out at sea and well away from the peninsula, there were no other boats around. As Chris began to pull up the anchor, I saw Dad with stealth creep up behind him. In his hand was his long antique wooden billy club. It was part of Dad's arsenal of weapons and he used it to stun and kill fish.'

Black, wooden and about one and a half feet in length, the police truncheon was used in the 1930s, but later became illegal because of the wanton, indiscriminate damage it can inflict.

'Catching Chris totally unawares, Dad began to pummel him rapidly, again and again and again with the truncheon. Chris didn't fight back at all but he fell to his knees, crawled into a foetal position with his hands and arms, trying to shield his head for protection. It was getting dark and the light was fading, but I could see and hear that the beating was fast and vicious. Chris yelled at Dad and told him to stop, but Dad didn't, he kept raining blows down on his skull again and again. His head, hands and arms were cut and his blood was flying all over the deck. I can remember the sound of the beating and it was horrendous. [Vince recalls Chris's skull fracturing with a sickening crack.]

'Hearing the screaming and shouting, Peta ran up from

the galley to see what was happening and shouted out loud at Dad to stop.

'Dad screamed at her in rage: "Get back down in the fucking gallery now or I will shoot you with the spear gun!"

'Chris tried to reason with Dad as he was being beaten and then screamed: "What's your game, what's your game?" I'd never heard that expression before – I guess it's an English one. Dad told me later that the billy club either slipped out of his hand from all the blood that was flying around or broke but the next thing he knew, he didn't have it. It had gone.'

Vince later confirmed that it broke from the impact of hitting Chris so hard.

'Vince and I were on deck, reeling in shock and blind fear, not knowing what to do or how to help. Chris was dazed and injured but stumbling as he attempted to stand up.

'I remember Dad then punched him very hard and sent him flying. I didn't realise at the time that Dad used a fillet knife that he had deliberately left on deck but it broke as it hit his sternum. Through the years, I have an image of Dad punching Chris in the chest.

'Chris cried out to Dad: "Please, please, I give up, I give up." At that point Dad was panting – he smoked constantly, and he was clearly beginning to tire from beating him with such force, but he showed no mercy to Chris, who was bleeding both from his head and upper body and in obvious pain.

'Dad and Chris were roughly the same height [5foot 7inches and 5foot 8inches respectively]. Chris was more slender and, in a fair fight, probably fitter, being 12 years younger and he surfed and swam, but Dad was of stockier build and had come from a lifetime of fighting. The day before, Chris had, of course, bested him when he was attacking me.'

DEAD IN THE WATER

Chris was badly injured. After a beating of such force with a weapon that, can wreak huge indiscriminate damage, it is probable that, in addition to a fractured skull, he would have suffered multiple broken bones, severe pain, concussion, vomiting and possible internal bleeding. Russell continued to describe the horrific event:

'When things had calmed down, Chris said to Dad: "Why did you do it?"

'Because you didn't pay me.'

'I agree, I agree. I am sorry, I was wrong. Absolutely, of course I will pay you.'

'Chris and Peta handed over the $500 in Thomas Cook travellers cheques* that they had agreed to pay at the outset of the journey.

'That evening, Dad could barely move from being in pain, having wrenched his back when beating Chris. Being a nice guy, Chris said, "Let me have a look at it for you," and then got a glass vial out of his medical bag and injected him with a strong muscle relaxant and it ended up knocking Dad out for the night.'

This was presumably an attempt on Chris's part to win over Boston by psychologically disarming and calming him down. Badly injured and incapacitated from Boston's bludgeoning, Chris was obviously hoping to retrieve the situation by winning him over with compassion and medical care. Had he been in a better physical state, he and Peta could have taken the dug-out boat that was on the deck and escaped whilst Boston was sleeping but then that would have been leaving two young kids on the boat with an adult who was sedated. It's probable that

---

*Pre-printed, fixed-amount cheques, they allowed the person signing them to make an unconditional payment when abroad.

Chris wasn't physically able to make the journey to shore and they obviously didn't appreciate that they were in the company of a psychopathic killer. Chris, with the contents of his medical bag, presumably had the wherewithal to knock Boston out for more than just one night, but he gave him the benefit of the doubt. Turning killer was not an option that he could ever have considered.

'That night, everyone went to bed in their usual places,' says Russell. 'Chris was bleeding a lot, and with Peta's help, tended to the cuts on his head and body. They huddled up together in the galley and were talking quietly but I couldn't hear what was said.'

MONDAY, 3 JULY 1978

'I remember Dad waking up in the morning, and it was like nothing had happened,' recalls Russell. 'He busied himself looking at maps and that's when he explained to Chris and Peta he needed to drop them somewhere very remote on the peninsula so that he could sail away before they could get to civilisation and report him to the authorities. He said he would drop them between the fishing village on the peninsula and the port of Puerto Barrios, thus allowing him a couple of hours to get away before they called the cops. Chris constantly assured him that they wouldn't go to the police or report the events to anyone.

'Then Dad told them that he was going to let them go and that they should pack their bags and put all their belongings on the deck. This they did without hesitation. I remember seeing their hastily packed duffle bags, Chris's medical bag and his boombox lined up on the wooden deck.

'That done, Dad then told them he was going to need to tie

them up, so it would take them longer to escape. He was very calm and reassuring, like it was nothing out of the ordinary, just the next logical step and part of the plan to drop them off and let them go.'

At this point Vince and Russell's account of the story varies slightly, the fog of almost forty years perhaps clouding memories. According to Vince, Chris resisted and Boston tackled him to the ground and tied him up with ropes that he had pre-prepared and left on the deck. After being beaten to a near pulp the day before, Chris put up little fight. Chris thus rendered helpless, Boston got hold of Peta and tied her up too. Vince recalls his father saying that he was going to tie them to a tree in the jungle so that their escape would be delayed. Russell's account is at variance with this as he says Chris and Peta, although far from happy about it, did comply as Boston said that he was only going to tie their hands in the front.

Russell says: 'When dad told him he was angry because Chris refused to pay him, I think Chris felt bad, like he realized he should have paid him for the trip up to that point. I think that's why he was agreeing to comply with my dad. It was weird and creepy dad telling them he needed to tie them up, but he assured them he was going to drop them off, telling them he just needed to tie them up so they wouldn't go to the authorities before he could get away to Honduras waters. Peta didn't want to, but Chris agreed, and assured her it would be ok, that dad just wanted to get paid.'

Boston then stripped Chris and Peta naked. 'Dad said it was to stop them leaving but I don't know why he did that,' says Russell. 'I remember them being nude and I found it very creepy and disturbing. Peta was protesting and crying. I have an abiding mental image of Peta in side profile, sitting up, her hands tied in front of her. Chris was badly injured but trying to reassure her that everything would be OK. I think he trusted my dad at that point that he was going to let them go, but by this stage, he didn't have any option other than to go along with Dad's plan. It was an evolution of Dad's, trying to make the situation believable but all the time revealing what his real intentions were.'

Originally it was just their hands that were tied. As day turned to dusk, Boston then tightened their bindings and bound their legs.

Vince says: 'Dad was really good at tying knots. It was second nature to him – it was like he had done it many times before. Dad kept Chris in the galley at the back of the boat and Peta down in the sleeping cabin in the front. He spent some time with her alone and I think it is likely that Dad sexually assaulted her. Later, he told me that he and Russ were going to watch Chris, and he said I needed to go into the cabin and guard Peta on my own. I went down there and she was tied up and naked. Who knows what he had done to her before that? When I was guarding her, I was crying and she kept telling me I was going to go to hell, and begging me to let them go. I really wanted to but I didn't know what to do. He would have probably killed Russ and me too if we had helped them to escape. I remember the bindings on their hands and legs were very tight and he left them both in that state all night long.'

Russell says: 'Dad constantly tried to engineer a situation in which Vince and I were accomplices and accessories to his crimes. It was very weird.'

DEAD IN THE WATER

Tuesday, 4 July 1978

American Independence Day dawned and the sun began to rise on what promised to be a typical hot, humid Caribbean day. There had been little or no sleep for anyone that night but as the light began to appear on the horizon, there was a flurry of activity on the boat.

Boston was busying himself in the galley, tying long pieces of heavy-duty, yellow nylon rope to some of the heavy engine parts that on the journey south he had bought in Dangriga (Stann Creek) to act as ballast and which Peta refers to in her last letter to her mother: 'We had to spend nearly a week at Stann Creek trying to get extra ballast. Finally, we were given about 700 lbs by a white Belizean who is the general manager of the Belizean Citrus Co at Pomona, about 12 miles from Stann Creek.'

Boston's expertise at tying knots ensured that there would be no chance of the ropes coming off. The job done, he put them to one side in two piles in the galley. No one asked what they were there for. He then got two white plastic bags with ties at the top, put two small holes in each and lay them to one side on the deck.

Tied up now for over twenty-four hours, Chris was in a very poor physical state, his skull fractured, his face, hands and upper body badly bruised and lacerated from the beating two days ago. Peta was in better physical shape but sobbing uncontrollably and mentally beaten.

Both were conscious and aware of everything that was happening but they were spiritually broken – worn down by Boston's psychopathic sick mind games that, by a process of attrition, had reduced them to total subjugation. Trusting and unsuspecting, they had been lured into the serpent's trap, only realising their wrong turn once his venomous bite was delivered but by then it was all too late.

Without untying them, he dragged them, one by one, to the deck – Chris from the galley and Peta from the small cabin in the front of the boat. Their few pitiful worldly belongings that they had packed the day before into their duffle bags in readiness for disembarking were waiting for them. Boston placed their enfeebled, bound bodies a small space apart on the portside of the boat, Chris at the back and Peta towards the front. Loosening the ties enough to allow him to dress them, but tight enough to prevent them struggling, he put a pair of green shorts and a canvas jacket on Chris and a pair of white pants, blue shorts and a T-shirt on Peta. He then further tightened the ropes around their wrists but this time behind their backs. Their legs fully outstretched before them were tied at the knees and ankles, allowing for no movement.

Russell says: 'Vince and I hoped at this stage that everything was moving forward to a resolution and Dad would let them go but then Dad's mood became even darker. When Dad gets weird, it's noticeable. I've been around him long enough to know that when he shifts, it's seriously dangerous.

'Dad was sailing up and down the coastline, taking the boat close into shore, and he taunted them by saying: "Hey, that sandy beach is a good spot to drop you guys." Chris constantly reassured him that they wouldn't go to the police. Peta was crying but didn't talk – I think she was in total shock. Chris kept telling her that it was going to be OK, that they were soon going to be set free. They could see the shoreline where Dad was pointing to.

'Then, as we were approaching, Dad suddenly announced that he would need to loop back round to get closer in for shallower water so that he could drop them off and they would be within their depth of water. He luffed the sails (to sail closer into the wind to add power to the boat) and started turning away from the shoreline.'

Boston, standing at the tiller, directed the boat out to open sea. Buoyed by his omnipotence, he and only he controlled whether Chris and Peta were to live or die.

Adding to their psychological torment, with a steeliness in his voice, he told Chris and Peta: 'I don't want you guys to see which direction I am going to sail in after I've dropped you, so I'm going to put plastic bags over your heads. It's OK, they have holes in so you can breathe.' Boston grabbed the pre-prepared bags that were lying on the deck, jammed them over their heads and tied them tightly around their necks.

Russell says: 'It didn't make any sense to me because we were in the lee of the peninsula towards the end and there was only one way we were going to sail away.'

Boston then jumped down into the galley and, one by one, dragged the heavy iron engine wheels up to the deck, clanging them onto the wooden deck as he pulled them up from the bowels of the boat. He positioned each set of leaden wheels next to Chris and Peta who, totally immobilised, had no option but to await their fate.

'Dad pointed to the weights and the ropes connected to them and with a demonic look in his eyes, he motioned for me to tie the weights to their legs. At the same time he said, but I knew he didn't mean it: "Russ, make sure those knots are loose so they can slip out as soon as we sail away." Dad made the comment about loosening their knots I think as a way to cover up the fact that he was tying a new rope to each of their feet. It was at that moment that I had the full realisation of what he was about to do. I shook my head, recoiled in horror and started to back away.

'Dad gave me a threatening, menacing look and mouthed,

"Tie the fucking knots, Russ! Tie the fucking knots!" I backed away and said, "No, no, no, Dad. No!"

'I don't remember him asking Vince to do it. I was in shock and it became a surreal blur of time and reality. Chris and Peta weren't saying anything at all.'

Softly, softly, step by step, Boston had, over the course of three days and two nights, mentally beguiled and physically and emotionally broken Chris and Peta down. He succeeded in overpowering them to such an extent that at the end, they were trussed up, incapable of any movement and with bags over their heads. Rendered totally incapacitated and petrified, they had no fight left in them.

Chris, horrifically injured but conscious, and Peta, in a state of shock and terrified, sat motionless and incapable of movement, awaiting Boston's ultimate act of sadism.

Boston then steered the *Justin B* further out to sea. As the bow pointed to the horizon, the only sound to be heard was the waves lapping against the hull and the sails flapping in the wind.

Russell says: 'We were by now well away from the peninsula. Dad said to Chris and Peta: "OK, we are right along the shoreline and it's really shallow so I'm going to push you guys off. It's not very deep so you are going to stand right up."'

Boston walked up to Chris and without pausing, callously lifted him off the deck and hurled him into the water, throwing the heavy engine parts after him.

'OK, here we go!'

'We were out in the middle of the ocean. I remember Vince and I standing there in total shock, not believing what we were witnessing. It happened so quickly,' says Russell.

Peta heard the impact from Chris being thrown into the sea

and the engine parts clanging on the deck before Boston hurled them in after him. Panicking and hysterical, she shrieked:

'Chris, Chris, are you OK? Are you OK?'

There was no answer.

'Dad replied in a calm, emotionless voice: "He's fine, he's standing up."

'Vince and I were standing on the deck. I could hear the blind terror and sheer panic in Peta's voice. I remember being frozen with fear and confusion. I was in a daze. I didn't know what to do or what would happen next.'

The two boys looked on helplessly as their father then walked up to Peta and, ignoring her screams, meted out the same treatment. Boston pushed her over the side of the boat as if he was throwing away something that had broken or was no longer of use.

Russell says: 'When she was drowning, she was screaming for Chris and I remember a huge air bubble came up in the sea through the plastic bag over her head, which burst. Then it was all over and there was nothing, they were both gone. The sea became calm and there was an eerie silence.

'I remember standing there dumbfounded and wondering what would happen next. Because he had beaten me three days earlier without provocation, I wondered if he was going to kill us. I knew they were dead, but death was hard for me to process at that point. Their belongings were still lined up on deck where they had placed them. I remember seeing Chris's beloved boombox next to his duffle bag. The boat was silent, with just the sound of the waves hitting the boat. There were no boats in sight, the horizon was deserted.'

Vince recalls that Boston looked at his watch and after three or four minutes turned to his sons and said in a flat, stone-cold voice: 'OK, they are dead now.'

Boston moved to the helm and started sailing.

Russell goes on: 'Vince and I didn't dare speak until, after a couple of hours, the silence was broken by Dad proclaiming: "You know I had to do that, they didn't give me a choice."

'We didn't reply. Later that day, Dad tried to justify to us what he had done. He said that the club either broke or was so slippery from Chris's blood that it had slipped from his hand and then when he stabbed Chris, the knife broke. When Chris said he gave up, [Boston] had no weapons on him at all. Dad reasoned that Chris, being 12 years younger, could have overpowered him but he chose not to and that was his choice. Chris could also have killed him when giving him the muscle relaxant. Dad's twisted, sick philosophy of the universe told him it was therefore OK to kill them because he'd given them a chance and they didn't take it.'

I asked Russell if he thought Chris and Peta knew they were going to die. Russell says: 'Dad had made us believe he was going to let them go. It was only when he luffed the sails, pulled the weights up from below, and announced we were along the shore when we so obviously weren't, that I realised what he was about to do. When it became apparent, I froze and didn't know what to do myself. I looked at them and I looked at the sea and how far out we were from land and I knew they didn't stand a chance. But Chris and Peta had the plastic bags covering their heads so hopefully they weren't aware. Dad told Chris to stand up in the water as he pushed him in, assuring him it was shallow. Because Dad seemed genuine until that point, maybe Chris didn't know until he actually hit the water that he was going to die. Peta immediately started shouting his name and totally panicked when he didn't answer and I think she knew.

'I have thought about what happened a million times since

and analysed how, between the four of us, we could maybe have done something. Dad had lost his diver's knife at the party in Hunting Caye and, unusually for him he didn't have a gun with him. The only scenario that would have worked, would have been if Vince and I had rushed dad at the same time, pushed him overboard, untied Chris and Peta before dad got back on board, and kept dad off the boat, sailing it to port with Chris and Peta, perhaps with dad in tow, on a rope tied to our dory. But I know the timing of that to work was near impossible. And I wouldn't be here now if I had tried and failed. It doesn't stop me from wishing I had though. Instead, the situation spiralled quickly out of control and we were all unprepared for what was going to happen next. Dad was a master of deception and manipulation. Chris was badly injured and incapacitated but I don't think he understood how far Dad was going to take it or the kind of person he was dealing with.

'Until Dad murdered Chris and Peta, it seemed that killing was something we were aware he was capable of doing, but I didn't realise the reality of it. Except for him beating me three days before, and beating Vince and I severely when I was six, I didn't know that he could be that extreme.

'I started to believe that if I thought about Chris and Peta each day, they would still be alive on some existential level and I could expunge some of my guilt for Chris saving me. I realise it's all terribly dark and sinister, and I don't want to downplay the severity of what Dad did, or the fear they must have felt from being in such a vulnerable situation. I'm certain it was absolutely horrendous and terrifying. A day doesn't go by when I don't think of how Chris saved me.'

* * *

AUTHOR'S NOTE: the bodies of Chris and Peta were discovered on 8 July. The autopsy carried out on 10 July estimated that they died between 1–3 July but their bodies were not refrigerated and with average temperatures of around 76 degrees F (24 degrees C) a high rate of decomposition (as noted in the pathologist's report) would have taken place following the recovery. Thus, their bodies lay undiscovered in the water for four days, meaning that Russell Boston's calculation of the date of their deaths as being 4 July would appear to be an accurate one.

Chapter Twelve

AFTER THE STORM

Boston waited two full days before he sailed the *Justin B* into the Guatemalan port of Livingston on 6 July, approximately 12 nautical miles from Punta de Manabique. It was two days spent steadying his and Vince and Russell's nerves. Two days in which he blackmailed, threatened and made them promise that they must never utter a word to anyone about what they had witnessed.

Russell says: 'Dad sheepishly explained that the reason he beat me, without provocation, the day before he attacked Chris was so that he could have a practice run in ambushing Chris. He wanted to judge the timing required to make an attack on Chris when he was pulling up the anchor at the front of the boat. Assaulting me was the dry run and I was the guinea pig.'

Boston told his sons that they needed to help him destroy or dispose of the evidence and if they didn't assist him, they would all be caught and killed. He went through all of Chris and Peta's belongings, separating into two piles the things he wanted to discard and those he wanted to keep. He weighted down Chris's medical bag and threw it overboard, first taking out the medical tools, like a pair of surgical scissors, which were engraved with C.Farmer. Boston thought these could be useful so he got a hot piece of metal and melted Chris's name off and kept them.

'Chris was passionate about his music,' says Russell. 'All of us, including Dad, loved listening to his boombox and his pre-recorded music, which he played like a DJ, from sunrise to sunset on the boat. I remember Frank Zappa's "Over-Nite Sensation" was a favourite of Chris's and whenever I hear that album, it brings back fond memories of him. Because our education had been pretty hit-and-miss, Vince and I were like sponges for knowledge and culture and lapped it up.

'Dad kept Chris's boombox and his music tapes and played them after he killed them but one album of Chris's that haunted him was *Animals* by Pink Floyd. Dad was very superstitious and the lyrics about the sad existence of someone who enjoys stabbing others behind their backs in the track "Dogs" haunted him, presumably because he saw parallels with himself. In the 1990s I made a cassette tape of music for Dad and slipped that track in deliberately so that he would contemplate the words and I remember Dad asking me why I had done that and he became angry.

'Ironically, Chris's boombox was lost overboard a couple of weeks later as a large freak wave hit the boat and knocked it into the sea. Dad, frantic to keep it, shouted at Vince to jump into the water and save it but he was too late, it was consumed by the waves and sunk. We all felt disappointment at watching it go under. I remember Dad superstitiously thought it was Chris reclaiming it!'

On entering the port of Livingston, Boston ran into some

trouble with the port authorities. They had arrived without visas and with their last destination being Belize, a country with which Guatemala had very uneasy relations, the port officials were not happy. Boston attempted to win them over by telling them that he was seeking refuge as the boat's motor had broken and he needed to get it repaired. After some haranguing, the *Justin B* was permitted entry and Boston arranged for the motor to be repaired in Livingston. Whilst there, he disposed of Chris and Peta's clothes by taking them to a local whore house.

Russell recalls that his dad started getting very jittery because he reasoned that if the bodies were discovered then the engine parts that they had been tied to may have been recovered from the seabed and could be matched with those that were still acting as ballast in the bottom of the boat. He said he needed to get out of Livingston and as fast as he could.

'Collecting the boat from the repair shop in the dock, he was in a great hurry to leave,' says Russell. 'I recall Vince had gone to buy an ice cream and had been gone quite a long time. Dad started up the motor engine and without waiting for him to return, he left! I could see Vince on the shoreline, at first strolling along and shouting to Dad to come back. Then, when he realised Dad wasn't going to stop or turn back for him, his pace became faster and faster until he was running at full speed and crying out to Dad to wait. Still Dad motored on along the shoreline and made no effort to slow down or stop. Realising that Dad had no intention of stopping, Vince, fully clothed, started to swim furiously out to the boat. Eventually, crying his eyes out, he caught up with us but Dad made no concession in slowing down. Whether Dad would have eventually gone back for him or not, we will never know. The fact that only days before he had so callously killed Chris and Peta, I don't think it would have been out of the question at all, had he chosen to leave him.'

Whilst in Livingston, Boston hired two male guides to help him navigate up the Dulce River and a girl Friday too. A Guatemalan outpost, the winding river is nestled between lush mountains and craggy cliffs, but its 43km are notoriously difficult to navigate, a task made even more treacherous at that time by the country being in the midst of a civil war. Boston wanted to carry out his plan to take the boat up the river to the mine at El Estor on Lake Izabal, which the manager at the party on Hunting Caye had invited him to visit. He was warned by the custom's authorities not to sail up the river's tributaries because it was bandit territory and highly dangerous. But that didn't thwart Boston, who told Vince and Russell: 'There must be something interesting up there if they are telling us not to go. Fuck it, we're going to go and take a look!'

It was to prove a bad move. Sailing the *Justin B* up one of the confusing network of tributaries one evening in the pitch dark, it got stuck in a large fishing net strung across the river and came to a grinding halt. Trapped, and sitting in darkness, Russell says that they could hear machine gun fire from guerrillas in the jungle either side of them and they were scared.

'I remember Dad saying that the guerrillas were shooting guns and I couldn't work out how gorillas could have weapons!'

Boston demanded that they turn all the lights out on the boat and sit tight and very quiet for the night. Eventually, the guns went quiet but as the sun started rising, Russell recalls that a party of Guatemalan soldiers streamed on to the boat: 'It was really frightening and we didn't know what to do. Dad apologised profusely for taking a wrong turn, saying he had got lost. Eventually, after a couple of hours and much persuasion, he succeeded in winning them over.' The soldiers eventually left the boat and the *Justin B* and its anxious passengers were allowed to commence their journey up the main river.

Coming to the end of the Rio Dulce and saying goodbye to the two guides and girl Friday, Boston took his sons to Castillo de San Felipe de Lara. Situated at the eastern end of Lake Izabal, it's an impressive Spanish colonial fort and a popular tourist destination. The fort was built to stop pirates entering the lake from the Caribbean when this part of Central America was an important shipping staging point. After the traumatic murderous events of the previous week, Boston and his sons were able to enjoy some downtime. They spent a day of leisure and sightseeing, captured in photos that Russell took with his camera, They then set sail across Lake Izabal (a massive inland lake, which Russell recalls being more like a sea) to the nickel mine in El Estor on the far northwest side of the lake. Here, they met up with the manager from the Hunting Caye party.

Russell says: 'Dad had this notion that it was going to be like Shangri-La. He thought that the adulation he had enjoyed at the party would be replicated in El Estor but it wasn't to be. In fact, for much of the time the manager was working and we were left to our own devices. We stayed in his house, which was just like the ones in America but this was in the jungle. We played with his kids and had a great time. We didn't want to leave but Dad, not receiving the kind of reception he was expecting at the mine, was eager to make a move.

'We arrived back in Livingston by 16 July because I recall Dad ringing my grandmother for my sister Vicki's birthday, and found that they had gone away on holiday.'

It was on returning to Livingston that Boston received some

good news. He rang his ex-wife, Kathe, who told him that his current status in terms of Californian law enforcement had changed and changed significantly... He learnt that the statutory rape charge with a minor that he had jumped bail and fled to Belize for, had been dismissed in April of that year. His defence attorney had successfully argued that because the girl was in a bar (the legal age limit for drinking is twenty-one in California), Boston had reasonably assumed she was twenty-one. The lawyer also cited the fact that she went to his house with the intention of being intimate, therefore making it consensual sex. This, in effect, meant that with the rape charge having been thrown out of court three months before, had he been told about it, Boston could have returned to the United States without fear of being arrested as long ago as April.

Russell recalls that Boston was angry and perplexed as to why his father hadn't given him this important piece of news when he had visited him in Belize back in April and had given him the money to buy the *Justin B*. 'Dad always blamed my grandfather for not telling him that the rape charge had been dropped. He said that, had our grandfather told him, he wouldn't have been in Belize in July to kill Chris and Peta. He would have been back home in California. So, he laid the blame for their murders at our grandfather's feet. Dad suspected that our grandfather kept the news from him out of malice because he himself had lost visitation rights to his own children when he divorced my grandmother in the 1940s. He believed that our grandfather was jealous that he still had control of us.'

Maybe it was also borne out of anger because Boston's father forfeited his bail bond when Boston fled California. We will never know the reason, but what we do know is that had Boston been told he was a free man and able to return to California in

April, he would never have been in Belize in July to kill Chris and Peta.

Russell recalls: 'Vince and I really loved our grandfather. He had a movie-star swagger, a deep voice and real charisma. He favoured Vince, who idolised him. When our grandfather visited us, he took Vince into Belize City to buy him a checked shirt and straw hat so he looked like a mini version of himself.'

Arriving back in Livingston, Russell recalls his father also had some other business to attend to: 'After Dad killed Chris and Peta, and he was ransacking their possessions, he found two letters that they had written to their families. He steamed them open and read them and then put them to one side. The letters mentioned that they were on the boat but they were not happy with what was going on, with my dad drinking all the time and acting crazy. My dad posted them, saying it was better for him that their families receive the letters to make them believe that Chris and Peta were still alive in Livingston. He deliberately left posting them until just before we were leaving.'

One of these letters was the one that Peta's parents received in early August with a Livingston postmark of 18 July, which temporarily alleviated our concerns for them. The other letter was not, as far as we know, received by anyone so was presumably lost, or maybe Boston changed his mind about sending it because it was too damning of him.

Abandoning his plans to sell the *Justin B* in Costa Rica, which to Chris and Peta he had claimed was the aim in going south, Boston left Livingston on 19 July and sailed back up the Belizean coast. Before the *Justin B* left port, like Chris and Peta before them, another couple boarded the boat.

Russell recalls: 'In Livingston, Dad had met another couple (of Scandinavian or German origin, I can't remember which), who wanted to travel to Belize. On the journey north, we ran into a huge storm. It was a very dark night and we were near the port of Dangriga (Stann Creek). High winds were whipping up the ocean waves and where they met the turbulent currents from the mouth of the North Stann Creek River, the boat felt like it was almost surfing over a cauldron of boiling water. We were used to storms but with the howling gale, this was frightening and eerie.

'The foreign couple became really scared and thought our boat was going to capsize so they grabbed the oars and began to paddle on both sides of the boat towards the shore. Dad joked that they looked like Vikings because of their stature and long blonde hair and the way they paddled. They didn't have visas to enter Belize so Dad offered to take them ashore under the cover of darkness. He took them one at a time in the boat's small dug-out canoe, leaving Vince and I alone on the boat. It wasn't unusual for Dad to leave us on the boat alone so I didn't think anything more of it. I can't even recall how long he was gone because I fell asleep.'

It was almost four decades later, during the recent investigation, Russell was to learn from the Sacramento Police Department, that his father had claimed to several people that he had murdered the 'Vikings' that night. He said he took them ashore, one by one, to a small, remote island off Dangriga (Stann Creek), where he tied them to a tree in the jungle, robbed them and cut their throats, leaving them to die.

By the time Boston returned to the *Justin B* later that night, Vince and Russell were asleep. In the morning, he chose not to enter the port of Dangriga, as might have been expected, but instead turned around and sailed south down the coast, entering the village of Placencia on 31 July. It was a fishing port that he had visited with Chris and Peta and which she had described in her last letter home as 'very pretty'.

Having already spent Chris and Peta's signed Travellers Cheques in Livingston, Boston wanted to cash in the unsigned ones that Chris and Peta had left over after paying him the $500 for their passage. He told Russell and Vince to practise writing their signatures on paper and to keep doing it until they got it right.

'I remember spending hours purposely doing it wrong,' says Russell. 'But he wouldn't let me go to sleep until I got it right. I can recall how to write Chris's idiosyncratic signature even to this day. I remember Dad being so happy as he left to go into town to spend the cheques.

'It was whilst we were in Placencia that Dad met a very shady Belizean, whose acquaintance he had previously made in Belize City. Together, they burgled a number of big boats that were anchored in the bay and got quite a haul. They agreed that the Belizean should go ahead and sell the stolen goods and they would then meet up again in Belize City to share the spoils. Dad boasted it was just like a scene from *Pirates of the Caribbean*.'

The *Justin B* then continued its journey northwards, entering once again the waters of Dangriga (Stann Creek), but this time the boat was reported by the harbour master as docking in the port on 9 August.

Arriving in Belize City on 11 August, Boston was furious because his partner in crime from Placencia didn't show up, as they had arranged. He became paranoid that his accomplice had been caught and that he would 'snitch' (one of his favourite words) on him.

On my visit to the States almost four decades later, Russell recounted to me how that night, whilst anchored off Belize City, his father told him and Vince about murdering their mother:

'Dad was paranoid about being caught and he said that once he was apprehended, Vince and I would be caught too and he couldn't allow that to happen. He told us that we had to die and that he was going to kill Vince and I the next morning. He assured us that he would make it painless and that he was very skilled at it.

'That night he was drinking heavily, and a lot more than normal, and he told us about all the people he had killed, including our mom. The murders ran into double figures. It was as if it didn't matter telling us because what would we do with the knowledge when tomorrow he planned to kill us? It was like some long, weird confessional.

'He told us that he had killed our Mom 10 years before, in 1968. This wasn't the first time I had heard this story. Our grandma had told us when I was aged seven and Vince was nine, but this was the first time that I heard it from Dad.

'In 1968, my parents were legally separated and Mom wanted to divorce him. Mom had an apartment in Sacramento and Vince and I were living with her. He told us that he persuaded our mom to get in the car by telling her that he wanted to talk things through with her. He took her to some remote location outside of Sacramento, but he has never told us where. While they were sitting under a tree talking, he announced that he was going to kill her. Mom begged him not to and he screamed: "Run, bitch!" She started running as Dad fired shots at her. He couldn't remember if he hit her on the back of her skull or the base but the shot didn't kill her. He described how Mom's legs jerked and jumped like a deer does when it's shot, and that he cradled her in his arms as she cried and bled. As she was dying, she said to him: "What about the kids, Duane, what about the kids?" Dad told us he "snuffed the bitch out" in a creek bed and it caved in on her and that she would not be found for a "million years". That night, whilst anchored off Belize City, he said to us: "If there is a heaven, you can go find your mother." He said the only person he regretted killing was our Mom.

'Dad then gave us a roll call of all the other people he had killed. I think it was to reinforce the severity of what was about to happen to us the next day, and if we didn't choose to escape, it would give him "permission" to kill us.

'The next morning, Dad said that my pet parrot, Salty, did not need to die with Vince and me so he told me to take Salty into Belize City and give the bird away to the "queers" as he called them. They were a couple of gay guys who owned a hotel in Belize called the Pasada Tropicana, a place we had stayed at a couple of times, and they had both admired my Amazon parrot.

'We were anchored near Belize City at the mouth of the river and he told me to use the boat's dug-out canoe. As I put Salty in his cage, Dad said: "I am going to kill you and Vince quickly but if you don't return, then I will kill Vince slowly and very painfully."

'"Dad, the canoe will be stolen if Vince doesn't come with me to watch it."

'"No, he's waiting here. You will have to take your chance with the canoe because he's not going with you."

'As I climbed into the canoe, he grabbed my arm very firmly and with his piercing blue eyes boring into me, he said threateningly: "It's not going to be painless for your brother so you had better come back."

'Full of heart-thumping fear, I took the boat and paddled it into Belize City. I hastily tied it off at our regular mooring, and ran a couple of blocks to the hotel and knocked on the door. I told them my dad wanted me to give them Salty. They thought something was wrong with my parrot and said the only reason my dad would give it away was if it was sick. To my dismay, they refused to take the bird.

'Not knowing what to do, I took Salty back to the canoe and to my amazement it was where I had left it, probably because it was still early in the morning. As I was paddling back to the *Justin B*, there were lots of boats sailing against me into the market. Convinced that Vince and I were about to die because I still had Salty, I had tears streaming down my face. I was bawling my eyes out and desperately paddling at the same time. I was begging out loud for God to do something, to help me. Then I started singing the Beatles' song "Let It Be" with the lyrics "When I find myself in times of trouble, Mother Mary comes to me." They have special significance for me because Mom's name was Mary. It was a cloudy morning and I remember a strong beam of light hitting me. I felt it was my mom helping me in my moment of need. I read that as a sign, so I paddled fast back to the boat because I wanted to tell Vince, before we died, that there was a heaven and Mom would be there waiting for us.

'As I rowed around the corner, I saw another boat tied off to the *Justin B* and I wondered what was happening. As I boarded the boat, I discovered that it belonged to a couple of Americans that we had met previously in Belize. Dad didn't refer to anything that had gone on before and didn't even ask why I still had Salty, but instead said: "Hey, look at this, Russ, these guys were sailing by and recognised the boat and stopped to say hello. They always wanted to buy the boat, so fuck it, I've decided to sell it to them! So, pack your bags, we are heading back home to the States."'

Boston, Russell and Vince flew from Belize City to Miami on 14 August, with Salty smuggled through customs in Chris's old camera case, Boston having sold his camera.

Belize was behind them... or was it?

Chapter Thirteen

BENEATH THE SURFACE

As Boston was never apprehended for Chris and Peta's murders and the case remained unsolved for approaching four decades, we naturally assumed that both Russell and Vince had remained silent and never reported their father's crimes. But we were wrong. Unbeknownst to us, the Framptons or Greater Manchester Police, they had contacted law enforcement agencies in America and the UK for many years. We were nothing short of astounded.

In the immediate aftermath of Chris and Peta's murders it is true, Russell and Vince were understandably silenced by their father's threat of death if they so much as uttered one word of what they had witnessed. Their murders, along with that of their mother, Mary Lou, were put in the same category – a family secret which should never be divulged to anyone. But, as they approached adulthood, and their father's control lessened, they understood the enormity and evil of what they had witnessed; it lay heavily on their consciences and as responsible citizens, they acted upon it.

In 1987, Russell, now aged twenty-one, attended a series of personal development seminars with Landmark Education in California. He recalls: 'I did an exercise where the assignment involved talking about a relationship with a girlfriend that had broken down. Randy, the forum leader, wanted to delve more deeply by asking me questions about my childhood. I answered them all, until he got to the part about my father, which I respectfully declined to answer. But Randy became like a drill sergeant, getting into my face and berating me for not opening up – I think he thought I had been molested, and by not answering, I was not going to move past it. I told him that I didn't talk about my father in public. He started yelling at me to get me to open up, saying I was a victim, and would I rather go through life being a victim? I told him that's not true, that I wasn't a victim – I just don't talk about those things. He asked me, "Do you think there's anything you can say that hasn't been said hundreds of times before in these seminars?" I said I didn't know, but I still wasn't going to talk about it. This just made him furious. He got nose-to-nose with me and started shouting and screaming, trying to break me down and open up. At one point, I heard an old lady from somewhere in the room yell, "Leave him alone!" But I still wouldn't talk about it. Finally, I calmly said, "I'm not going to talk about it in here, but if you really want to know, I'll tell you after class." He calmed down, gave me the number of his hotel and told me to call him. I called him that night and told him straight up that my dad was an outlaw and a criminal, who had murdered several people, including my mother and two British tourists in front of me and my brother when we were kids.

'Randy was quiet for a moment, then he said, "Yes, you're right, you shouldn't talk about that." And then he hung up on me.

'I had finally had the courage to tell someone outside of my inner circle, and this was his response. I felt betrayed and crushed. It was a massive thing for me to tell him. I wanted him to say, "Yes, tell everyone, tell the authorities, put your dad in jail, go into witness protection if necessary, but do what needs to be done!" But he didn't say that.

'The next day, several people who had witnessed him trying to get me to talk about my dad the previous day came up and asked me what he had said. I told them he said I shouldn't talk about it. Dumbfounded, they asked me what it was about. Strangely though, after telling Randy, I felt it opened the door and was a turning point in my life. For the first time, I felt able to open up to a number of people in my life about Dad. It was liberating.

'At the next seminar in the series I unburdened myself to an Anaheim police officer in front of one of the other seminar attendees, a girl who has remained a life-long friend. I told the cop because I knew he would be legally obliged to tell his superiors, who would then act on the information. I felt sure at this point that Dad would finally be investigated and brought to justice. I was shocked, however, when after listening to my story, he dismissed it as "family gossip and hearsay". I felt like no one would listen to me and I discussed my frustration and disappointment with Vince at some length.'

Not put off course, the following year, in 1988, Russell was attending a yacht convention in Long Beach with Boston's ex-wife, Kathe and Burt, her husband at that time.

'Kathe was talking to me about the time Dad kidnapped their son Justin in 1979 for six months. She said the police had informed her at the time that my dad was suspected in the disappearance and murder of two British tourists in Belize, and she asked me if Dad ever mentioned them to us.

'I replied, "Yes, he killed them."

'"What! He told you he killed them?"

'"No, he did it in front of us."

'I then told her exactly what we had seen.

'Kathe was naturally shocked and asked me if I'd be willing to tell the authorities and I said yes, of course. Later, Kathe told me she had relayed what I had told her to a friend of hers who lived in Toronto and worked for the Royal Canadian Mounted Police (RCMP), and had previously worked for Scotland Yard. Kathe told him what I had told her. She said he called an FBI agent he knew in Washington, D.C. We were given a case number of #435035, and Kathe told me he had contacted England and they were investigating the case. I don't know if that case number was from the FBI or Interpol, or Scotland Yard in England.

'At this point, Vince and I fully expected the case to go forward and we discussed at great length what I would do if, in the event, Dad was questioned and released and he was made aware of the fact that I had turned him in. There was absolutely no question that he would kill me. Dad had no idea where Vince lived at that time or how to find him so, for that reason and that reason only, we agreed he should be the point person and represent us both. Astonishingly, I never received a call nor received any feedback from the RCMP, FBI nor Interpol despite them having my contact details and full information on what happened.

'Vince has told me on numerous occasions that the police maintained that there was nothing that could be done in regard to our mother, because even with a "Jane Doe" [unidentified body] whose DNA matched Vince's and mine, without a witness or a confession from our father, it would be just hearsay.' It was only in becoming estranged seven years ago, following conflict over multiple family issues, that Vince and Russell stopped jointly devising ways of bringing their father to justice.

'I think almost every meaningful friendship and relationship I have had over the last thirty or so years, I have been totally open and honest about my dad, my background and what I know. I have felt that no one in authority was ever going to apprehend my father or take mine and Vince's allegations seriously or even just sit up and take notice. As a consequence, I have spent literally years and years searching for Chris and Peta's families on the internet but never found you.'

In 1982, on reaching sixteen and having been on the receiving end of a severe beating from his father, Vince decided to join the Navy. This being his first opportunity to escape the clutches and influence of Boston, he contacted London's Scotland Yard to tell them that four years previously, he had witnessed the cold-blooded murder of two British citizens and he gave Chris and Peta's full names. Vince and Russell didn't know that Chris and Peta were from Manchester and, as citizens of the United States, it was understandable that they assumed that Scotland Yard operated and had jurisdiction throughout the whole of England. Unbelievably, Vince was told that there was no file and they were not traceable. Up in the Northwest of England, none of this reached our ears. After Inspector Sacks was moved off the case we heard nothing more from Greater Manchester Police or Sacramento Police Department after July 1981.

Again, in 2002, and on several other occasions, Vince made several strenuous attempts on his and Russell's behalf to alert the authorities to the fact that they were allowing a serial murderer to remain free and at large in the community but each time he contacted the Sacramento Police Department, Interpol or Scotland Yard, he was told that he needed hard evidence. It seemed no one on either side of the Atlantic was prepared to do any digging, join the dots and work out jurisdiction.

In 2012, with his health beginning to fail (a combination of advancing years and hard living) Boston had given up, for the short term, living an itinerant life split between the Baja California Peninsula in Northwestern Mexico and California, and he stayed for a couple of years in Russell's mobile home in Roseville in Placer County, Sacramento. Russell had inherited the home from Boston's mother when she died in 2009. Occasionally cared for by a friend of his mother's, Boston complained to her that he had no friends. So, on 12 April 2012, just after his seventy-first birthday, she made him a Facebook account to help him locate some of his old high school friends.

It was this Facebook account which Vince spotted in 2012, just as I was to do three years later. He saw that it publicly displayed a list of Boston's friends and it announced that his father was back living in the Sacramento area. Vince contacted Sergeant Robert McCloskey of the Sacramento Police Department and implored him to investigate. He told him in great detail about his father's admission of killing his mother and that he and his brother had witnessed the murders of Chris and Peta.

Attempting to establish the voracity of Vince's claims, Sergeant McCloskey contacted Interpol in London but, once again, they said they had no file or trace of Chris and Peta. In March 2013, Sergeant McCloskey wrote back to Vince saying: 'Interpol has included London [Scotland Yard] in our requests in an attempt to determine/confirm the identities of the alleged victims, who were UK nationals; however, they too are having difficulty locating information about this case. They

Above left: Chris Farmer and Peta Frampton in the summer of 1977, the year before their fateful trip to Central America.

Above right: My brother, Dr Chris Farmer: 'with him around, life always seemed that bit more exciting and edgier'.

Below: A happy day: my parents with Chris and Peta following Chris's graduation ceremony from Birmingham University Medical School in July 1977.

Above left: The last known photograph of Chris and Peta together before they left for Australia in early December 1977; this was taken on the day before their departure.

Above right: Chris (standing) and Peta (sitting) with the girlfriend of the owner of the *Norma* – the boat which took them from Belize City to Caye Caulker and the Great Blue Hole. The picture was taken by Boston from the deck of the *Justin B*. *(© Russell Boston)*

Below: Photographed by Boston using Russell's little 110 camera, Chris is pictured with twelve-year-old Russell (left), proudly displaying his catch of the day, and thirteen-year-old Vince (right) at Blackadore Caye. *(© Russell Boston)*

Above: Chris sailing the *Justin B*.

(© Russell Boston)

Below: The two crosses that were erected in Puerto Barrios Cemetery, Guatemala, to mark their graves, with the misspelling of Peta's surname.

Above left: Silas Duane Boston, the family man. Taken at the request of Boston's mother, Mary Evelyn Sellers Boston, at Sears Stores, Sacramento, in October 1978, some two months after returning home from Belize. Left to right: Russell (twelve), Vince (just turned fourteen) and Boston's disabled daughter Vicki (fifteen), who was not present on the boat. This is a rare photo of Boston, who had an aversion to his picture being taken.

Above right: Russell Boston.   *(© Russell Boston/Facebook)*

Below left: Vince Boston.   *(© Vince Boston/Facebook)*

Below right: A photograph of Boston, taken in Sacramento in 2012, which he used as his Facebook profile picture. He was 71 by then, and 34 years had passed since he had murdered Chris and Peta.   *(© Facebook)*

Left: A vintage 'nightstick' similar to the billy club that Boston used to hit and disable Chris.

Right: Heavy metal machine parts, identical to the ones Boston tied to Chris and Peta before he threw them overboard.

Above: Russell (left) and Vince (right) with their grandfather, Russell Boston Senior, on his visit to Belize in April 1978, some three months before Chris and Peta were killed.

(© Russell Boston)

Left: Russell Boston and me in Emerald Bay, Laguna, California: July 2017.

Right: The infant Russell with his mom, Mary Lou – Boston's third wife, whom he killed in September 1968. *(© Russell Boston)*

Left: Mary Lou and Silas Duane Boston; he was never to be charged with her murder. *(© Russell Boston)*

Above left: Head of the GMP Cold Case Review Unit Martin Bottomley flanked by Detective Constable Michaela Clinch (left) and Detective Sergeant Julie Adams (right).

Above right: With FBI Special Agent David Sesma and Victim Specialist Carol Watson (right).

Centre left: Pictured with me (centre) from left to right: (AUSA) Jeremy J. Kelley; (FBI SA) David J. Sesma; (US Attorney) Philip A. Talbert; (AUSA) Matt Segal and Detective Amy Crosby.

Below left: The certificate presented by the US Department of Justice, bearing the poignant words: 'On behalf of those who can no longer speak for themselves'.

Below right: The timepiece in memory of Chris that was presented to me by Philip A. Talbert, on behalf of the US Department of Justice.

Left: Discovering Boston, Russell and Vince on the internet, I felt sure that I could get to the truth if I just drilled down far enough.

Right: With my 25-year-old son Charlie, who met me in California after a back-packing tour of Southeast Asia.

Left: Our mother, Audrey Farmer.

asked London if it was possible to initiate inquiries with the appropriate government officials to check Embassy records in order to communicate with surviving family members of the deceased, not to mention possible repatriation records of bodies to the UK. Apparently, London has completed these checks and have been unable to locate anyone that matches the descriptions with anyone reported missing in the UK. However, without more information it is difficult to know for sure. They would need date of births and/or the location the couple were from in the UK. London stated that they are doing some additional searches at the National Archives to see if there were any news reports around the time of a missing couple.'

It was England that was the stumbling block which prevented Boston's sons from taking the case against their father forward, not just once but several times. Records show that an enquiry was also made to the UK's National Crime Agency. Set up in 2010, it is a national law enforcement agency and, similar to the work of the FBI in America, operates across both regional and international borders. A joined-up national network, it was established with the express intention of avoiding oversights such as this from happening.

When the enquiry, initiated by Vince, came in from Sacramento Police Department in 2012, like Interpol, the National Crime Agency reported they had no trace of Chris and Peta. In their defence, the agency had only recently been established and the file which Greater Manchester Police had held in 1978 had been lost. But it was sloppy work; whoever investigated the enquiry failed to do so properly. Being a British doctor, a fact which Vince did relay to the police on several occasions, Chris was eminently traceable. All it required was a simple call to the General Medical Council, and the police would have been able to quickly confirm that Chris was removed from the register on confirmation of his death in 1979. It's one of the greatest ironies of the case that Chris was very traceable all along.

With all the files that had once belonged to Interpol, Greater Manchester Police and Sacramento Police Department seemingly lost, and Vince quite understandably not knowing what part of England Chris and Peta came from, the investigation in 2013 once more came to a grinding halt. Clearly frustrated that his father's heinous crimes had again been so negligently overlooked, Vince, out of desperation and to his credit, in March 2013, wrote to Sergeant McCloskey: 'I wonder why Interpol or Belize never questioned or talked to my brother and I as we were eyewitnesses. Also, there was Chris's blood on the boat from when Dad beat him with the club. Interpol and or the police never followed up. Doesn't it seem like my dad is the luckiest murderer in the world? He has gotten away with all these crimes for so many years and might never be caught. I did what I could. I am not sure what to do next. Is there anything else that I can do from my end? *America's Most Wanted*? Put an ad in *London Times* with Chris's information and picture? Can we get a warrant and tap my dad's phone and get him to confess? I wish there was more I could do.'

So, despite Russell and Vince's attempts to bring their father to justice, their efforts came to nought, leaving a serial killer to roam free for decades.

It was our visit to Greater Manchester Police in October 2015 that reconnected law enforcement in this country with Sacramento Police Department and put Chris and Peta's names back on the radar, and thus traceable. Without that, all of Sacramento's enquiries would have resulted in nought.

BENEATH THE SURFACE

At exactly the same time as we made our first visit to GMP, Detective Amy Crosby of the Sacramento Police Department's Missing Persons Unit was looking at the case file of Mary Lou Boston from 1968 and deduced it had been very poorly investigated. I called Greater Manchester Police on 5 October and on 12 October we had a meeting and on 13 October, Amy spoke to Vince. Amy could see from her records that Boston's sons had made several attempts to report their father over the years but it hadn't been enough to bring about a conviction.

Amy says: 'I started working in this unit in May of 2014. In 2012, Vince had contacted Lt McCloskey [who was at that time a homicide sergeant] to inquire into the missing person case of Mary Lou and also to report witnessing the homicides of Chris and Peta. McCloskey documented what Vince reported to him in a homicide information report. That was the report that I reviewed and started conducting my follow-up investigation on. There was enough detail in what Vince had reported to Lt McCloskey in 2012 for me to believe that he was telling the truth about the murders. If Boston was capable of murdering Mary Lou and Chris and Peta in cold blood, what else had he done? I knew he was a very bad man – I wanted to find out just how bad he was. It bothered me that Boston had got away with these murders for so long. I started digging and the more I dug, the deeper the rabbit hole became. By then, I was on a mission.'

In late February 2016, Interpol put the two police forces on either side of the Atlantic in direct touch with each other. Greater Manchester Police's Michaela Clinch spoke with Detective Amy Crosby in Sacramento and they held weekly web conference meetings to liaise on how the investigation was progressing on both sides, in preparation for Boston's arrest and forthcoming trial.

It was at this point that we discovered a very startling fact: Boston was on Sacramento Police Department's radar for something totally separate from Chris, Peta and Mary Lou's murders. And it was for this reason that Detective Amy Crosby had Mary Lou's missing person file, dating back to 1968, on her desk in October 2015 at exactly the same time as I had made contact with GMP.

The reason was this: From 1976 through to 1986, California was plagued with an unidentified serial killer and rapist who went under the media epithet of The Original Night Stalker, the East Area Rapist, the Diamond Knot Killer, and since 2013, the Golden State Killer (GSK). He wasn't known to be the same person until DNA connected numerous cases all over California, decades later. He is believed to have committed 50 rapes and murdered 12 people across 15 jurisdictions from Sacramento down to Orange County. Knowing they had the GSK's DNA, the FBI decided it was time they tried to catch or identify him. In the autumn of 2015, the FBI created a task force that reached out to the police jurisdictions in all the counties where his attacks occurred, in the hope that some cold case file, which was overlooked decades ago, would hold the key to identifying the perpetrator.

Law enforcement was asked to look for crimes or a perpetrator whose modus operandi had similarities with what was known about the GSK: tying people up, specifically couples, assuring them they would ultimately be released if they complied, then killing them; rape; murder; a history of violence; blue or green eyes; lived in East Sacramento in 1976 and 1977; military training and possibly a Vietnam veteran; attendance at American River College (a community college in Sacramento); had access to several different kinds of vehicles which were spotted near the crime scenes; someone who may have had a real estate connection; painting or construction skills; a tattoo on his left forearm that looked like a bull or had horns; athletic or had skills in climbing or jumping fences; a cat burglar and skilled at breaking into homes; skilled with weapons, guns and a good marksman; spoke through clenched teeth when angry; connections and ties to not only East Sacramento but also specific areas in Southern California, etc.

Russell says: 'When Detective Amy Crosby made contact with me in January 2016, I was completely forthright and told her everything I knew about my father with unbridled honesty. At the end of the conversation she cautiously asked if I had any samples of my father's DNA in the things he left with me – an old toothbrush or something. I said I might have, but asked her why they needed it, because there would most likely be no DNA of Dad's from the murders of my mom or Chris and Peta. Amy told me they were looking at him for some other unsolved crimes, rapes specifically, which happened in the mid to late seventies in Sacramento. I asked her if she was talking about the East Area Rapist and she was a bit stunned then asked me how I knew about it. I told her it was all over the news in Sacramento during that time period.'

Russell adds: 'Because of my mom's case and the notes pertaining to the details of Chris and Peta's murders, my dad quickly rose to the top of the list of suspects. His modus operandi of tying Chris and Peta up, luring them into a false sense of security by assuring them that they would be OK if they just complied, they would be let go, all matched perfectly with the GSK's technique from the same time period.

'Throughout my upbringing, my father had lots of people who came in and out of his life. He liked to have flunkies as he called them, lookouts and assistants in his burglaries and such. Most didn't measure up to the skill and precision he expected of them, and he'd end up running them off or threatening to kill them. He seemed constantly on the lookout for someone he could teach and join him in his endeavours. For instance, in the early 1980s, a friend of Dad's worked for a real estate agent in Carmichael and got him a job as a handyman. Dad and his friend would go in and repair toilets, hot water heaters, decorate or fix whatever was broken. It was a good way of learning the owner's schedule and obtaining a set of keys which they could then duplicate. Weeks later they would return to rob them.'

Russell wasn't the only person to suspect his father. In late 1977, the East Area Rapist had phoned one of his victims and his voice was recorded on an answering machine as saying, 'I'm gonna kill you.' This chilling message was broadcast in California, in 2013, in an attempt to flush out the identity of the rapist. On hearing this message, Vince thought that his father might indeed be the East Area Rapist: 'The recording was really creepy. The guy was disguising his voice and it's more like a grunt. My dad has a very deep voice and when he gets mad, he grinds his teeth together. It sent shivers down my spine and I just wondered could it be him? Dad was an accomplished burglar and used to come home with all kinds of stuff. He would break into people's houses and he and his friend would break into trucks, steal a bunch of things and sell them. He had these Halloween masks, rubber masks, and he would wear them when breaking into people's homes – I think one was orange and one was green, like a Frankenstein. They were rubber latex that covered the whole head with holes for eyes and the mouth. He was very crafty, he would plan it all out. He said he tied up this old lady with duct tape. Dad would come home with all kinds of stuff.'

Although the GSK originally targeted women, either alone in their homes or with children, he later preferred attacking couples. Read the description below, from Wikipedia, of the GSK's modus operandi and it takes one back to the events on the boat and how, over the course of two days, Boston lured Chris and Peta to their deaths with his sick psychological mind games. The GSK's standard procedure was to break in and awaken the occupants, threatening them with a handgun. He would start by assuring them he only wanted money, and if they complied, they wouldn't be harmed. By doing this, it lulled his victims into a false sense of security. Victims were bound with rope. The female victim was made to tie up her male companion with bootlaces or ropes. He would separate the couple, often stacking dishes on the back of the male and telling him that if he heard the dishes rattle, he would kill everyone in the house. Meanwhile, he would rape the woman repeatedly, who he tied up, in another room. The intruder at times spent hours in the home, ransacking closets and drawers, eating food in the kitchen, and then coming back to utter more threats to the victims, who were often unsure as to whether he was still in the home.

With such compelling similarities, it is little wonder that in early 2016 Boston came under the microscope and rose to the top of the FBI and police's lists of prime GSK suspects.

The cynic in me is left asking, had it not been for Sacramento Police Department pursuing Boston's possible link with the extremely high-profile case of the Golden State Killer, would Chris and Peta's case have ever stood a chance of being reopened, especially given that it was almost four decades old? How much were the police and FBI motivated by the thought they could solve a serious multiple crime case and reap the glory and public relations kudos? It's a fact that despite the abomination of Chris and Peta's murders, the case had been so easily overlooked and seemingly, so quickly forgotten on both sides of the Atlantic.

What we do know is that we were truly blessed with the calibre of the lead detective on the ground in Sacramento, Amy Crosby, and her highly skilled investigative team, who all worked the case with such diligence.

Extrovert and vivacious, with a shock of long blonde corkscrew curls, when Amy enters a room, she has presence. Growing up in a small, sleepy rural town in Northern California, she has been a police officer for 26 years. She has spent 16 of those as a detective, specialising in elder and dependent adult abuse investigations, domestic violence and child abuse cases and works now in the Missing Persons/Warrants Unit.

Fortunately blessed with a phenomenal memory, Russell sat down with Amy in early 2016 and they spent many days sifting through every event and contact of his father's that he could recall, which Amy and her team then extensively researched. Both were determined that this time, Boston was not going to get off. Incredibly, the police have three large files totalling 2,000 pages, detailing the crimes, including numerous murders, Boston is suspected of committing over a period of five decades. A highly volatile, dangerous character, supremely clever at covering his tracks, he'd slipped the noose throughout his life.

However, Boston's fortunes had, the previous year, thankfully started to change. Aged seventy-five, his health poor and with nowhere to live, he was low on steam and options. After a lifetime spent on the run, Boston was finally running out of road.

Exhausted from living an itinerant's existence between Mexico and California, he had travelled to Eureka, a seaport city in

Northern California, some 310 miles northwest of Sacramento. Recognising he needed to seek help, he turned up, dishevelled and dirty, on the doorstep of the ex-wife of a deceased partner in crime, whom he hadn't seen for over 30 years. He was too incapacitated to even to take a shower so she suggested driving him to Eureka's Seaview Rehabilitation & Wellness Center. Before he agreed to go, knowing that he wouldn't be allowed to take them into any healthcare facility, he entrusted her with his highly treasured stun guns, saying that he would be back for them when he was better. Installed as an in-patient in the nursing home, Boston found himself, for the first time, not a prisoner but certainly exposed and a sitting duck for law enforcement.

Making the five-hour journey from Sacramento on 16 February 2016, it was to Eureka that Amy and her colleague, Detective Janine LeRose, drove to interview Boston. He was now firmly in their sights and they were armed with Vince and Russell's damning eyewitness statements of events on the boat.

Entering the side room, they found a man who looked much older than his years. His hands and limbs were riddled with arthritis and, although he could walk, he chose to use a wheelchair. Boston must have been shocked at the announcement of the detectives' arrival but if he was, he didn't show it. His circumstances might have changed, but his arrogant cocky personality hadn't. Amy described him as: 'Cognitively sharp as a tack'.

Beset by ill health and the ravages of old age he may have been, but he was still the same hard-core evil criminal that he'd been all his life. 'Boston was adept at playing "the game", which is why he had evaded justice for so long,' says Amy. 'It is very difficult to deal with someone who shows no empathy and no remorse because you can't tap into them in any way. Despite having full mental capacity, when I interviewed him about Chris and Peta, he at first said he didn't know them and refused to talk about them. After further questioning, he admitted to knowing them but he laughingly and arrogantly dismissed the case as being out of the jurisdiction of the Californian law authorities. He wasn't prepared to, and said he didn't have to, answer to anyone.'

Amy and Janine were unsuccessful in extracting an admission of guilt from Boston but their visit to Eureka was far from wasted. Crucially, Boston admitted to owning the boat, the *Justin B*, in 1978, which was to prove a vital tenet of the prosecution team's future case against him.

Moving the interview on from the events in Belize, Amy then asked him point-blank the question to which all the law-enforcement agencies throughout California wanted the answer: 'Are you the Golden State Killer?' Boston replied that he wasn't.

Anticipating his denial, she continued undeterred and asked him for a saliva cheek swab for DNA matching with the known sample of the GSK's, collected from one of the scenes of crime. Boston put up no resistance but was savvy enough to know that in California, police can take a DNA sample from any person who is arrested on probable cause for a felony offence.

The interview concluded, Amy and her colleague travelled back to Sacramento where Boston's DNA was fast-tracked in the laboratory for DNA matching in what they felt would be an affirmation of a foregone conclusion. When the result came back, it astonished not only Russell but many in the Sacramento Police Department and the FBI: it was negative.

In June 2016, because law enforcement had still had not found or identified the GSK, the FBI launched a $50,000 reward for information that would lead to his arrest and conviction, in the hope that some member of the public would realise who he was, or have the courage to come forward.

It was, therefore, with much more than just an enquiring mind that on 25 April 2018 I read news reports that a man suspected of being California's elusive Golden State Killer – 72-year-old former police officer, Joseph James DeAngelo – had been taken into custody after police used DNA testing and an online genealogy database to track him down at his home in Citrus Heights, in Sacramento. Even though the GSK's crimes were committed over 5,000 miles away, because 76-year-old Boston had previously been prime suspect, I was fascinated with news of DeAngelo's arrest.

Suffice to say that the Californian capital of Sacramento, a city built by the gritty pioneers of the Californian Gold Rush, possessed in the 1970s and 1980s a very disturbing dark underbelly of crime and violence which spawned more than its fair share of rapists, robbers and murderers.

But to return to our case, in ruling out Boston from being the GSK, the police and the FBI knew that he was a serial killer and needed to be prosecuted, but how were they going to do it now? Things were looking gloomy and once again, the appalling thought that Boston might never be brought to justice started to creep into our heads. With an entire task force of the FBI, Sacramento PD, Sacramento Sheriffs as well as Greater Manchester Police, the police had finally focused their attention on him, yet still we were back to square one. They could not leave a known serial killer free, especially when he had been allowed to commit a litany of serious crimes for five decades.

Russell once more sat down with Detective Amy Crosby and this time delved even deeper into every single crime his father had committed, in the hope of finding something that would bring him to justice or a jurisdiction that would stick. Although Boston was known to have committed multiple crimes, many of them were decades old and therefore difficult to prove. For instance, the FBI could corroborate that he was responsible for a hit-and-run traffic accident on Lemon Hill Avenue in Sacramento, in 1972. The victim had been killed and the incident was reported in the local newspaper, the *Sacramento Bee*. Amy Crosby was able to locate the article describing the 10 June 1972 hit-and-run traffic death of Marshal Williams, but because it had been misfiled under the traffic and not the murder crime section, it had been purged and the police did not have the jurisdiction to pursue it through the courts.

The police came to the conclusion that with two living eyewitnesses, their best chance of securing a conviction was by charging Boston with Chris and Peta's murders. A successful prosecution would mean that he would either get a life sentence or the death penalty. But the next thorny question was, who would stand up to the plate and take jurisdiction?

Enter legal eagle, Prosecuting Assistant Attorney Matthew D. Segal. A Harvard graduate (cum laude), in 2014 he was made chief of the U.S. Attorney's Office's Special Prosecutions Unit for Eastern District of California. Possessing an intellectual aura, Matt is a great communicator and quick thinker; you sense every word he utters is considered and measured. Thankfully, he is also very tenacious. Others less driven might well have given up, defeated by the complexity of the case, but not him. He told Greater Manchester Police's Martin Bottomley that the case had got a hold of him and he constantly devised ways of prosecuting Boston even when he was on the treadmill at the gym!

Greater Manchester Police went into discussions with Matt and his team about the feasibility of extraditing Boston to the

UK, and Michaela Clinch and Julie Adams were put on standby to go over to California to interview him.

Lawyers for Great Britain's Crown Prosecution Service became involved but disappointingly, reported back with their findings in April 2016: 'The advice is pretty unequivocal that section 4 of the Suppression of Terrorism Act 1978 provides jurisdiction to try a non-British national for homicide committed abroad, where it is a European Country that has signed the European Convention on the Suppression of Terrorism 1977. Clearly this would not apply to Guatemala. A footnote on page 10 refers to the Territorial Waters Jurisdiction Act 1878, however again this relates to offences on the open sea or within the "waters of Her Majesty's dominions... ", therefore has the same limitations as the Merchant Shipping Act 1995, which didn't provide jurisdiction as it applies to international waters.'

Looking for any option open to them, they then looked at section 9 of the Offences Against the Person Act 1861, but again found it to be wanting. The UK neither had jurisdiction to try either the offence itself or offender. In summary, the UK did not have jurisdiction under any law that was in existence in 1978. Not only were GMP and the American prosecution team disappointed, we were crestfallen in the extreme to hit yet another brick wall. How sweet it would have been to have made Boston make the trip to England to stand trial.

Undeterred, Matt and his team then looked into extraditing Boston to Guatemala to stand trial, but again they ran into legal problems, plus a reluctance to try a near forty-year-old cold case. Belize also said they didn't have jurisdiction because even though the murders happened on a Belizean boat, and theirs was the last port the boat departed from, the murders happened off Guatemala. The FBI also said they had no jurisdiction, because again, the murders happened in another country with no ties to the US.

The legal team concluded the only way they could claim jurisdiction was if the murders happened in open water, and most importantly, were committed by an American, on a boat owned by an American, with registration or proof that the American was indeed the owner of the vessel at the time. The FBI started searching for records in Belize for the boat and its provenance, but all their records from that time period had been destroyed by a fire and were long gone.

They were left with only one option and that was to prove that Boston had owned the boat by showing ownership through witness testimony, including, for example, Peta's letter, the Belize harbour master's crew list and verbal testimonies of Russell and Vince. Using this as a basis for claiming American jurisdiction, the case began to gather momentum.

Matt says: 'Homicide cases are rare in federal court, and I was lucky enough to have an attorney in my unit, Heiko Coppola, who had been an Oregon state homicide prosecutor before joining us. Once Mr Coppola and I had assessed that we had jurisdiction and could put on a legally sufficient double-murder case, I added Jeremy Kelley to the team and we worked as quickly as possible to direct the investigators to what evidence we thought was necessary for charging Boston. We were constantly balancing the urgency of initiating prosecution against the need to ensure that we had gathered enough admissible evidence to prove our case if Boston demanded a speedy trial.'

On 26 April, the prosecuting attorneys Matt Segal and Heiko Coppola sought assistance from the FBI in helping them in their investigation and in particular, the complex task of tracing leads in the UK, Guatemala and Belize.

Chapter Fourteen

THE PEARL IN
THE OYSTER

Quite astonishingly there were more surprises to come, and one in particular we could never have imagined. Whether it was the stars in the constellation aligning at the right time or just a bizarre set of coincidences, we will never know but for once the wheel of fortune spun in our favour... It was 16 September 2016 when Russell made a truly remarkable discovery.

On my visit to California the following year, Russell Boston described what happened. He told me how, over the years, he had secretly retained evidence from Belize, which, when added to his testimony, he hoped would one day bring his father to justice. He could never have imagined at the time just how crucial this evidence would prove to be.

Escaping the long arm of the law, Boston on his frequent trips to Mexico often visited Russell at his home, southeast of Los Angeles in Huntington Beach. He would offload unwanted belongings and, at the same time, take the opportunity to bribe his son for money, cars, or even a bed to sleep in. If that didn't work, he'd threaten to harm or kill Russell's neighbours until he got his way.

'Many a time, he'd stop by my house on the way to Mexico and say, "Do you want this shit? I'm throwing it in the trash." Dad spent his life running away and would pull up stakes and escape in the night at the drop of a hat. When we were children, he would often tell us, "Pack a box" and then hand us a cardboard box,' explains Russell. 'Everything we wanted to bring with us had to fit in that box. That usually included our clothes, personal items, drawings, toys, etc. He would also reduce his own belongings in those situations for a faster getaway. Important things he'd store with our relatives – his mother, his father, his aunt, etc. – and he'd retrieve those later. That's why I have several of his things now.'

Living in the same house for 23 years, Russell held onto all of his father's belongings that he had deposited. What the legal team really wanted was any proof that Boston had owned the boat. Russell was unsure if he had anything but he did recall that he had at one time kept the boat's flag with his dad's handwritten '*Justin B*' on it and he mentioned it to Amy Crosby, who was very keen that he should find it. And so Russell set about the business of searching through absolutely everything that belonged to his dad.

'Dad discarded several things throughout the years. One of them was a vintage leather briefcase with old papers, IDs, business cards, address books, etc. I knew I'd saved years of junk and items my father had intended to throw in the garbage, but I didn't know if I had the ownership proof they needed. I had the original photos from Belize and Guatemala, and even the actual 110 film negatives they came from, showing a chronological timeline of photos from northern Belize, to when we met Chris and Peta, to Blackadore Caye, where the photo on the boat of me, my brother and Chris was taken, and then the photos of San Felipe Castle in Guatemala, with Chris and Peta absent. However, all of that was circumstantial.

'Of all the items my dad left with me which linked him to killing Chris and Peta, the most significant was Chris's music collection. Chris had painstakingly recorded his treasured vinyl records onto cassette and in his own handwriting, he had labelled each one with the band, album and songs. He used to play those cassettes on our boat all the time, and lovingly described the songs, lyrics, influence and significance of each one. Dad kept Chris's cassettes, and I'd always known those could one day be used as evidence against him, if compared to Chris's handwriting. So, when he discarded those, I scooped them up and put them in storage. I moved two years before my dad was arrested and most of my dad's discarded belongings were still packed away. I spent weeks sifting through old boxes and crates until I finally found my father's old briefcase. Inside it, wedged between a pile of junk, was a small, folded-up scrap of paper. When I unfolded it and saw the title of the boat, with my dad and grandfather's signatures, handwritten and stamped and dated, I knew I was on to something.'

Both Russell and Vince were subpoenaed to attend the Grand Jury on 13 October 2016 at the US Courthouse and Federal Building in Sacramento. Some seven hours away from his home in Laguna, and, wanting to deliver the document in person, Russell waited until then to hand over the critically important document.

'To be honest, at the time I didn't appreciate just how important it was. I felt that with everything else going on in the case, that it was no longer that significant. Until, that is, I drove to Sacramento to appear before the Grand Jury. I met with the FBI, Sacramento PD and Federal Prosecutors in a conference room prior to my testimony. I had brought along my dad's briefcase and a box of original photos, negatives, driver's licences, IDs, etc. When I handed them the boat title, they actually jumped up out of their chairs and high-five'd each other with cheers you'd expect from die-hard fans witnessing a World Cup winning goal, as opposed to stoically reserved investigators in suits and ties. I was eager to continue showing them the next items I was pulling out from the briefcase, but they were still standing around me, looking at each other with wide eyes and open mouths in unbridled disbelief. It was at that moment that it dawned on me what that scrap of paper meant.'

The receipt was evidence that at the time of Chris and Peta's murders, Boston was the owner of the boat. Being a citizen of the United States, this made the *Justin B* the property of a US citizen and thus maritime and territorial laws of the US would apply and a case could be brought against Boston under the federal jurisdiction of the California Department of Justice. The thorny question of jurisdiction was nailed once and for all.

Aware that Boston had evaded justice for so long, and knowing how much of a slippery, conniving character he had proved to be, all the law enforcement agencies were scrupulous in their collection of witness statements and the gathering of evidence in order to make sure the case was as watertight as possible for the forthcoming trial. Everyone was determined that this time, Boston wasn't going to slip the net.

Although almost forty years had elapsed since the crime, the

FBI used their worldwide network of agents to trace witnesses for the forthcoming trial. It was quite remarkable the lengths they went to. Alicio Palacios, one of the *Bomberos* (ambulance men) who had recovered Chris and Peta's bodies from the sea, was traced. Now living in New York, he clearly remembered recovering their bound, decomposing bodies weighted down with the engine parts. The FBI also tracked down the Guatemalan doctor, Dr Cuéllar, now aged ninety, who performed and wrote the autopsy report in July 1978. Plus, Alberto Mahler – the acting Belizean harbour master who in a most crucial piece of evidence, replied to my parents' letter of enquiry detailing that Chris and Peta had been on the *Justin B* when it left Dangriga (Stann Creek) but were not present on the boat's return journey. And, Sergeant Kelly of the San Rafael Police Department, who had interviewed Boston at the request of Interpol in 1981, was also traced.

With all these witnesses in their twilight years, including my mother, aged ninety-one, former Chief Inspector Sacks aged 81 and Boston himself, aged seventy-five, it seemed like the forthcoming trial was to be a gathering of senior citizens! Both my mother and Peta's oldest brother, Blaise, were asked to give a statement of events as they had occurred back in 1978. Sadly, Peta's mother and father had passed away and her older sister Rocki, died suddenly at the age of 64 in early 2014 from a subarachnoid haemorrhage, a type of stroke.

There was one piece of vital evidence missing from April 1979 and that was Chris and Peta's dental records. The prosecution team had a detailed record of an unequivocal positive identification from when their corpses were exhumed but unfortunately the dental records had over the years been lost. The prosecution team, sensing the defence team might make capital out of this lost document, requested the FBI to locate and, once again, exhume Chris and Peta's bodies in order that they could be photographed and sent to the FBI laboratory in Quantico, Virginia, for analysis.

Mum, Nigel and I, and Peta's surviving family members, were all asked to provide DNA samples to Greater Manchester Police to send to the FBI. The aim was to compare DNA samples, taken from Chris and Peta's skeletons, and match them with the surviving members of their respective families in order to provide up-to-date evidence that they were indeed Chris and Peta. It was intended that their bones would then be returned to Guatemala for reburial.

The FBI's agent in San Salvador was duly tasked with seeking permission from the Guatemalan law enforcement agencies to commence the exhumation in Puerto Barrios Cemetery in early autumn 2016, using the assistance of Forensic Anthropology Department at Chico State University, California and the Fundacion de Anthropologia Forense de Guatemala.

Knowing the approximate location of burial, the FBI offered a very handsome $1,000 reward to any cemetery worker willing to join in the grisly search for their bodies and successfully locate them. To identify the boundaries of the search, the FBI consulted with the head of the cemetery and referenced a map of the graves (the term 'map' is used loosely here as much of this part of the cemetery is dilapidated, owing to the work of grave robbers). They also used the photographs of Chris and Peta's simple crosses on their gravesites, taken by Pastor McClure, and his description of their final resting places contained in his letter to my parents in 1984.

The task of finding them was, however, to prove extremely difficult because the crosses had long gone, either blown away with the impact of the frequent hurricanes that blow through that part of Central America or removed by human hand.

It was a bizarre feeling when one afternoon, whilst working in my office, an email pinged into my inbox from Michaela Clinch at Greater Manchester Police. It contained the picture of a worn silver ring, bearing a turquoise and coral bird motif.

Did this belong to Chris or Peta? It may well have done as both had a love of silver jewellery, and throughout their courtship they had bought each other numerous rings and matching silver pendants, not dissimilar to the one that was staring back at me from my computer. Maybe they had bought it during their travels in Mexico? Sadly, neither our family nor Peta's were able to identify it. Nowadays, with modern methods of communication it would be extraordinary not to receive photographs of loved ones travelling abroad but back then, the last photos we had of them were those taken just before they left the UK. I looked for some time at the ring, once loved and worn by someone now lying in the cemetery. What was its story? It served to emphasise and symbolise the bizarre, macabre nature of the situation.

The search party were greatly hampered by the fact that many additional bodies had been buried at the site since 1978. Unfortunately, the lead law enforcement agency, i.e. the local and national Guatemalan authorities, prevented the FBI from conducting as thorough an exploration as they would have liked and the search was eventually called off in early November 2016. The plots of their graves were known to have been in swampy ground, close to a river course, so it is possible that over the decades their bodies had been washed away. That the FBI even attempted to locate them was a measure of their determination and dedication to cover all bases, and for this I salute them.

Finding the following description on the internet not long after, I gained an appreciation of the impossible task they were faced with. The disorganised, rambling hellhole and God forsaken place that is Puerto Barrios Cemetery is not for the faint-hearted:

Excerpts from an article by Oswaldo J. Hernández originally published by Plaza Pública, 2014

A UN report puts Guatemala amongst the top five most violent countries in the world, with 40.6 murders for every 100,000 inhabitants. It's difficult [in the UK] to imagine a life without death. However, in the world's fifth-most violent place – it's strange, but true – there are places without homicides, with just one murder in a decade. Then there are others where death is overflowing. You just need to spend a few hours on a highway to see these contrasts – from Sibinal, San Marcos, to Puerto Barrios, in Izabal, for example.

Puerto Barrios: hot, humid, 36 degrees. A city-port in northwest Guatemala that greets visitors with the colours red, green, blue, pink, yellow and grey. These are the colours of the tombs in the cemetery, visible when entering this town, which for three years now – according to police statistics – has ranked as number one for violent homicides in Guatemala. Death greets you in Puerto Barrios.

'What never ends here are the dead.' Upon pronouncing this, the voice of Cesar Barrera – caretaker of Puerto Barrios Cemetery (shadow of a beard, small eyes, small body) – resembles an EVP recording.

THE PEARL IN THE OYSTER

Cesar Barrera, caretaker of Puerto Barrios Cemetery, photographed by Oswaldo J. Hernández, going about his work in 2014.

Cesar is in charge of coordinating burials. He's the gravedigger, the head of the municipal cemetery in Puerto Barrios, although he says he doesn't like the word 'gravedigger' at all – it gets on his nerves. He prefers (and asks) to be called the 'handler of affairs of the deceased', the one who keeps everything in order. But sometimes it's difficult, he says, sweating. For two years now, between 60 and 70 people are buried in Puerto Barrios Cemetery every month. Simply saying the number wearies Cesar, who is now immobile under the hot noonday sun.

'Today, we buried one. Someone killed him for stealing a motorbike. This week, we buried two others. A woman who died of natural causes. Another one murdered, if I'm remembering right.'

According to statistics, Puerto Barrios is the

municipality with Guatemala's highest murder rate. 'People are killing each other here,' says Cesar. For this municipality that borders Honduras, the mortality rate was the only one in Guatemala to reach three figures in 2013. There are 106,722 [at the time of writing] people living in Puerto Barrios and 137.74 murders for every 100,000 inhabitants, a statistic resented inside the cemetery.

'On average, I bury some six or eight murder victims every month,' Cesar says slowly. Now he's become a guide in this town of gravestones. He wants to show me the most recent graves, the ones he remembers were violent deaths. Between the multi-coloured tombs, the dried-up and plastic flowers, Cesar signals, explains dates and names, recalls robberies, revenge killings, bullets, stabbings and bodies cut into pieces. This is his territory. But he confesses the cemetery is also a dangerous place: 'They rob here, they open the graves, they look for valuables, like good teeth. If someone is killed violently, after their death they keep experiencing violence. That's how it goes,' he laments, passing a destroyed grave, half a pile of bones lying outside its resting place. 'I don't touch them, that's up to the Public Ministry,' he adds.

The sun finally sets when Cesar stops at the edge of the cemetery. We've walked for more than an hour. During this time he has recalled a great deal of Puerto Barrios' violence, which, at the end of the day, he seems to carry on his shoulders, supporting himself on a stick. We've arrived, exhausted, at the place where those without name are buried, the unidentified who die in Puerto Barrios and are claimed by no one. 'About 15 in two years,' says the gravedigger. No one knows who they were. Now they rest in the farthest corner of the cemetery, where there are no colours, no flowers, no visits. Just Cesar, standing in front of the heaps of earth, where he explains that the space here is disputed; there's no more room in the cemetery. Those buried for free in this corner (usually it's 280 quetzales a year for a grave) will have to be moved to leave this patch of ground for those who do have someone who remembers them.

'They'll go to the mass grave.'

'Why is there violence in Puerto Barrios?' I ask at this far corner of the cemetery.

'For drugs. For contraband. Because we're a port, a frontier. Because someone owed something to someone. Because there's few rich people and a lot of poor. Because you've also got to defend yourself,' Cesar theorises.

Chapter Fifteen

CAUGHT... HOOK, LINE AND SINKER

At the age of seventy-five, after a lifetime spent on the run, Silas Duane Boston's luck eventually ran out. On 1 December 2016, he was arrested and charged with the murders of Chris and Peta. Some 14 months after I had first tracked down Boston and his two sons, Russell and Vince, on Facebook, his loathsome past had finally caught up with him.

In the absence of finding Chris and Peta alive, it was the best news that we could have possibly hoped to receive. Not once in all the 39 years since their deaths did we ever believe we would hear those words: 'Silas Duane Boston is in custody'. It was better late than never.

Even his arrest wasn't straightforward. We had been told that since reopening the case, he was under surveillance at his nursing home in Eureka. Boston had housing and medical rights as a military veteran because he had served in the United States Coast Guard for a short period of time in his teens before being kicked out for falsifying his documents. Because this was a Federal case, it was the responsibility of the FBI and not the police to arrest him. As planned weeks in advance, the two burly arresting FBI Special Agents, David Sesma and Marcus Knutson, arrived unannounced at the Seaview Rehabilitation & Wellness Center, but when they asked for Silas Duane Boston, they were told he had checked out! Just three days before, he had moved to the Paradise Ridge Post Acute Facility, 1633 Cypress Lane in Paradise. Some 200 miles from Eureka, Paradise is located in the Sierra Nevada foothills above the Northeastern Sacramento Valley. Had he been tipped off about an imminent arrest? Was this his last swansong? We will never know.

After a 12-hour round trip, David Sesma and Marcus Knutson arrived in Paradise and were told by staff at the facility that he was staying in bed 18B. Armed with the double murder warrant, they approached Boston, who because of arthritis was in a wheelchair in the hospital lobby, having a cigarette. He was wearing diapers and Sesma said: 'he appeared not to be in great physical shape but he had all his mental faculties'.

Was he surprised? If he was, he didn't show it but even he must have wondered how on earth he could be arrested for a crime he committed almost 40 years go. The interview with Detective Amy Crosby in February of that year had flagged up to him that the police were once more on his trail and this time closing in on him. Knowing his status was 'hot', Russell believes that his father had started to grow his grey hair and beard to disguise himself in readiness to flee to Mexico again, but his health never improved enough.

The Special Agents advised Boston that he was under arrest for the disappearance of Christopher Farmer and Peta Frampton in 1978. He made little or no comment when they placed handcuffs on him. Complaining that he couldn't hear what they were saying, they took him to collect his hearing aids from his bedroom. From the staff, they obtained a copy of the medication he was required to take.

When he walked he wobbled and he had to be lifted into the FBI's transport vehicle to take him to the Chico Resident Agency of the FBI in Chico. Here, he was interviewed, videoed, and given a sandwich. He was shown pictures of Chris and Peta but denied knowing them. Questioned further, he then changed his story to say that he did recall meeting them in Belize and that they had been passengers on the *Justin B*. The FBI officers employed various methods of interrogation including playing to his ego but Boston did not waver from his standpoint of innocence. They said that the families wanted closure but he lacked all remorse. On hearing that his sons had given witness statements against him, he was said to be livid, and particularly with Russell. The interview lasted two hours and Boston then requested an attorney.

He was then transported to the Sacramento County Main Jail where as a high-risk prisoner he was fully shackled. Sesma noted that when they were booking him into the jail, he had a 'ton of medical conditions'.

It was Sesma who wrote the affidavit for the arrest of Boston. Working for the FBI for 18 years, his extensive experience extends from criminal matters involving violent gangs, drugs, the sex trafficking of children, international kidnappings to homicides and complex financial crimes. He has been consulted on many cold case homicides and violent crimes. Boston was in expert hands.

Shortly before the arrest, my family and Peta's family were asked if we wished to seek the death penalty but advised that were we to do so, it could greatly protract proceedings. Personally, I would like nothing more than to have seen him wiped from this earth. What possible good can come from keeping such a sick deviant alive? But Nigel and I felt the ultimate decision should be Mum's: she chose to opt for a life sentence. At the age of ninety-two, having waited almost 40 years to see Boston arrested, she naturally wanted justice to be served as quickly as possible. That aside, her decision was no surprise to us, knowing that she has never believed in an 'eye for an eye' philosophy. Mum felt that in seeking the death penalty she would be stooping to Boston's level of the gutter. She was content that if convicted (and with such compelling evidence, he surely would be), he would spend the remainder of his life in jail and that would present greater suffering, contemplation and recognition of his evil than being sentenced to death could ever do.

On 2 December 2016, Boston appeared in front of U.S. Magistrate Kendall Newman in a federal courtroom in Sacramento. Brought into the courtroom in a wheelchair, he had a flowing white beard and long grey hair past his shoulders and was dressed in a rumpled orange jail smock.

'Can you hear me all right, sir?' U.S. Magistrate Kendall Newman said, and prepared to read out the murder charges that in America carry life imprisonment or the federal death penalty. Boston nodded.

His federal public defender, Douglas Beevers, asked: 'Boston is in frail health. Can he be spared from being shackled when being moved inside Sacramento County Jail or brought to court?'

Magistrate Newman replied: 'The shackles will be used, as is the norm with any dangerous inmate, and looking at the charges in this case, I find that fully appropriate.'

Boston was charged on two counts of premeditated maritime murders of Chris and Peta and remanded in custody. As he had demonstrated so many times in the past, he was a major flight risk and, coupled with the severity of the charges, he was denied bail and taken back to his cell.

In contrast to British law, the American judicial system allows the affidavit, drawn up by the FBI for Boston's arrest, to be made available to the public. Released the day after his arrest, the 27 pages detailed some, but not all, of the painstakingly gathered evidence. Much of its supporting evidence originated from the documents that had lain in Mum's bureau for 37 years plus the damning eyewitness statements of Boston's sons. It served to highlight the difference in the American and British judicial systems because such a detailed document would never have been released in Great Britain for fear of prejudicing any future trial.

With California eight hours behind, I received a phone call from GMP's Martin Bottomley early the following day to say that it had been published. Despite it being a Saturday morning, he wanted to alert us to the potentially distressing content of the document which was now available for all to view on the internet. He also prepared us for the fact that it contained a never before seen picture of Chris with Vince and Russell, taken on the *Justin B*. Russell had emailed the photograph of Chris on the boat to Amy Crosby in January 2016 after he had given his statement and this photo became a vital piece of legal evidence for the prosecution team, because it was visual proof that Chris had been on board the *Justin B*. Martin told us that the picture had already been splashed on the front page of the Northern Californian newspaper, *The Sacramento Bee*, which over the course of the following week, was swiftly replicated by a plethora of British and international publications.

Naturally, we had never seen the photograph, which had

been in Russell's possession. You can therefore understand the effect on my mother, Nigel and I when we saw this picture for the first time. It is most likely the last photograph taken of Chris before he was killed. Sometimes, a picture really is worth a thousand words.

Chris looks happy and how we would like to remember him. The boys look angelic, relaxed and well cared for... in fact completely at odds with how I would have imagined them to be. With Russell proudly showing off his catch of the day, it all seems so normal and relaxed. I can only imagine how events on the boat must have taken a very sudden turn for the worse.

On that cold winter's Saturday morning, huddled around the open log fire, our two dogs dozing at our feet, I read the affidavit out to Mum whose eyesight is failing. The cosy surroundings of our Oxfordshire home, could not have provided a greater contrast to the scene of horrific events in the Caribbean some 38 years previous. A stranger happening upon us might have thought I was reading a chapter from some horror story.

The affidavit included details of some of Boston's other crimes and also referenced a Bryan Logsdon – a good friend of Russell's from High School days in Bishop. Logsdon had spent a year travelling with Boston in Mexico in the early 1990s.

Russell was later to explain to me how this had come about: 'Bryan had fought as an army ranger in the first Gulf War and in the invasion of Panama. He was between jobs and Dad invited him to go down to Mexico and hang out in Baja. When Bryan accepted, I pulled him aside and warned him not to go. I told him Dad had killed people in the past, but Bryan, who had just fought in two wars, said he wasn't scared of him. I warned him to watch if my dad's mood shifted because he would become devious and uncontrollably violent.'

Whilst in Mexico, Boston bragged to Logsdon that he had killed Chris and Peta and described in graphic detail the sadistic enjoyment he'd derived from murdering them. He said he found it 'funny' when he threw Peta overboard. The plastic bag that he had placed over her head and tied around her neck burst and you could hear her screaming through the bubbles that came up whilst she was drowning. Boston told the story with relish and was laughing because he had got away with it. He said the lesson he had learnt from killing them was that you should always: 'Gut someone when you are going to throw them in the water because otherwise they are going to bloat and float to the surface.'

Russell says: 'When Bryan returned from Mexico, he was shocked and for the first time, I think he fully appreciated just how evil my father was. He knew Vince and I had been going to the authorities for years and were told repeatedly there was nothing they could do in regard to my mother, nor Chris and Peta, so he knew he had no chance of convincing the authorities when they had continued to ignore two eyewitnesses to a double murder. We both knew that his testimony would be dismissed as hearsay.

'Bryan started to tell me about what Dad had told him about killing Chris and Peta, and my mom, but I stopped him and said, "I know, I warned you before you went to Mexico about him and what he'd done." I should have let him finish but I didn't want to hear it. It was literally only after reading the affidavit, detailing Bryan's police statement, that I learnt that that night when Dad took the German/Scandinavian couple (whom he called the 'Vikings') ashore in Dangriga, in the storm, that he had in fact killed them, two weeks after killing Chris and Peta. I had never even suspected him. As far as Vince and I were concerned, he had taken them ashore and that was the end of it. Bryan was going to tell me about this couple but I had stopped him because I didn't want to hear it.

'When Bryan returned from Mexico, he said to me, "I've killed people in two wars because my government told me it was my job, and none of those people I killed deserved it as much as your father does. If they can't stop him, I will. I'll take him out into the desert and plant him." At the time, I was shocked. I told Bryan that if he killed my father it would make him a murderer, putting him in the same category as my dad, and that vigilantism has no place in a civilised, modern society. I felt it wasn't Bryan's job to take my father out of circulation, and I explained to him it was the job of our government and law enforcement.

'After reading the affidavit and hearing for the first time that he had killed the second couple, combined with the callousness in Dad's recollections of killing my mom and Chris and Peta, I now understand why Bryan felt so strongly that Dad should die. I didn't at the time, and still don't believe in vigilantism, but I do understand the frustration of knowing a killer is unstoppable and free to harm more people while the authorities turn a blind eye.'

Stunned, I finished reading the affidavit to Mum. Reading and re-reading the affidavit and its summary in subsequent newspaper reports over the following days only served to further underline Boston's evil.

8 December 2016 was a nerve-racking day for us, spent as it was waiting to hear from GMP, who were relaying news to us from the Sacramento courtroom. With the time difference, we knew news would only come later that evening but it didn't stop our anticipation. I was cooking supper for the family when I received a call from Martin saying that Boston had

been indicted and a status hearing was set for 10 January 2017. That evening, we raised a glass to Chris and Peta and the hope for a successful conviction.

15 December 2016 found us back in the Northwest with Greater Manchester Police for a video conference call with key members of the Californian prosecution team, the FBI and Sacramento Police Department, who were assembled in a meeting room in the Robert T. Matsui Courthouse in Sacramento. Prosecutor Matt Segal told us that Russell Boston had handed over to the Grand Jury as evidence in October 2016 two cassettes of pre-recorded albums – Santana's *Welcome* and Pink Floyd's *Animals* – that he had found in his dad's briefcase. The legal team wanted to use these as exhibits at the trial to provide further evidence that Chris and Peta were passengers on the boat. I was asked to find the original vinyl albums, which Chris had recorded them from before leaving the UK for Australia. Searching through boxes and boxes in my loft that weekend, I fortunately found the two albums. Rather run the risk of them being lost or broken in the post, I took them up to Manchester and handed them over to the police in person.

Conscious that all the main participants of the case were elderly and time was of the essence, Matt urged us to send letters to the American judge requesting an early trial date.

My mother's letter was read out to the judge in the status hearing on 10 January 2017: 'I am writing to ask if you will please consider setting a date as soon as possible. My husband and I were very involved in the search for them and we did all we could to establish how, why and who killed them. It was a matter of great sadness that my husband, Charles, died three years ago, never knowing the truth surrounding their deaths and that their murderer was never brought to justice.

'I am, myself, now almost 92 years old and Silas Duane Boston is 75. Taking all this into account, there may be little time left for justice to be seen to be done.

'The brutal manner in which my son's life was taken has left an enduring and very painful gap in my family's life, which no amount of time will heal but I will derive a sense of closure from knowing that his killer has been apprehended and appropriately sentenced.

'Aside from the trial, I have always believed that Boston's sons held the key to unlocking the crime. I would dearly like to speak to Russell and Vince Boston about my son and what happened on the boat and I understand from the British police that one of them has expressed the same desire to speak to me. Naturally, that cannot happen before any trial for fear of prejudicing the witnesses.'

I too wrote a supporting letter: 'Chris was a much-loved brother who died in the most tragic of circumstances; I am aware the autopsy report shows he suffered brutal injuries and was killed in a most heartless and shocking manner. We have spent 38 long years not knowing why he died. It is a question that has plagued my family all this time...'

'It is a fact that much of the evidence that was sought back in 1978 (e.g. the Belize Harbour Master's report; the discovery that their bodies had been buried unidentified) was gathered by my parents. They were both heavily involved in the case and without their diligence and efforts it is unlikely that a prosecution would be possible today.

'My mother will be 92 in February 2017. She is very sound of mind and in reasonably good health, but naturally she is frail. At that age, every day is a bonus. She has said that making the journey from our home in Oxfordshire, England, where she lives with my family and I, to travel over 5,200 miles to Sacramento is the very last thing she can do for Chris. The 12-hour plane journey from the UK to California, plus over six hours driving and waiting/check-in time will naturally be a very long one for my mother, but she has said she would rather die in America and know that she has done her best for her son than not go at all. I am sure you will understand when I say it would be the ultimate tragedy, were my mother to die before the trial. It is largely for my mother that I want to see the perpetrator of this crime punished. As his mother, the greatest loss was hers.

'A less important factor, but still one that I would be grateful if you will please take into consideration: I believe the weather in spring in Sacramento will be much more clement for her advancing years than in the height of summer.

'Furthermore, the man accused of these murders, if he is found guilty, will have evaded punishment for this crime for almost four decades. He is himself 75. The earlier he stands trial and a verdict is delivered, the sooner we will truly know what happened over 38 years ago; if found guilty, the more promptly the accused faces justice and receives the appropriate sanction from the Court, the better for all...

'Lastly, and perhaps most significantly, we have waived our right to seek the death penalty in order that this case may be expedited in the hope that this is within my mother's lifetime.

'If, after taking all of these factors into consideration, you are able to set an early trial date, then please rest assured that my mother and I are ready to get on a plane at 24-hour notice.'

Matt Segal requested that the judge set a trial date within six months saying: 'Christopher Farmer's survivors want to see a trial badly enough that they are willing to travel to Sacramento at risk to the elder Mrs Farmer's health. Given her advanced age, justice delayed may be justice permanently denied.'

In reply, Attorney Lexi Negin, one of Boston's federal public defenders, said that the defence required extensive time to prepare the case and complained that Boston, who had health issues, was suffering in Sacramento County Jail 'and is not getting the care he was getting in the nursing home. Our position is that we will be ready for trial someday.'

'That's incredibly unhelpful,' answered Judge Mendez.

Pressed for a date on when the defence would be ready, Negin suggested the autumn of 2018.

'That's not going to work,' Mendez replied.

Whilst declining to rule on the prosecution's motion, the judge suggested he would most likely set a trial date for autumn 2017. 'I think both sides can anticipate this trial will take place this year,' he said.

The next court appearance was set for one month later on 14 February 2017.

To try to bring the trial forward, Matt Segal asked if Mum and I and David Sacks, the detective in charge of the case in 1978, would make the journey to Sacramento to give evidence at a pre-trial hearing. This was partially to help secure an early trial date but also to get the evidence in the bag in case any of the witnesses died or were unable to travel when it came to trial. Naturally, we said yes.

We were offered the option of the prosecuting and defence teams coming to the UK and setting up a mini courtroom in Greater Manchester Police's Nexus House with a video link to the courtroom in Sacramento, where Boston would be present. However, we were told that it would have greater impact if we were to make the journey to America and give evidence. For Mum, there was only one choice: she was going to America.

After talking to Martin Bottomley for over an hour one evening, I apologised that he was having to work so late on the case and he said: 'No problem, this isn't work, this is a passion.' The dedication of everyone involved in helping us secure a conviction, never ceased to amaze us.

When Boston was arrested, the story immediately broke in the media. Watching it spread online was like watching the concentric circles rippling out from skimming a stone in a pond. Large swathes of the American and British press and television channels covered the story, as well as, more surprisingly, countries such as France, Canada and China. We hadn't expected so much international interest outside of America and Great Britain.

Within 24 hours of Boston being indicted, we had a newspaper reporter on our doorstep. Well-dressed and in his forties, he explained, almost apologetically, that he was from a well-known British tabloid newspaper and he was interested in getting our comments about the case. We had been advised by the police and lawyers not to give interviews so we declined to comment. He then asked if we would be interested if money were involved. After some persuasion, he left.

Greater Manchester Police released a statement on our behalf: 'GMP's Cold Case Review Unit have been working with the families of Christopher Farmer and Peta Frampton for over a year since relatives asked us to reinvestigate these tragic events. Since that time, we have worked closely with Interpol, Sacramento Police Department, the FBI and the U.S. District Attorney's office. This inter-agency cooperation has led to the two murder indictments being issued by the U.S Grand Jury.

The families of both Chris and Peta now await the outcome of a trial and would ask for privacy in the meantime.'

But it didn't stop the British national newspapers, such as the *Daily Mail* and *The Times*, covering the story extensively, updating it each time there was a court status hearing. (See, for instance: http://www.dailymail.co.uk/news/article-4034422/ Yachtsman-boasted-murdering-British-couple-Caribbean-son-told-friend-beating-stabbing-drowning-funny.html; https://www.thetimes.co.uk/article/yacht-murderer-betrayed-by-his-children-dhp2wdds0.) One touching and unforeseen consequence of the press coverage was that several of Chris's friends, from Manchester Grammar School and Birmingham Medical School, read the press coverage, and went to some considerable effort in tracking us down and getting in touch. One of them even called round at my parents' old house in Cheshire to speak to neighbours to find out where my mother had moved to since Dad died, and another of his friends rang the GMP Cold Case Review Unit to get our contact details. It was heartening to know that Chris hadn't been forgotten – he would have been amazed and humbled

.

Chapter Sixteen

LAND IN SIGHT

The rollercoaster of emotions, so much a feature of this case from 1978, still had some more unexpected twists and dives. With our hopes buoyed at the imminent prospect of going to California to give pre-trial evidence, we were then hit by another tsunami of disappointment.

Boston failed to appear at the status hearing on 14 February 2017. Unbeknownst to the prosecution team, he had fallen ill the day after his last court appearance on 27 January and was hospitalised, due to apparent complications from heart and liver disease. Boston's attorney, Lexi Negin, said she was informed by Sacramento County Jail officials that Boston had been hospitalised for nearly two weeks for 'a very serious condition', adding: 'We are unsure if he is talking or conscious.'

Jail authorities wouldn't reveal where Boston was being cared for, but he was reported to be suffering 'complications of liver failure and congestive heart-failure'. Giving us some ray of hope, Negin said that Boston's condition might not be life threatening: 'he could be back in jail in a few weeks.'

In a written motion, Matt Segal requested that the depositions be taken in open court, arguing: 'There is no better evidence than sworn, cross-examined testimony taken under court supervision. Given the witnesses' current ability and willingness to travel, there is no practical reason why their depositions cannot be taken under the conditions that the law most favours.'

Boston's defence attorneys argued that any pre-trial depositions should be conducted in private and not introduced into the record until the trial began.

Because Boston wasn't in court, District Court Judge John A. Mendez said he was unwilling to rule on the prosecution's motions to grant permission for pre-trial depositions and to allow them to be held in open court. He scheduled a hearing for two weeks time on 28 February 2017 to get an update on Boston's medical condition and consider an anticipated motion by prosecutors to allow the depositions even if Boston couldn't be present in court.

He concluded: 'I understand your concern for the witnesses and the mother of the victim. I understand what is going on here. Both sides have serious needs.'

Out of hospital, Boston returned to federal court on 28 February and we were delighted to hear that the judge sanctioned us, plus David Sacks and the Guatemalan pathologist, Dr Angel María Vásquez Cuéllar, to go to California to give depositions in April or May.

The judge agreed that the prosecution team could interview the witnesses and record their testimony for potential introduction for trial and the defence was allowed to cross-examine us. The depositions were to be conducted at a location to be determined by the lawyers and a federal magistrate to be available to answer procedural questions by phone but not physically present. He set a potential trial date for seven months hence, on 2 October, but said he was uncertain whether the case would be ready to begin with jury selection by then.

Boston was described as having a pungent smell because since entering jail he had displayed a reluctance to wash, apparently a not uncommon trait of prisoners wanting to make themselves even more objectionable. He was equipped with headphones to help his hearing, but complained that he was having trouble following the discussion.

'Were you able to hear me, Mr Boston?' Mendez asked.

Boston nodded to the judge, but indicated he couldn't hear his attorney, Lexi Negin: 'I couldn't hear her,' he said, fumbling with his headgear. 'Hello? Hello?'

'He is taking a lot of medication,' Negin said. 'Mr Boston is good today. I don't think there is any issue today. But it is an ongoing medical issue.'

6 May was set as the date when the UK contingent were to travel to California, accompanied by Martin and Michaela, to give our pre-trial evidence. We eagerly anticipated the day arriving when we would be stepping off the plane in Sacramento. It was a surreal concept to grasp that we were now within weeks of coming face-to-face with Chris and Peta's killer.

But the rollercoaster hadn't stopped turning - the unthinkable happened. Boston, who had turned seventy-six on 20 March, took a grave turn for the worse. On 5 April, he had started to refuse his medication and treatment and by mid-April, he was re-hospitalised in a far more serious condition than in February.

Suffering liver and heart complications, Boston, dressed in the distinctive orange boiler suit reserved for high-security prisoners, was moved from Sacramento County Jail to the City's UC Davis Medical Center in the presence of two burly armed guards.

'There has been more dire information about this hospitalisation,' Boston's Defence Attorney Negin told the court on 19 April. 'If he weren't in custody, he would probably be referred to hospice care.'

We were totally shocked and dismayed to learn that the defence team then filed a 'declaration of doubt' that Boston was competent to face trial, suggesting his health was fast deteriorating, impairing him both physically and mentally.

'The Court finds that reasonable cause exists to believe that Mr Boston may presently be suffering from a medical condition that has caused a mental disease or defect rendering him mentally incompetent to the extent that he is unable to understand the nature and consequences of the proceedings against him or to assist properly in his defence. The Court orders that Mr Boston be committed to the custody of the Attorney General forthwith for placement in a suitable medical facility for a psychiatric or psychological examination and treatment.'

'The law requires him to be mentally present during court proceedings,' Judge Mendez responded. 'If he is in and out of awareness in terms of his medication, he may be physically present, but mentally he is not there.' He ordered a medical competency evaluation for Boston but the challenge was that Boston would need to be airlifted to a medical facility in the federal prison system as far away as Illinois or North Carolina for an appropriate evaluation. Negin said Boston was in no shape for such an excursion.

Our much longed for, and highly anticipated trip to Sacramento was cancelled. It was crushing. Bitterly disappointed,

I wrote the following letter to Judge Mendez imploring his help: 'To hear the news yesterday that Silas Duane Boston might not be fit to stand trial was nothing short of devastating for us as a family.

'Since I first made the phone call to Greater Manchester Police with the findings of my internet research and the whereabouts of Boston and his sons, Vince and Russell, on October 5th 2015, the fight for justice for my brother Chris and his girlfriend, Peta, has become an all-consuming personal crusade. To receive this news is therefore a massive blow. If it is that Boston doesn't stand trial, the ultimate sadness is that the wheels of justice just didn't move quickly enough for us. It is particularly tragic when, for 37 years, those wheels barely moved at all.

'This last cruel twist of fate is, of course, nowhere near the pain of losing Chris but it's a very bitter pill to swallow when we were reaching the last hurdle and a trial was in sight. Mum, in particular, has taken the news badly. It has been a very sad, long journey to this point, but she was more than mentally and physically prepared for making the trip on May 6th in the hope that at the age of 92 she would see her son's killer brought to justice. When Boston threw, like jetsam, their tortured bodies alive into the waters of the Caribbean he thought they would not be missed. He could not have been more wrong: Chris was a much-loved son and brother as keenly missed today as when he first went missing.

'I know the Head of the Greater Manchester Police Cold Case Review Unit, Martin Bottomley, and California Prosecution Attorney, Matthew Segal, and their respective teams have done absolutely everything within their powers to bring Chris and Peta's merciless, barbaric killer to justice and for that, as a family, we are eternally grateful. Leaving no stone unturned, they have, after almost 40 years, quite unbelievably given us knowledge of why they were senselessly murdered. They have all gone the extra mile for us and we are indebted to them. It would be the ultimate tragedy if this case were to falter now.

'I appreciate that Boston's state of health is out of everyone's hands but if anything can be done to bring about a prosecution, please rest assured that my mother and I are ready to jump on the next plane to America without any notice. Our visas are all prepared. If, in the end, Boston holds the ultimate "get out of jail free" card and dies before he faces trial, he will have trumped us all. So near and yet so very far and that truly hurts.'

Chapter Seventeen

DEATH ROLL

(Death roll: the boat rolls from side to side, becoming gradually more unstable until it capsizes.)

By April 2017, time was fast running out for both Boston and the prosecution team who, having gone to extraordinary lengths to construct the beyond all reasonable doubt case against him, like us, were eager to see him convicted.

The gravity of Boston's failing health was fully apparent on admission to hospital. After a life spent consuming an excess of rum, heavy smoking and illegal drugs, he was now paying the price with congestive heart failure coupled with liver and kidney failure.

The medical director of Sacramento County Jail had previously examined Boston and predicted with medical intervention he would most likely live at least until Thanksgiving in November, and maybe well beyond. Meaning that he would have made the provisional trial date of 2 October 2016. However, with failing kidneys, he was dependent on dialysis. Fully aware that the prosecution team were planning a pre-trial in early May, Boston must have concluded his game was up.

On 5 April, he told his doctor that he didn't want to live and that he wanted to exercise his right to withdraw medical treatment. That included no kidney dialysis, no food, feeding tube nor anything that would prolong his life.

A domineering, controlling personality throughout his life, he played his last card and extricated himself from proceedings on his terms, thus ruling out having to face justice. It was the equivalent of a skipper scuppering his boat on the rocks.

It seemed the last cruel twist of fate that at this final hurdle we should be denied a few meagre crumbs of justice. I cannot begin to describe a greater conflict of feelings. Yes, we wanted him to die but at the same time we willed him to live, at least long enough to stand trial to face us and his wicked, evil crimes. We were desperate to have our day in court and witness the full judicial process so that punishment could be meted out. We wanted to face the monster that had so brutally and gratuitously killed Chris and Peta and tell him that his actions had brought a lifetime of grief upon so many.

Close to dying, he lay shackled to his hospital bed in a side room with two armed Marshals, assigned by the Federal Prosecutors and the FBI, standing to one side of the bed. His breathing was laboured but he was *compos mentis*. That he was shackled, despite the fact his health was failing fast, denotes just how dangerous a criminal he was deemed to be.

After weeks of refusing medicine and food, Boston drifted in and out of consciousness whilst his kidneys and liver failed and his bladder backed up with a urinary tract infection. A simple cure with modern antibiotics, but without it, his abdomen festered and rotted from the inside. Pus and bacteria ate away at his organs in a chain reaction of decomposition whilst still alive.

The day before he died, Boston's chosen next of kin, his son Russell, visited him. He would later describe to me in detail his visit: 'There were things I wanted to say to him that I had never been able to say before because he would have killed me. It was now or never, so with time against me, I rented a car and drove to Sacramento.

'I was stunned and frustrated that he was allowed to die before he could answer for what he'd done. Had he continued taking the medication for his kidneys, I'm convinced he would have been alive for the trial, and most likely several more years. It was a shock to everyone involved that he was able to exit that way. It was Dad giving his last "fuck you" to us all. I didn't understand how he was allowed to basically commit suicide. It made no sense to me that he was allowed to check out on his terms, as his right, but the rights of society and his victims were disregarded.

'They called me as his next of kin, because he had been unresponsive for a couple of weeks, and now was dying and unable to make his own decisions, those decisions were now passed to me, but it was done when he was so far gone. There were no decisions to make anymore. I asked the doctor why I wasn't called sooner, when I could have forced him to be on dialysis and his meds, but I never got a logical answer as to why they waited till he was past the point of no return. It was extremely frustrating for me, but apparently they were legally obliged to honour his request. It was ridiculously too little, too late. He'd told me for years he would kill himself, but he never had the balls, until of course he was arrested and he knew his game was up.

'I wanted him convicted, and I wanted him to answer for his actions. To finally, once and for all, make a statement regarding what he'd done to Chris and Peta, my mom and the countless other people he'd killed, as well as for him to hear and be fully aware that his selfish actions had caused immeasurable pain and suffering for his victims and their loved ones. I also wanted him to tell us where he killed and buried my mom. I realise now he most likely wouldn't have felt remorse for what he'd done, but I still felt it was important for him to be forced to hear from others just how senseless his actions were.

'I had made sure the police knew absolutely everything he'd done, including all the crimes I had overheard him talking about to his partners in crime. I was fully aware he would know exactly where that information had come from. I gave them every shred of evidence I could muster because I wanted him to be aware and accept that he didn't have a glimmer of hope that he'd ever walk out of jail a free man. I wanted him to know his goose was cooked and his only option was to surrender and answer to the prosecutors for what he'd done... on everything.

'On the day I arrived, his body and mind bounced back one last time. I'm told it's the body's last-ditch attempt to survive, which happens when the final moment is near. He was alert and sitting up, aware and interacting with his doctors by answering their questions with nods and gestures. Even repeatedly winking at the cute nurse he'd flirted with weeks before.

'When I walked into the hospital room, he leaned forward, grimacing and glaring at me. He was seething with me. I started crying. He looked like he wanted to leap out of bed and get me.

'He gave me his clenched-teeth, signature evil glare. I had always thought that one day he would look at me this way when he was in court, or after his conviction, from behind prison bars or safety glass, when I could explain to him that it was his actions that had put him there, not me. I wanted him to have the realisation that he didn't make one bad decision, he'd made a lifetime of bad decisions that harmed so many people. I wanted to tell him that if he wanted to be mad at me for snitching on him, that's his right, but it wasn't my snitching that put him behind bars, it was his actions and countless bad decisions.

'It was a huge relief to be able to talk to him. I desperately wanted him to tell me where I could find my mom's body, as one last sliver of humanity and to try to make some amends for all that he had done to us and others.

'I said, "I love you, Dad, and I forgive you for what you have done. I will never understand the choices you have made in life and you're not coming back from this. Answer this before you go, I beg of you to tell me where our mom is buried."

'Dad looked at the Marshals guarding him as if to say, "You don't expect me to tell you in front of them, do you?" Then he looked down at his legs, which were shackled, and his festering body, then he stared back at me as if to say, "You put me here, you fucking snitch!" He didn't speak at all. According to the Marshals and doctors, the last time he had spoken was two weeks previous.

'He refused to answer, even though he was fully aware and glared at me. I know his last conscious thoughts were of me facing him, begging him to tell me.'

The not knowing where their Mom's body is buried has tormented Vince, Russell and their sister Vicki for 50 years. Russell says: 'I always thought Dad killed her at Last Chance Mine in Foresthill, Placer County but it's a bit far from Sacramento, and I don't know that Mom would have gone that far with him. My uncle Kevin, Dad's brother, said that my dad told him that he killed her near Yuba City in an almond grove but we don't know where she is.

'I was just shy of three years old when she died, but I've always held tightly onto the few images I have of her. A white Chevrolet Corvair is one of the memories I have of my mom... the Corvair is parked on a street in Sacramento, with large maple leaves on the ground around it. I just remember those tail lights of that car and associate it with Mom. But like a copy of a copy of a copy, I no longer know if the memories I have of her are actually just memories of the memories I've held onto all these years.

'Vince once asked Dad where he buried her and Dad asked angrily, "Why the fuck do you want to know? Do you wanna turn me in?" Vince said, "I just want to put flowers on her grave," to which Dad said, "It washes out and floods, you'd never be able to find it." I stayed with Dad for four hours that evening, during which time my sister Vicki spoke to him on my mobile so that she could say goodbye to him. It crossed my mind that you and your mom would have liked to have spoken to him too.

'Even though he didn't answer, I know he heard me. He was fully aware and tracked me with his eyes the entire time. I then left the hospital for the night.

'When I returned the next morning, his mouth and eyes were open and he was unresponsive. He was once again pulled down by his self-imposed ballast. Still physically shackled to his bed with arm and leg restraints, his body writhed. His dry mouth was agape as his breathing was reduced to hours of sporadic gasps of air. His eyelids were frozen open as his tearless eyes stared into the abyss, which awaited his arrival.

'I drove the seven-hour journey back to Laguna Beach that afternoon and, as I got home, I received a call from the hospital to say he had died.'

Boston was defiant and remorseless to his last gasp of breath. There was no admission of guilt or deathbed confession. The Marshals who guarded him described him as 'controlling with an evil glare right to the very end'.

Back in England, I was kept constantly informed of Boston's slow descent into death by the detectives from the Cold Case Review Unit. I felt in limbo, waiting for someone I knew to die. But thankfully I didn't know him, I knew *of* him.

Boston died late afternoon on 24 April 2017 – the same date as his mother eight years before. It was just three weeks short of Mum and I flying out for the pre-trial hearing and five months short of the provisional trial date. After 39 long years, for approximately four months sweet justice had been in our sights. With two strong, independent eyewitnesses, we were confident the prosecution team would secure a guilty verdict, indeed we felt it was ours for the taking. For Mum who, along with my father, had played such a pivotal part in the hard-fought battle to ascertain the truth, seeing Boston stand trial represented final closure and this was cruelly snatched from her grasp.

In the end, Boston played his greatest Houdini trick of all and, in choosing to exercise his right to stop medical treatment, he effectively took himself out of the frame and committed suicide, exiting life on his own terms and so avoiding the consequences of his actions – much as he had lived his life.

The only satisfaction we could derive was the fact that he was arrested, denied bail, died in custody, charged with Chris and Peta's murders, and was awaiting trial.

The day after he died, it was painful to read on Sacramento County Jail's website the euphemistic word 'released'. In that, there was no justice – death was too good for him. US Attorney Phillip A. Talbert of the Eastern District of California made the following announcement: 'Although the recent death of Silas Duane Boston will require us to dismiss the case against him, that dismissal in no way reflects our view of the evidence gathered in the course of our investigation. We were prepared to present that evidence to a jury and to meet our burden of proof at trial. Our hearts go out to the victims' surviving family members who were not able to see Boston brought to jury trial in this case. Nevertheless, we remain thankful that the hard work of our law enforcement partners allowed the allegations against Boston to be presented to a grand jury and brought to light in an indictment. We are particularly grateful for the persistent investigative efforts of the Sacramento Police Department's Cold Case Review Unit, as well as the diligent work of the FBI and the Greater Manchester Police Department. The conclusion of this case in no way diminishes their hard work and commitment to justice.'

Combined with a chilling inability to feel remorse or pity, Boston's personality as a master of deception, a smooth operator and an excellent actor, perfectly fitted the stereotypical personality of a psychopathic killer. When Russell was told that his father was dying, he contacted Professor James Fallon, a neuroscientist at Irvine School of Medicine, California University, who is currently conducting research into the brains of psychopathic killers to determine if they are hardwired differently.

He believes there are genetic markers in some people's DNA which may give them a predisposition to becoming a serial killer. On his father's death, Russell contacted the university again to go through what procedure he was required to follow. Wanting to derive a positive out of his father's life of barbarism and killing, Russell asked Sacramento County Coroner's Office for Boston's body to be donated to Irvine School of Medicine.

Unfortunately, red tape got in the way and the body was not able to be transferred soon enough, but Russell was at least able to get DNA swabs.

Russell says: 'I hope, through the diagnosis of his DNA, that some good can come from him. My dad left a trail of death and destruction behind him and people who hated him. He burned so many bridges, simply for the sole purpose of harming those who were unfortunate enough to cross his path. He cut up and burned the clothes of his exes after they broke up. Those ones got away lightly, whilst others he wanted to kill and, in some instances, he succeeded in doing so. There was no reason to do it, other than to scorch the earth around him.

'I was sad he died because I never got answers to my questions about my mom and I would trade anything to have had him go to trial. Visiting him in hospital was the first time that I spoke to him from my heart because I had been so fearful of him. It was liberating to stand in front of him. Shackled, and with Marshals either side of him, I could say things which in the past would have caused him to kill me. It was only some days after he had died that I realised how much I had been in fear of him. The relief I felt when I knew Dad could no longer show up, bribe me, extort money from me, and threaten me, or others, if I didn't comply, was intense. When the weight lifted, it was incredible. The monster was dead.'

Chapter Eighteen

HANDS ACROSS THE SEA

With the death of Boston, Prosecuting Attorney Matt Segal kindly offered us the opportunity to learn more about the case, which, had it gone to trial, would have been revealed.

Mum and I naturally jumped at the chance, so one day in May 2017, bathed in warm, early-evening sunshine, we drove for the last time to Greater Manchester Police's Nexus House. With the imposing building looming into view, my thoughts returned to when, some eighteen months earlier, we had first made the journey, full of such high hopes and nervous anticipation, never fully daring to believe the police would reopen the case.

We gathered with Martin Bottomley and Michaela Clinch in the same large airy meeting room in which we had first met. This time, the meeting was less formal and we warmly embraced each other and gave thanks for all the many hours of work and commitment they had given to our case.

Greetings done, Martin clicked on the large wall-mounted TV and, via the video link, we connected to Matt Segal in

Sacramento and the now familiar faces of his team, assembled in the meeting room, 5,500 miles away. The team included Amy Crosby, and the FBI agent, David Sesma, who had arrested Boston.

Privacy laws prevented some of our more searching questions from receiving answers but we were able to gain more information about the twisted character of Boston and his ill-spent life. What was staggering was the depravity and extent of his crimes. Chris and Peta and Mary Lou were by no means isolated cases. The consequent suffering that he alone had wrought had left a trail of destruction and scarred so many lives. The ultimate tragedy was that he was allowed to freely peddle his evil for five decades and unbelievably evaded justice right up until five months before his death.

Fear of prejudicing the forthcoming trial had prevented us up until now from making contact with Boston's sons but with his demise, there were no holds barred. Through Detective Amy Crosby, we were put in touch with Russell Boston and from my home office in Oxfordshire, Mum and I had a three-and-a-half-hour Skype call with him on 19 May, the eve of what would have been Chris's 64th birthday.

Both of us had vowed to be as empathetic as possible, recognising that it can't have been easy for him to pluck up the courage to talk to us. And like us, Russell is a victim of his father, not only for the physical and mental abuse he inflicted on him for so long, but also for killing his mother. The only parent he has ever known is one who, at best, treated him with zero regard and at worse, threatened, on countless occasions, to kill him.

With a mixture of anticipation and nervousness, I clicked my computer's video camera on to see for the first time 'in the flesh' Russell Boston. The man whom my brother died defending, one of the last three people to see him and Peta alive and an eyewitness to their horrific murders. We had, of course, already seen his Facebook picture but that did little to prepare us for actually talking to him. In contrast, because I had used an anonymous Facebook account when I first contacted him, he had never seen our faces before, so he was seeing us for the first time. We were conscious that he too must have a thousand questions for us.

The face that greeted us was friendly, warm and open. As we introduced ourselves, he was quickly overcome with tears, admitting that he wasn't prepared for finding the experience 'so emotional, so quickly'. In his early fifties, slim, casually dressed in a T-shirt, and pleasant looking, I tried to look for some family resemblance to his father but fortunately, couldn't see any. It's perhaps wrong to judge a book by its cover, but on seeing his face for the first time, both Mum and I warmed to him and liked him. His strong American accent served to emphasise his strangeness to us, as I am sure our English accents did to him.

What struck me throughout the conversation is the fact that he is a total stranger to us but through his father's diabolical evil, our families are now inextricably linked. Despite our very different lives, spent living on opposite sides of the ocean, there is an invisible thread that connects us. As Boston's victims, we all have that dubious distinction of belonging to the same ghastly club.

Mum and I were, for the most part, composed. Indeed, it felt as if we were taking the role of counsellors, absolving Russell of any remorse that he claimed to have that Chris had died for him whilst he himself had lived. Our empathy was sincere; we do indeed feel immense pity for him and sorrow that he lost his mother and has lived so many years cowered by his dominating, murderous father. We wanted to like him and we did. Hopefully, it was a cathartic experience for him.

The conversation flowed. Russell recounted the gruesome events on the boat as they had played out. We reassured him that we bore no grudge against him or his brother Vince and only had pity for them witnessing such a horrific scene. It made painful listening but both Mum and I had a need to know.

It was certainly the strangest and most unusual conversation I have ever had or am ever likely to have in my lifetime. I respected the fact that he made no attempt to brush any of it under the carpet but instead, he met the subject head on with bare-faced honesty. He didn't in any way try to excuse his father's actions (how could he?) but I sensed, understandably, that he wanted to shield us from the pain and fear that Chris and Peta went through in their final hours. Mum and I came away emotionally drained but grateful for his first-hand account.

Typical of the sincerity he had displayed to us, on the death of his father he had written an open letter to his friends and acquaintances on Facebook:

When my father was arrested on December 1, 2016 and the newspapers posted his story on December 2, I started getting calls and emails from friends and strangers. Some of my dad's past and actions have been questioned, understandably. To those who know me, I've always been honest about my family, while also striving to avoid being a victim or complaining about things I couldn't change.

As some of my friends may know, my childhood was unconventional. I was raised by my grandparents, and partially by my father, who was an outlaw. He made some very bad decisions in his life and career path which often harmed others. I wasn't dealt the best hand when it comes to family, but I've made up for it with my choice of friends and how I live my life. At the age of 12 he told us he was driving my brother and I to Belize. I didn't have a clue where that was and I thought he meant Brazil. At that age, I didn't have a choice in where he took us.

At 51 years old, I'm pretty sure I'd know by now if I have a propensity for crime or killing. I've done my best to figure out why my dad turned out the way he did, and always strive to do the opposite. I'm not a criminal, I don't do drugs, I don't hate, nor do I hold animosity towards others. I'm overprotective of women and children, and I do my best to make the world a better place. I've been questioned as to why I go out of my way to be nice to strangers or others, sometimes to the point of seeming insincere. It is my way of balancing out the harm and pain my father inflicted on the world. With that, please learn from his choices and, when given the option, always be kind to others. If you're ever in a relationship or situation where it might seem like harming someone is an option, choose the path of kindness, communication and understanding. If you have any questions, please private message me and I'll do my best to answer. Please don't hesitate to ask me the awkward questions. If you're wondering it, most likely others are too.

Russell.

With the trial cancelled, we were denied the opportunity of thanking those on the other side of the pond who had worked so tirelessly on the case. So, in July 2017, I flew to California to give personal thanks. It's a trip that Mum would have dearly liked to have made too and was, of course, prepared to do so, had the trial happened, but approaching ninety-three, she appointed me as her ambassador.

I was delighted to meet up with my 24-year-old son, Charlie, in Los Angeles who was returning from a three-month backpacking tour of Southeast Asia. We hired a car and I appointed him my driver for the trip. We drove the Interstate 5 to California's capital city of Sacramento, absorbing along the way the magnificent views of the San Joaquin Valley and enjoying the opportunity to chat about his recent travels and his return to England for the start of his graduate job in the City of London.

On arrival in Sacramento, we were stunned by the city's beauty and diversity. In amongst the majestic skyscraper buildings of the Wells Fargo Center, the U.S. Bank Plaza, the Renaissance Tower and the Bank of the West Tower is the district of Old Sacramento, which harks back to the city's Gold Rush era, with wooden sidewalks and wagon rides.

Waking up on the morning of 27 July in our hotel rooms, opposite the California State Capitol building, Charlie and I, with great excitement, made our way to the Robert T. Matsui United States Courthouse, where all the video conference calls between the prosecution team and Greater Manchester Police had taken place. A famous Sacramento landmark, our eyes only needed to look to the skyline to see its imposing 18-floor structure soaring high above us. Its buff-coloured Indiana limestone turns at ground level to dark-green polished granite that mingles with the tree-lined streets of downtown Sacramento. A sweeping arc of tinted blue-green glass mimics the flow and passage of the nearby Sacramento River.

Escaping the searing 36 degrees centigrade heat, a welcome blast of cool air conditioning hit us as we entered the cavernous and hallowed sky-lit rotunda lobby. There was a reverential hush, befitting the solemnity and formality of the courtrooms and judicial chambers; a dignified and impressive representation of the United States judiciary.

Passing through tight security, Charlie and I then made our way up to the offices of attorneys Matt Segal and Jeremy Kelley, and minutes later, we were joined by Detective Amy Crosby. After the web conference calls, it was a surreal experience to meet them in the flesh. We had an informal chat about the case and its hasty and unforeseen disappointing end, before Matt then took us down in the lift to a boardroom, where around fifteen people had gathered.

In entering the room, I was stunned and honoured. Matt had organised a surprise reception for me and following a short speech, United States Attorney for the Eastern District of California, Philip A. Talbert, presented me with a certificate to thank me for pursuing justice and a travel clock in memory of Chris. Humbled both by the reception and the thoughtful gifts, as my mother's ambassador, I thanked them for all their hard work and dedication to the case and attempted to describe just how much that meant to my family.

It was a very special day and like no other. As guests of FBI Special Agent David Sesma, Charlie and I were then taken to the Sacramento Field Office of the Federal Bureau of Investigation in Roseville, which had been opened just eight months before. Bristling with high security, the three-storey, 122,385-square-foot building is state-of-the-art and spectacular.

The formidable building was as awe-inspiring inside as it was outside. After a brief tour, David returned the evidence to me that would have been used as exhibits in the trial. In a plastic bag were Chris's last few worldly belongings. They included two of his much-treasured music cassette tapes that had travelled thousands of miles, had been in Boston's possession for 38 years and were now here in my hands. The thought fleetingly crossed my mind, were they the last things on this earth to have Chris's DNA on them? Although technically now belonging to Russell Boston because they were last in his possession, he gave permission for them to be returned to us.

Also returned were the two vinyl albums, Santana's *Welcome* and Pink Floyd's *Animals*, which we had handed in to Greater Manchester Police and they had sent over to America to match with the music cassette tapes. There was a birthday card that he had sent me and some of his medical school case notes, both of which we had sent as examples of his handwriting in order that a writing expert could match it to that on the back of the cassette tapes. It was all evidence that the prosecution team had sourced in order to prove that Chris and Peta had been on the boat. They were our last tangible connections to Chris.

Such was the FBI's interest in the uniqueness of the Boston case that David told me some months later said that he and Amy Crosby had been asked to make a presentation at a homicide training conference in Las Vegas for 800 delegates from across the state at the California Homicide Investigators Association in February 2018.

The day was rounded off with a visit to the Sacramento Police Department to give my personal thanks to Amy Crosby and her team, who had all done so much to bring Boston to justice. I also had the opportunity of meeting Lieutenant Bob McCloskey who, in responding to Vince's damning testimony of his father in 2012 and 2013 had done his level best to investigate but had met a brick wall when the investigation got as far as London. It was an extraordinary day and one I will never forget.

We left Sacramento that evening and via a stopover in San Francisco, Charlie and I then travelled south, taking in sections of the scenic Pacific Coastal Highway, circumnavigating the urban sprawl of Los Angeles and arriving, two days later, in beautiful Laguna Beach. Aside from thanking the investigators, I very much wanted to meet Russell Boston.

Our long Skype call earlier in May of that year had been an icebreaker but it was no substitute for meeting him face-to-face. Any fear that I might have had of awkwardness dispersed within minutes and we embraced each other as if we were friends. There was a sense of familiarity. The warmth and openness that Mum and I had felt when talking to him on Skype was there in the flesh and although complete strangers, I felt at ease in his presence.

After meeting Russell at 9am at our hotel in Laguna Beach, we walked to a local supermarket and bought bagels, ham and cheese and ate them on the sidewalk at the beach. Conversation flowed naturally and we spent the rest of that day and into the evening talking about myriad things – the lives we lead, careers, family and relationships. Inevitably, our conversation turned to Belize and his father. He was honest and open and said there was nothing that I couldn't ask him about what he had witnessed... and I did.

Maybe I felt I had an understanding and affinity with him because we are of similar ages but over and above that is the fact that both our families are now connected by the pain and suffering that his father has inflicted.

Russell has been treated like no child or adult should ever be treated, made even more heinous by the fact that it was at the hands of his father. His upbringing must undoubtedly have left scars, but if I was expecting to meet someone who is traumatised and imbalanced, I would have been very wide of the mark. Russell is a gregarious, well-adjusted human being with a warm, forgiving heart and generous soul. Given that he received spasmodic education, spending most of his younger years on the run with his father, he is intelligent and articulate.

In truth, given his traumatic life, I was expecting him to have turned out, at worst, a protégé of his father or at best, a bitter and twisted soul but neither of those apply to him. He has borne his losses and hardship well; he has turned his back on anger and hate and instead chosen a path of love and humility. He is a good role model for forgiveness and acceptance of life's hardships and pain.

When I asked him how someone who has been brought up by such an immoral, evil character as Boston could turn out so 'normal', he said: 'I always did the opposite of Dad and whenever I felt conflicted, I asked myself what my mother would have wanted me to do and be and I chose that path.'

He talked about the overwhelming relief he felt that his father was no longer in his life. For the first time ever, he felt free. He said that he could now breathe without fear that his father was somewhere in the background and about to show up. He regretted, however, the timing.

'I never anticipated that Dad would kill himself – I figured he was too selfish to do that. I had hoped that he realised his goose was cooked and that his only option was to trade information for some comforts in prison. I always thought I would have a chance to talk to him after he was convicted, and ask him about my mom but that wasn't to be.'

Russell and I met up for a second day in which he showed us some more of the sights of Laguna and its beautiful coastline. He was an excellent tour guide. I told him that I would like to be able to reciprocate by showing him London and my hometown of Oxford and introduce him to my Mum, who I know would welcome the opportunity to meet him. By the time Charlie and I arrived at the airport for our return journey to England, I felt I was saying goodbye to a friend. If we had to meet in these most terrible of circumstances, I am happy that Russell is the person he turned out to be. Even if we never meet again, I hope that we will stay in touch if only through Facebook. I wish him only the very best.

Chapter Nineteen

THE SPAWNING GROUND

So where did the roots of Boston's immoral sick personality lie? Is it nature or nurture that makes a psychopath? Were there any signposts in his early development and upbringing to suggest that he would become such a demonic human being?

Meeting him in Laguna, Russell Boston was generous in sharing with me his vivid recollections of his depraved father's reckless and lawless life and his family's history. He spoke openly and with complete frankness.

Silas Duane Boston was born on 20 March 1941 in Shasta County Hospital, Clear Creek, Rural Shasta, in Northern California to working-class parents, Russell and Mary Evelyn Sellers Boston, who divorced shortly after he was born. He attended Elk Grove High School in Sacramento County. Hillbilly, redneck, white trailer trash, he fitted a variety of epithets – Boston was all of those and much, much more.

The seeds for his vile character were sown from an early age. Russell explained: 'Dad came from a broken home and claimed he was abused and beaten. He felt his mother was a tramp who betrayed him and she was the source of his serious psychological issues of abandonment and betrayal regarding women. He started stealing when he was a child because, he said, his mom left him alone for days at a time to be with her latest boyfriend and he had to feed himself.

'Dad claimed he made his first kill when he was just eight years old. He enjoyed throwing rocks at passing railcars and he was proud that on one occasion he made a direct hit with a hobo passenger, who slumped to the floor. After that he got a thrill and a lust for killing.'

No academic, Boston was nonetheless cunning, savvy and streetwise and as tough as snakeskin. He had a fierce sense of pride and would rather see everything go to hell than suffer humiliation. His volatile temper could go from zero to murder in a heartbeat. He was a tyrant and a master of manipulation, ruling his immediate and extended family with a rod of iron. Physically and mentally abusive, those with whom he came into contact were said to live in constant fear of him, and he repeatedly threatened them with death if ever they thought about exposing the crimes he so often bragged about. The majority colluded in silence for fear of retribution either by him or his network of 'outlaw' contacts with whom he did 'business', such as burglaries, hijacking, smuggling and drug deals.

Marital breakdown, adultery, domestic violence, alcoholism, murder, sexual deviance and burglary characterised Boston's life. Like a serpent, he could disguise his evil core well. Outwardly, he could turn on the charm and charisma at the flick of a switch; inwardly, he was cold, ruthless, with no hint of a moral compass.

Russell told me: 'When he wasn't showing his dark side

he was well liked by those around him. He was a superb conversationalist and very successful womaniser, a gift he used with devastating effect. All my life I've been stupefied by Dad's ability to attract women. My grandmother called it the "Boston Charm", which she said Dad inherited from his father. He was able to schmooze and charm women of any walk of life and always had a plethora of girlfriends and wives. A misogynist, he had a cocky confidence, which he combined with a physiological trick of insulting women, who then craved his attention and validation. I can't tell you how many times I saw him blatantly degrade women, only for them to come crawling back to eat out of his hand afterwards.'

Believed to have been married a staggering seven times, and siring more children than anyone can count or remember, Russell, perhaps not jokingly, says there is a village in Mexico where all of its inhabitants look like Boston! Boston always protested that he wasn't a rapist, saying 'I can get any chick I want.' He had a conveyor belt of women who fell prey to his 'charm' and despite his timeworn, haggard appearance and violent, abusive character Boston had several girlfriends right up to the point he died. He was also an outspoken racist, yet he had Afro-American girlfriends aplenty. One of his favourite sayings was: 'The only thing worse than a nigger is a nigger lover, and the only thing worse than a nigger lover is a snitch.'

Whilst Boston might well have been hardwired wrong, as Russell suspects, nurture undoubtedly had a large part to play in the twisted monster he turned out to be. One doesn't have to look further than his parents for the root of his total lack of moral agency.

The matriarch of the family, Boston's mother, fostered a culture in which her son could do no wrong and had to be protected at all costs. When Russell and Vince spoke to their grandmother about their father's crimes they were told that it was a family secret, which they were forbidden to talk about. '"He's my son," my grandmother said and that dogma took precedence over absolutely everything. It was non-negotiable,' Russell explained to me.

'My grandfather is not without blame either – in fact, he was more wicked than my grandmother. He killed federal agents during the Prohibition in 1920–33, who were searching in the mountains of Oregon and Idaho for people making illegal whisky. He was never caught for killing, but he did serve time for forging a cheque, taking a woman over state lines for immoral purposes, and for beating a prison guard almost to death when he was escaping. He used to tell Dad horrible things about my grandma after they divorced. My grandparents' influence was a textbook catalyst for creating a psychopathic serial killer.

'It was common knowledge throughout my family that Dad had killed our mom in September 1968. When the *Justin B* was anchored that memorable night off Belize City and he intended to kill Vince and I the next day, he told us how he had killed Mom, but my grandmother had already told me when I was seven. She wasn't one to sugar-coat things – she was an odd one and would talk about anything and everything. She said she needed to tell us so that it was no longer a mystery and because she didn't want us to think that our Mom had abandoned us. Dad, however, gave us more details. I remember Vince having terrible nightmares after Belize.

'After Dad killed Mom, he sought help from his aunts (Grandfather's sisters, Grace and Mildred), and they removed Mom's clothing and personal items from her apartment and took them to a local thrift store to make it look as though she had left. Dad came to my grandmother's house in Roseville the day after he killed Mom. Divorced from my grandfather, she was married to a man named Mark Sellers. Mark spotted the blisters on his hands and said, "Duane, what happened to you?" Dad started crying and told him what had happened. Mark said: "Don't tell your mom, it will break her heart," so initially they lied to my grandmother, saying that my mom had left.

'My grandmother couldn't understand why Mom would just leave like that because she knew she loved us. Mark kept sending her on wild goose chases, saying: "Oh, I saw Mary Lou working at this store over there," and my grandmother would drive over and frantically look for her. After several months, my grandmother said: "Duane, what happened to Mary Lou?" He finally told her. It was then that Dad gave my grandmother my mom's box of jewellery, high school scrapbook, mementos, drawings and photos.

'Wanting to know more about my Mom, I spoke to my great-aunt Grace but she said she didn't know much about it and then clammed up completely. I knew she knew but I didn't want to hold an old lady's feet to the fire so I stopped asking her about it. I also asked my grandmother why my Mom's murder was kept a secret within the family and told her that, had she reported him, he might not have gone on to kill others, but all she said was, "We're family, we don't talk about it, Russell."

'Within days of Mary Lou going missing, a missing persons report was filed with the Sacramento Police Department by her younger brother, Jeffery Venn, who told authorities her disappearance seemed particularly out of character given "she was a devoted mother to her three children and could not stand to be away from the children for any period of time".' Jeffery told police that Boston was acting uncharacteristically 'nervous and jittery' and said he didn't want to get involved if Jeffery contacted the police.

The missing persons report also noted that a .22 calibre rifle with a scope, said to be Boston's favourite possession, was missing. Boston told Jeffery he had traded it in: 'For some junk items he wanted'. Jeffery reported this to the police plus the fact that a couple of shovels in the back of Boston's truck had fresh soil on them. He told them that when he himself had questioned Boston about them, he explained it by saying that he had lent the truck to some friends to go deer hunting. Boston had never lent his truck before and he was not the sort of person to lend anything to anyone, said Jeffery.

Mary Lou's mother, Helen Venn, was also interviewed and she described how her daughter was just eighteen years old when she and Boston had run away to get married. In further incriminating testimony, she said that she didn't like or trust her son-in-law. She complained that he avoided work but always had money and he would spend it on himself and not his three children. Most damning of all, she said that he had threatened to 'blow her head off'. Despite all of this highly compelling evidence, quite shockingly their accounts were discredited and police investigators concluded that Mary Lou Boston's disappearance: 'Does not appear to be a legitimate missing person case because the couple are having marital difficulties and the wife has left the husband'.

'They even threatened to charge Mom's brother, Jeffery, and her parents for harassment if they kept bothering the police. Jeffery later committed suicide supposedly because he never got over the loss of his sister who he was close to,' says Russell.

Boston worked at this time as a driver for two different ambulance companies including the Metropolitan Ambulance

Company in Los Angeles County. Vince recalls: 'I know that he collected a lot of photographs from dead people. Like this guy hung himself from a tree in his backyard and he had his tongue sticking out and my dad would keep all of those pictures in a scrapbook and show them to us kids. It was full of his gore and stuff.'

Both Russell and Vince are naturally dismayed at how the Sacramento Police Department in 1968–70 comprehensively botched the investigation into their mother's disappearance to the point of absolute negligence.

Russell says: 'So many times, the police could have, and should have, stopped him. I still don't know why it took so many decades to connect the dots about my father.'

Vince says: 'The almost non-existent way in which they "investigated" my mom's murder was a travesty. If they had properly investigated and locked Dad up then, he wouldn't have been free to destroy all the lives that he subsequently did.'

He added: 'Mom's family used to send us letters and gifts but Dad had left explicit instructions not to let them contact us. My grandma and my dad had a weird bond and they would fight over our welfare money. One time when he was extremely drunk, he came to pick us up from her house but we weren't there, so he kicked in her glass door. She made him pay for that when he sobered up. She was pretty tough and they would get into big screaming matches. I found letters that he wrote to her over the years. He would say: "I miss you so much, Mom". Really nice sweet letters, but when we were around he would call her a "cunt" or a "bitch" but I don't think she was ever in fear that he would kill her. She would always cover for him. She put us in Sunday School and was a Christian and didn't want him to do these things but knew he was a law unto himself.

'My grandparents were divorced and Dad would run away from home a lot and run to my grandpa's house, to whom he was close. My grandpa knew what was going on and basically groomed him to be a criminal.'

Just how shockingly complicit Boston's parents were in their son's crimes was revealed during the investigation. In spring 2016, Russell gave Detective Amy Crosby a key to the mobile home that his grandmother had left him when she died in 2009. Seeing if she could glean any further evidence, she made a truly remarkable discovery. Taped to the back of a drawer in Russell's grandmother's bathroom cabinet, Amy found a letter in her handwriting, dating from 1978 and addressed to both Boston and his father. The grandmother had concocted an alibi to give to the police if they were questioned about Boston's nefarious crimes. It mentions Chris and Peta but also, the German/Scandinavian couple that Boston called 'Vikings', whom he had boasted to Bryan Logsdon on their road trip in Mexico, he had killed off Dangriga (Stann Creek) by slitting their throats, just weeks after killing Chris and Peta.

The FBI took this very seriously, particularly after Russell found a small scrap of paper in amongst Boston's belongings from Belize with a German address on it. The FBI in Sacramento instructed its agents in Berlin to investigate if any German, who had travelled in Central America in 1978, had been reported missing. The search identified three possible people. They did indeed trace a German citizen who was in that region at that time but the FBI was unsuccessful in linking Boston to the murder of any Europeans beside Chris and Peta.

It is Russell's belief that the address on the scrap of paper belonged to one of the many German tourists who travelled on the boat before the 'Vikings' were passengers, but it did not pertain to the couple that Boston killed. The fact that the 'Vikings' are included in his grandmother's alibi, along with Chris and Peta and his Mom, leads Russell to believe, that his father killed them. If that is the case, there is some family in Germany, or possibly Scandinavia, whose loved ones never returned and they never learnt of their fate. For all we know there might be relatives of other victims who, like us, have spent decades searching but weren't as fortunate as us in getting answers.

'My grandmother was more than just negligent, she was complicit in Dad's crimes,' says Russell. 'She partially helped to raise us, to keep us out of foster homes, and I am grateful for that, but if she and other family members had gone to the police in regard to my Mom, the world would be a much better place.'

Not only did Boston's parents fail to instil any morality and ethics in their son, they sheltered and protected and aided and abetted him. Between the pair of them, they were highly instrumental in moving Russell and Vince around so that the police could never question them about events in Belize. They have to take a large share of blame for the evil misfit Boston turned out to be and for helping him avoid capture for almost all of his life.

Chapter Twenty

BOSTON, THE DESTROYER

(Destroyer – originally, torpedo-boat destroyer; a small, swift, and powerfully armed warship)

Nearing the end of his life, Boston confided in Russell that he had killed a staggering 33 people. Russell believes this number to be accurate because his father never shielded him from knowing the kind of person he was. Assuming that number is correct, it puts Boston in the category of being one of America's most prolific serial killers. He also holds the dubious distinction of avoiding capture for one of the longest periods of time. Starting from Mary Lou's murder in 1968, 48 years elapsed before he was finally arrested in 2016.

In our face-to-face meeting, Russell told me about his childhood and growing up with his father. With their mother dead, he and Vince had a chaotic upbringing: 'In 1969, one year after killing Mom, Dad went to Vietnam as a volunteer private contractor "for fun", with his brother, Kevin. He told us the people he killed in Vietnam didn't count because they were "gooks" [foreigners, especially Southeast Asians] and it was war. There is a photo in our family photo album that Dad took of a dead, mangled body in Vietnam, and in the white margin, Dad wrote: "Kill for peace, war is fun".'

Boston spoke of Vietnam as a shooting gallery, and enjoyed describing the carnage. He reminisced about fun pranks to play, such as separating tracer rounds. Tracers, built with a small pyrotechnic charge in their base, are usually loaded as every fifth round in machine gun belts in order to light up the trajectory of the bullet. Boston filled his machine gun with just tracers, then shot people with what he described as a rocket powered road flare.

On returning to California, he took control of the boys but in 1970, Russell aged four, accidentally ate some pills that his father had left lying around. He was taken to hospital to have his stomach pumped. At the same time, Boston spent six months in jail for stealing guns so the two boys were placed in foster care. Russell describes it as: 'The one and only time that I experienced anything like a proper childhood.' But this was not to last – the foster parents had two daughters, whom they favoured over Vince and Russell in winning races and games. The boys made a mild complaint to their social worker, who overreacted by moving them to a long-term foster family. The new family were harsh and the mother would regularly beat them. Out of jail, Boston visited Vince and Russell and when they told him about the beatings, he decided to take the law into his own hands [as he was to spend a lifetime doing] and he took them back into his care, saying he couldn't do a worse job. Vince, along with his elder sister, Vicki, was raised largely by their grandmother, interspersed with occasional stays with Boston.

Vince recalled: 'He would walk around nude all the time and

he had a lot of pornography that he would leave lying around, Swedish erotica and weird stuff like that. One time, hidden under a blanket, he took us to an adult movie that was playing at a drive-in. Dad would often hit us with a belt but he didn't do anything sexual to us. We all knew what he was capable of. He would just party and give us a little bit of money and tell us to go to a friend's house. That was his idea of raising us – letting us wander the streets.'

Russell says: 'That I had an unconventional childhood is a massive understatement,' he says. 'All my life, my father dragged me around when he was running from the law, with no regard for my education or well-being. I was left to fend for myself, often knocking on the doors of neighbours for food. He taught me how to fish and forage for food but it wasn't unusual to go days without eating, and as a child, I learned how to ignore the hunger pangs.

'Dad loved terrifying us. When I was eight, he took Vince and I into the Trinity County Mountains. He told us the story of Bigfoot [in North American folklore, a hairy, upright-walking ape-like creature that lives in the wilderness, akin to the yeti of Tibet], and how he lived in the woods, dismembering people, ripping off their limbs, which were seen floating in the river by picnicking families. After going into gory detail, he told us to bring firewood in from the barn. We begged him to let us wait until sunrise, but he forced us out. In the darkness, we heard a large animal growling and moaning in the trees. As we lugged the large box of firewood towards the house, Dad jumped out of the forest and ran towards us, snarling and pretending to be Bigfoot. He laughed and laughed over that one.'

Relating what a first-class marksman his father was, Russell told me how he could shoot pistols and rifles with pinpoint accuracy from either hand: 'Dad invariably carried a firearm, either in a holster or in his vehicles. He also had an assortment of weapons – clubs and truncheons, like the one he beat Chris with, maces, knives and a folded Buck knife in a leather belt holder. He had "stash" places at home to store his guns and stolen items. In our house on 57th Street, Sacramento, he pulled up the carpet in his room, took a thin blade and cut away the seams in the wooden floor underneath. It was an irregular shaped section of the floor, about a foot wide. Then he reinforced it with a frame, boxed it in and used magnets to keep it shut, in case the authorities showed up with a search warrant.'

As adults, both sons despised their father in equal measure, but their responses were polar opposites. Both reactions are plausible and understandable. Russell, being the youngest and possibly more malleable, retained contact with Boston up until 2014, but Vince, after being severely beaten by his father, at the age of sixteen joined the Navy in 1982 to get away.

'Once I joined the Navy, I had my own money and independence,' explains Vince. 'I didn't need Dad anymore. He came to my boot camp graduation in San Diego and he was really nice to me but I wasn't buying it. I didn't talk to him for over a year and then he came up to Washington, where I was stationed. He kept asking me for money, but then it was a car he wanted. I took money out of my account and bought him a car just to get him out of my hair. He didn't come back to me for money after that.'

Boston's killing spree continued well into the eighties. Vince describes how he found out from his half-sister – Boston's daughter Alicia (whose mother, Colleen was Boston's girlfriend in 1986–8) that he was involved in a murder of a Mexican national in Ensenada. He got in a fight with a preacher and told him in front of Colleen and other witnesses: 'I'm going to kill you tomorrow.' Boston rigged the preacher's car so that it would split in two whilst he was driving and just as he had threatened, the preached died the following day. It was reported in the local Mexican newspaper and Boston proudly gave Russell the newspaper article reporting the accident.

Vince says: 'Dad moved to Southern California in the nineties. I visited him in Santa Ana to see if he had changed and to give him another chance but it soon became apparent that he was the same old person, so I was out of there. That was pretty much the last time I talked to Dad.'

Turning sixteen in 1982, Russell attempted, like Vince had done, to break free from his father's clutches. He had the chance to live in the small town of Bishop, in the foothills of the Sierra Nevada mountains. A family friend observed that he was missing a lot of schooling and offered him the opportunity to stay with her and her 16 year old daughter, so that he could attend high school there. Russell was keen to accept because it promised more stability than he had experienced in his entire life.

Russell says: 'Dad finally agreed, but he had one stipulation: he would continue to receive my welfare money and food stamps. If I wanted to be on my own, I had to work and buy my own food, clothes and keep myself. Whilst I lived in Bishop, Dad lived in Baja, Mexico, but because it gets so hot, unbeknownst to me, he spent the summers up in Northern California, on the coast where he could camp, fish and be out of sight. Eventually, the welfare office in Eureka withheld my welfare cheques, insisting my father show me to them in person to prove I existed and was living with him.

'He turned up in Bishop one day without notice. I'd been swimming with my girlfriend, Melanie, and, as I got out of her car, Dad's girlfriend was waiting for me. She insisted I got into her car, saying it was very important. She drove me to the far side of the Indian Reservation, where I was living, and I saw my father sitting in his truck, waiting for me. Drunk, he started telling me what a wonderful time he was having in Northern California, fishing and camping, like he and I used to do. He wanted me to join him. I declined and said I was happy in Bishop. I explained I had a job as an illustrator for a local wildlife magazine and was working for a sign painter. I had just accepted a competitive internship with the US Forest Service to work in their graphics department and get on-the-job training to be a commercial artist. I told him I only had one more week of summer school to complete, and then I'd jump the entire junior high school grade. The more I resisted, the angrier he became, and he started babbling about the family I was staying with: "Who the fuck are these motherfuckers, turning my flesh and blood against me? How dare they keep my son from me! I'm going to kill every motherfucking last one of them!"'

Russell described how his father then took out his pistol, unloaded all the bullets, counted them and reloaded. The entire time he was doing it, Russell begged him not to, but Boston kept grumbling through clenched teeth he was going to 'fucking kill 'em all'.

Knowing that he would, in a heartbeat, kill each and every one of them, Russell reluctantly relented, saying: 'OK, OK, I'll go with you, but please let me go home and put some clothes on.

'The only thing I was wearing was a pair of swimming trunks. He said I could buy more clothes in a thrift store. It was Sunday afternoon and no thrift stores would be open until the following day. He said the family would try to stop me and then he would be forced to kill all of them. He finally relented, on the one condition that he would park up under a tree, down the end of the street, and if I wasn't back by 11pm, he would kick the front door in at 11.01pm and shoot every "motherfucker in the house". I went home, grabbed my belongings and slipped out without even telling my girlfriend I was leaving.

'In silence, we sped north on the winding mountain roads, the sun filtering through the trees onto my dad's old pickup, and I felt unbelievably sad. Stopping only for gas, we drove for 12 hours straight to a government welfare office in Eureka. Dad ushered me inside and stormed up to the desk of a social worker and yelled, with everyone looking: "Here he fucking is! I told you he was gathering firewood, fishing and shit, now give me my fucking cheques!" The social worker fumbled through some paperwork before handing him an envelope. It was at that moment that I realised I would never escape him. No matter what I did in life, he would always be there with his hand out, threatening to harm or kill people if I didn't comply.

'By this time, I totally despised him and I didn't want to be around him. Dad threatened, and almost succeeded, in killing me several times. I put it in the category of a bad storm, and once it passed, I learned to recognise the warning signs on the horizon in order to survive future storms. He said I was worthless and he wanted to take me up into the hills and put a bullet in my head but I wasn't worth the cost of the bullet. He kept following me around, tormenting me and trying to encourage me to talk back, so that he could "justify" attacking me. Wise to his ploy, I stayed quiet and went about my business.

'There were many times I wished I was far away from him but Vince and I had been to the authorities so many times and been ignored. As an adult, I realised the police couldn't, or wouldn't, stop him so I took it upon myself to protect the world from him. I explained to Dad that he didn't need to harm people, that if he ever felt the necessity, there was always another way and I made him promise to call me first. I always maintained an open-door policy, giving him cash, buying him vehicles, giving him a sofa to sleep on. I received his mail and military retirement pay cheques for him.

'When I was nineteen, Dad and a friend of his had sex with two underage girls. Dad was afraid that they would go to the police and they would haul his friend in for questioning, and he would in turn be implicated. So, as he had promised, my father called me in advance to tell me he was about to kill. I managed to make him see that it was totally senseless because he would then be even more under the spotlight. Thereafter, I felt I was the backstop between him and others he wanted to kill. He called me a couple of times and I talked him down from killing, so I naively thought it worked.

'I can't count how much money Dad extorted from me, or vehicles I've bought for him. I became weary of it, like a parent dispensing tough love on their teenager, who constantly has their hand out, and one time I politely refused to buy him two expensive metal detectors that he said he needed in his quest to find gold in Baja. He immediately threatened to knock on the doors of my "silk drawer" neighbours, his expression for wealthy people, then beat or kill them for the funds he needed. There was no doubt in my mind that he meant it. I relented, maxed my credit cards and bought him two Gold Bug-2 metal detectors.

'From an early age, he tried to coax me into following his ways but I adamantly refused. It angered him, and he perpetually made derogatory jibes about me, saying that I thought I was too good for it, or I was too much of a coward. One time, when I was in Sacramento with Dad, his friends asked how I had turned out to be so normal and Dad said he did all the bad stuff, so that Vince and I would know what not to do. It angered me so much that Dad took credit for us. It wasn't because of him we turned out OK, it was *despite* him.'

One might question why Russell chose to have anything to do with his father, but he was the youngest and, at the tender age of twelve, he had witnessed at close hand the brutal murders of Chris and Peta, who had stepped in to defend him from being beaten to a pulp. Remember that shocking, life-changing event, and it then becomes understandable how he spent his whole life attempting to placate his murderous father, subjugating himself to his every whim in order to stop him hurting or taking anyone else's life.

'I wanted to insert myself in between him and anyone he wanted to destroy,' says Russell. And that is exactly what he spent most of the next four decades doing. 'I hated Dad as much as Vince did, but if I found myself feeling hatred or anger, I'd push it out of my head. I've always believed that hate only harms the person who is hating by eating them up inside.'

In 2012, Boston was living in Mexico and, with his health failing, he wanted to return to the States. Russell drove him up to his grandmother's house in Roseville, Sacramento, that Russell had inherited from her on her death in 2009.

'Everyone warned me not to let him stay, but I felt it would stop him from being in a position where he needed to harm or kill. He was by now old and crippled and I stayed with him for a month, but I quickly realised he was going to do what he had done all his life: it was his nature and he could never change.'

Sitting in the living room one day and complaining about

the neighbours, Boston articulated to his son his theory of the universe and explained his 'justification' for taking life. Russell thought this was an ideal opportunity to capture his words and pass them on to the police. So, he hit record on his iPhone.

'Well, I could fucking kill the neighbours, Russ. It wouldn't bother me at all, you know that. I've killed people and haven't lost a minute's sleep over it. You can't, Russ, you're not made that way – you don't think that way. But I can,' Boston told him.

'Dad put his hands out in front of him and said: "It's just there, it's just there."

'Dad had a "code" that he had to adhere to, but he would bend it to suit himself and the situation he found himself in. The universe gave him licence to kill and that was reflected in events that did or didn't happen, or, if the person that he wanted to kill didn't take the "chance" that he had given them. If the universe wanted someone to die it would dictate whether it happened or not.

'After abducting [his son] Justin in 1979 and losing visitation rights, he planned to kill his ex-wife, Kathe. He drove to San Rafael with his gun, but when she came out of work and took a left instead of a right, he decided it was fate telling him not to do it.

'He was more than willing to kill Vince and me when he thought we would be questioned in Belize for witnessing Chris and Peta's murders but fate intervened that day when some people who were passing by made an offer to buy the *Justin B*, which he accepted.

'Dad occasionally went out of his way to protect kids or old people, if he felt someone was harming them, but he had no qualms about doing home invasions against old people, tying them up and smacking them around for valuables. I don't know the extent he and his crew abused them. I heard them talking about it afterwards, without specifics, but I know they were tied up and "motivated" to divulge where their money and valuables were.

'Dad was an absolute psychopath. He had feelings. I saw him cry on occasion and there are certain things he got sentimental over, but he was an insane dog that needed putting down. He should have been taken out of circulation a very, very long time ago.'

Boston's abuse of his son continued right up until he died. In January 2014, he sold the home that Russell had inherited from his grandmother in Roseville and had allowed his Dad to stay in. As a consequence, Boston was evicted and Russell lost the house that to this day is the subject of a court case, with him trying to reclaim the property.

'Regardless of the financial loss, I was heartbroken. My grandmother's home was a time capsule of my past and things I held dear. It was filled with mid-century furniture, artwork and belongings, but also all of our childhood homework, drawings and loved items, such as our *Star Wars* T-shirts. It was an entire timeline of who we were. My grandmother had given me a box with some of my mom's things, but she kept her larger drawings, paintings, letters and mementos. I lost it all.

'After Dad sold my property, its contents and my vehicles, he moved to Placerville, 40 miles from Sacramento, and kept a low profile in camping grounds.

'Before Dad left, he and I fell out because he had been talking to his cousin, Narvell, who had got wind that Vince had been going to the police about Dad. Thinking that his phone was bugged and his call was being recorded, either by me or the police, he rang me and said in his familiar, deep drawl: "Russ,

Narvell says that Vince was trying to turn me in for some shit! What the fuck! He's trying to turn me in for something with the people on the boat in Belize. Why the fuck would he say that? I don't know what happened to them! They just left – you remember that, don't you? And, he's trying to say that I had something to do with your mom. Why would he say that, Russ?"

'It was Dad trying to cover his ass – he was no idiot. He was flabbergasted that Vince was trying to turn him in and that I hadn't told him.'

In mid-March 2014, Russell received several messages from his father saying he was in San Diego and was about to return to Mexico: 'Russ, I've got a box of your grandmother's things. If you don't want them, I'm going to throw them in the fucking dumpster!'

'It was my Achilles heel – he knew I was sentimental and would take the bait to pick up her belongings. I made arrangements to go down on March 20th, his birthday.

'He looked like he was one hundred years old, but he was seventy-three. The booze, drugs, fights and his vile existence had taken its toll on his body and, living in a campground, he could barely open the door of his motorhome. I took him to lunch at a Mexican restaurant and listened to him ramble on about how he sold my property and possessions, even though he said it didn't belong to him. I listened, but all I could hear was a lifetime of lies and selfish manipulation. He had totally abused me and betrayed my goodwill. I didn't let him know how much I despised him and was disgusted. I asked the waitress to bring him a cake with a candle and, blowing it out, he started to weep. Following lunch, I dropped him off, and he acted like everything was wonderful again and all of his wrongdoings had been swept under the carpet. I drove away and ignored his calls, until they eventually ceased.'

Returning to Mexico in 2014, Boston retained contact with his daughter, Vicki. Mentally disabled and living in a care facility, she is aware her father killed their mother but she has forgiven him.

Russell says: 'After devoting his life to burning all the bridges, he came in contact with, and scorching the earth around him, Vicki was one of the very few people who still accepted Dad's calls. He told her how nobody loved or took care of him.'

Russell, as Vicki's guardian, was able to keep some tabs on where his father was. He learnt that Boston spent several months in Mexico but then took a bus back to California. A couple of months later, he got a call from the ex-wife of one of Boston's partners in crime, who said his father had turned up on her doorstep demanding help and that she had taken him to the convalescent home in Eureka to access medical treatment. As Russell was his next of kin, she said he needed to help him. Russell politely declined, saying he had had enough.

'I didn't talk to Dad on the phone, nor see him again in person until April 2017, when I drove up to Sacramento. Dying, and strapped to his hospital deathbed, I will never forget how Dad leaned forward and glowered at me with his menacing eyes. If he could have killed me, I know he would have, in a blink of an eye.'

Chapter Twenty-One

THE PERFECT STORM

The fact that the only time Boston faced prosecution was five months before he died at the age of seventy-six reveals just how much of an accomplished survivor he was. His was a fight-or-flight response and it worked.

When he was arrested on 1 December 2016, there was no shortage of reports stating he was a volatile, very dangerous criminal, who consistently threatened and was suspected of murder. And yet the only time he appeared on the police's radar was when he made a mistake whilst drunk. He literally got away with murder, not just once but countless times.

His arrest and ultimate downfall in 2016 was only facilitated by his failing health (which allowed the police to finally catch up with him) and the fact that he had permitted two eyewitnesses to his murderous crimes to live. If he showed any humanity in his sick depraved life it was that he couldn't quite bring himself, despite threatening it several times, to kill his own flesh and blood.

DEAD IN THE WATER

How did such a prolific psychopathic killer dodge justice for five decades when his crimes were known to so many people, including several law enforcement agencies? That is the perplexing question that I keep returning to.

Highly intelligent, and blessed with a devastating charm, he was a master of deception and manipulation. This was coupled with his demonic controlling personality which imbued everyone in his acquaintance with terror. Fear of retribution, which stopped nothing short of death, certainly played a large part in preventing some people from coming forward to report his crimes.

It's doubtless unfair to compare the robust, regulated systems and computerised checks and balances that are in place today with what happened four or five decades ago. Thankfully, Sacramento Police Department and Greater Manchester Police now operate very differently and bear little or no resemblance to the organisations that were in place in 1978. But it's undeniable that his campaign of terror was aided by a system that comprehensively failed its victims. When his crimes did occasionally appear on the Sacramento Police Department's radar, the investigation was bungled or overlooked. The indisputable fact remains that had the police properly investigated Mary Lou's disappearance in 1968, Chris and Peta, and countless others, would not have died, because Boston would have been in jail, serving either a life sentence or on death row.

That Boston never stayed in any one place long enough was a devious, well-executed ploy. His modus operandi of repeatedly fleeing south to Mexico when police investigations were 'hot' proved highly successful. There appears to have been a systemic breakdown in communication and poor leadership between the different Californian Sheriffs' Departments involved in investigating his trail of vicious and varied crimes. This extended from the reporting of his first crime in 1961 through to the shambolic investigation into Mary Lou's 'disappearance' in 1968, continuing on to Chris and Peta's murders in 1978 and his multiple other crimes in the 1980s, and maybe even beyond.

Indeed, it seems there was a chronic lack of joined up thinking, co-operation and communication between all the different law enforcement agencies, both internally and externally and on both sides of the Atlantic in the 1970s and 80s which meant that within a shockingly brief timespan, Chris and Peta's murders literally dropped off the radar, without trace.

Even accepting the fact that their murders happened prior to the days of computerisation, it was a massive fail that neither Interpol nor Greater Manchester Police had apparently archived their case notes or indeed, possessed any written note of Chris and Peta's murders from 1978. This was, after all, a horrific double killing of two British citizens not some petty theft report. When Vince contacted Scotland Yard in 1982, just four years after they were murdered, either Scotland Yard failed to investigate properly or they couldn't find any trace of the crime. How can that possibly be? Where did the file at Greater Manchester Police headquarters go? Did Scotland Yard not think of contacting Interpol about an international murder? And if they did, where did the file of original documents, that was said by San Raphael's Police Department to be in Interpol in Washington's possession in 1981, go? No wonder that my parent's continued desperate enquiries fell on deaf ears and why, after summer 1981, we were never to hear from a single soul at Greater Manchester Police or Sacramento Police Department again.

No one can accurately determine how many people Boston killed after Chris and Peta but we have his sons' testimonies that there were several others. With his wanton and wholesale disregard for others, inflicting pain and taking life came easy.

There were serious fault lines in the investigation carried out by GMP in 1979. Although a journalist and skilled at interviewing, my father was not a trained detective. It therefore seems remarkable that he was permitted to conduct telephone calls with Russell Boston (father) and Boston himself. Also, given that Boston was the last to see Chris and Peta alive, and therefore the prime suspect, it seems incredible that the British Consulate in San Francisco interviewed him initially and not the police. [Perhaps what's even more surprising is that he agreed to subject himself to these interviews when it wasn't mandatory. Maybe in some sick and bizarre way he enjoyed the notoriety to reinforce his sense of control and empowerment.]

In 1978, as indeed it would seem to be true still to this day, Interpol often proved itself an unnecessary hurdle to cross when expediency dictated that it would have been better to cut through the red tape and crack on with directly contacting law enforcement personnel across national boundaries. Now and then, I am sure Interpol does give legitimacy and open doors but, in our case, it was found sadly wanting on several occasions and severely hindered progress.

Even today, the protocol for police forces in the UK is that most international contact has to be initiated and channelled through Interpol, as evidenced when, following my visit, GMP first reached out to Sacramento Police Department in October 2015. It took a staggering five months before GMP and Sacramento PD had any direct contact at all. This is apparently abnormally quick and it was only because Sacramento Police

Department initiated contact with Interpol at the same time as GMP, that contact was made within this time span, as normally it can take twice this length of time. Where the international crime involves a criminal who is known to have been on the run for 50 years and is aged 76, is that really acceptable? In the global village we live in today, where instant and constant communication is a facet of everyday life, a wait of five months is an anachronism, particularly where the fighting and prevention of criminal activity is concerned.

When Vince went back to Sacramento Police Department as recently as 2012, the case was again overlooked. When the enquiry came in from Sacramento Police Department to the National Crime Agency, had they picked up on Vince's information that Chris was a doctor, with just one simple phone call to the General Medical Council they could have traced Chris and the case could have been re-opened four years earlier.

Lastly, it seems astonishing that Vince and Russell's strenuous and credible efforts to report their witnessing of two horrific murders were time and again overlooked... no matter how old the case was or how scant the evidence.

Understandably, Boston's sons still have a lot of unanswered questions and unresolved anger for the way the authorities chose to ignore them.

Vince wrote to me to say: 'I am so sorry for your family's and the Framptons' loss. I have been trying to find your families for years. There was no trace of Chris or Peta, at least none that I could find. I called Scotland Yard in 1982 when I was sixteen and first joined the Navy. I have been calling and writing to Sacramento Police Department for years about the murder of my mother – I wanted to see this brought to justice as well. I contacted everyone I could think of, including FBI, Interpol and the Belizean and Guatemalan authorities. I spent hours in libraries in search of news accounts about Chris and Peta from 1978 but there was nothing.

'I am extremely upset that it has taken the authorities so long to believe me and make an arrest. I am trying to piece together what happened and why it took so long. That the Sacramento Police Department dropped the ball in 1968 is an understatement. The almost non-existent way in which they "investigated" my mom's murder was a travesty. If they had properly investigated and locked him up then, he wouldn't have been free to destroy all the lives that he did subsequently. I know that we can never bring our loved ones back but maybe we can figure out what went wrong to prevent something like this happening to other families.'

Russell feels equally strongly: 'I am disappointed that the FBI, in releasing a 27-page affidavit at the time of our father's arrest in December 2016, chose to put information and details out in the public domain that I didn't even know (and shouldn't have known before testifying), yet they failed to say that Vince and I had been going to the authorities over the decades. They instead chose to say that we were too afraid of our dad. Absolutely, we were afraid, because there is no doubt he would have killed us but we still went to the authorities. When it fell on deaf ears, I stepped back and let Vince be the point person, because Dad didn't know where Vince lived, but he did know where I lived. I figured the authorities would have to talk to Dad first and unless they arrested him in that meeting, he'd promptly kill me and then head back to Mexico. There was never any doubt about that.

'They asked me at the Grand Jury testimony on October 13th 2016 whom I had previously told about my father and his crimes, and I gave them a long laundry list of people, including the authorities. The only reason I can think why they left those details out of the affidavit is because people would ask why nothing was done all these years and why it took the authorities so long to apprehend a serial killer. I don't want revenge or punishment but I would like some answers. Lessons need to be learnt, so it doesn't happen to other families. If the authorities keep sweeping it under the carpet, it shows they didn't learn and it's business as usual.'

As a family, we are grateful for the efforts that Vince and Russell Boston made to inform the authorities and, like them, we are appalled their protestations fell on deaf ears for so long.

I am not a believer in pre-destiny per se but there is an element of me that thinks if your number's up, your number's up. Who would have thought that a boy and girl, born in a nondescript suburb of Manchester in 1953, would grow up and travel to Central America, walk into a bar on a remote island off Belize and meet Boston, an American without even a scintilla of morality or humanity, who would prove to be their nemesis? There's a real sense of 'There but for the grace of God... ' When Chris and Peta's stars aligned with Boston's Death Star in June 1978, it was as if two alien worlds collided.

As a humanist, I am not given to fanciful interpretations, but I can certainly understand why someone might think that it was divine providence that brought about the solving of this complex case some 38 years after everyone thought it was long buried. It seems we had to wait that long for the tide of good fortune (if you will excuse the pun) to turn in our favour. So many of the circumstances surrounding the case's resolution are based upon pure coincidence and in the end, it was all the pieces of the jigsaw converging in 2015 that brought about Boston's arrest in

2016. GMP's Martin Bottomley used the word 'synchronicity' to sum up the following events:

The launch of the FBI's task force in the autumn of 2015 to catch the Golden State Killer in the hope that they would solve the case by June of 2016 – the 40th anniversary of the GSK's first attack. The fact that Boston was at one time the prime suspect for the GSK series of crimes was possibly the only reason that the Sacramento Police Department took the time, trouble and money to look at our case again after 38 years. I believe it was certainly the initial driver and once they knew just how bad and guilty Boston was, they knew this time the facts could not be ignored and they would have to find a way to prosecute him.

Peta's lengthy descriptive letters proved invaluable. Writing to her mother to say that they were on a boat called the *Justin B* that was *owned* by Boston was the key to unlocking the seemingly insurmountable problem of deciding which country, if anyone, had jurisdiction. Russell finding the 38-year-old receipt for the purchase of the *Justin B*, made that key turn.

Boston posting Peta's letter to her mother following their deaths to divert the finger of blame from himself – had he not done so, we would never have known they were on his boat.

My father requesting the Belizean harbour master's report stating Chris and Peta were on the *Justin B* when it left Dangriga (Stann Creek) on 29 June 1978 but not on it when the boat put into Livingston on 6 July, nor when it returned to Dangriga on 9 August.

Our private investigator, Alphonso de Peña's chance meeting with the Catholic priest in January 1979, telling him two unidentified bodies had been buried in Puerto Barrios Cemetery seven months previous.

My epiphany in the field in October 2015, when I felt sure

the internet held the key to finding Boston and his two sons on Facebook. Boston creating a Facebook page in 2012, made him discoverable to the world and more specifically... me. My taking this internet research to Greater Manchester Police put them back in touch with Sacramento Police Department after a gap of almost forty years.

The extraordinary turn of events when, finding there were no case files in the Greater Manchester Police archives, we discovered that the detective in charge of the case in the 1970s had a file copy in his garden shed.

Who would have believed that almost four decades on there were photographs of Chris and his music tapes still in existence? They represented valuable evidence that he and Peta had been on the boat.

All these coincidences coming together would not have been enough without the professionalism, dedication and tenacity of the agents who picked up the cudgels and drove the case forward. We were fortunate and blessed with the investigating teams on both sides of the Atlantic and it was an Anglo-American special relationship that truly worked. We are under no illusion that without their combined Herculean efforts and skill pushing the case forward, it would have floundered again.

Chapter Twenty-Two

JOURNEY'S END

This book is testimony to my family's enduring love for Chris, whose tragic death has defined and shaped us. Time moves on and heartbreak becomes heartache; the intense stabbing pain of bereavement gives way to numbness and a reluctant acceptance until finally, some sort of normality is established. My family's life is divided between what happened before we lost Chris and what happened after.

Life goes on, as indeed it should, but scratch beneath the surface and the scars of loss and the knowledge of how much richer life would have been, had they lived, are still there to this day. Russell and Vince Boston, who grew up never knowing the love of a mother, share the same pain. Just as there is no greater love than that of a mother, there is no greater crime than a parent killing and depriving a child of its other loving parent. In choosing evil, Boston's actions left a trail of destruction, not just for my family, the Framptons and his own two sons and daughter but also for other bereaved families who will never know the fate of their loved ones.

This book has been cathartic to write. For so long, I was unable to talk about the pain of losing Chris, preferring to keep it bottled up, but the journey of discovery has been liberating. Talking about his story still, at times, brings me to tears but I realise it is part of the human condition and it is better to let those tears flow.

Retracing Chris and Peta's footsteps through Mexico and Belize (albeit via the internet) has been fascinating and hearing again Chris's cassettes recording his travels and listening to all the seventies music he loved has brought me close to him again.

Sadly, there was no tidy ending. I can't deny that we were bitterly disappointed to be cheated of justice at the last hurdle but we derive solace from the fact that Boston was charged and in custody awaiting trial when he died. Chris and Peta's ghosts have finally been laid to rest and I am grateful that this has been within my mother's lifetime. Coming to live with my family when my father died, I know just how much the unanswered question of why Chris was tortured and murdered has plagued her for almost half her life. I am only sorry that Dad died in 2013 without knowing. It's the nature of life that we all die in the middle of a story, indeed many stories, but this was my family's biggest story and my father was robbed of knowing the ending of something he had strived for, for almost four decades.

Dad was immensely proud of Chris studying medicine (as he himself had done) and seeing his degree through to completion (where he himself hadn't). He would have been even prouder to know that his son was a humanitarian who stepped in to stop a child from being beaten and possibly killed. Chris was a doctor to the last and, despite having been badly injured by Boston, he still gave him the benefit of the doubt and treated him. Always seeing the best in people, Chris was a great exponent of how you should do unto others as you would have them do unto you. As Russell says: 'Chris and Peta weren't a couple of drug dealers that my dad killed at a whim, they were worthwhile human beings.'

Every life leaves an echo but it is only an echo and, as life moves on, it becomes increasingly faint. Very few people leave a lasting footprint on this earth; most are only remembered by the next one or two generations. In the course of researching this book, Mum and I went through drawers of dusty old sepia-tinted photographs looking for some of Chris, and I frequently asked who so and so was. With today's digital photography and so many images now locked away on computers, it's a sad fact that those who have died will become even more anonymous. I would like to think that telling his story will, at least, keep the memory of Chris alive for my three children, who never had the pleasure of meeting him. He would have been such a fun and exciting uncle, for sure. Whether it is a concession to Mum and I or not, they have shown great interest in Chris's life and death, and for this I am grateful.

Gap years are now commonplace and most young people aim to travel and taste adventure before university or before they settle down, just as Chris and Peta did when they departed for Australia in 1977. If this story makes just one person think before they place themselves in a potentially exposed, vulnerable situation then it will have been worth it. There can be fewer more isolated places than a lone yacht out at sea. Literally, no one can hear you scream.

Ironically, it was Chris and Peta's great love and appetite for life that brought them into contact with Boston: they lived their lives rather than existed. For Chris, the spirit of adventure was sown when he learnt to sail on our family holidays in Anglesey.

Just as he always wanted to sail that bit further than anyone else, he was eager to venture off the beaten track. Mark Twain's outlook on life was Chris's: 'Twenty years from now, you will be more disappointed by the things you didn't do than those you did. So, throw off the bowlines. Sail away from safe harbor. Catch the trade winds in your sails. Explore. Dream. Discover.'

Adventure and exploration were in Chris's blood and that lust for life should be embraced and encouraged in us all. Risks are part of life and it would be a very sterile existence without them. As a parent myself, I would dearly love to bind my three children to me and keep them safe. When my son, Charlie, took off on his own adventure in the sumer of 2017, backpacking in Southeast Asia, I had to steel myself from discouraging him. I remember when he was born I hoped that he would inherit some of Chris's idiosyncrasies. In his love of travel, dedication to work and easy manner, I think he has.

Much as we want to keep our children safe, without seeking new horizons and taking some risks there can be no growth or development. The internet and social media make the globe accessible to us all but that's not getting out there and seeing, tasting and learning about the world for oneself. Ironically, it wasn't Chris's love of sailing that killed him and Peta nor a native of Guatemala, but a chance meeting with a murderous itinerant psychopath. Thankfully, such people are rare, but they can be encountered anywhere.

It's my belief that Chris and Peta signed their death warrants as soon as they stepped onto that boat. Russell and Vince should never feel any sense of blame for what happened: a deeply disturbed sadistic personality such as Boston possessed was always going to find an 'excuse' to kill two defenceless, innocent tourists carrying their worldly possessions. The foresight he displayed in waiting a week in Dangriga (Stann Creek) to get motor engine parts for ballast meant that he was probably planning their murders well in advance and maybe as soon as he met them.

Learning of his death and writing to my parents, Chris's best friend, Rick Henshaw, captured the essence of my beloved brother: 'There is no danger of me forgetting Chris. He changed the way that I saw the world. Chris's outlook on life of: "Nothing ventured, nothing gained" means he would not have wanted us to regret his whole-hearted attitude to living. It would be too easy to say "if only... " but Chris would not have been Chris without doing what he did. With his death, we are all the poorer and it is impossible for me to try to express what the loss of a trusted and admired friend, who had a lasting effect upon my outlook on life, means to me.'

As the poet John Donne said: 'No man is an island entire of itself.' When Boston threw Chris and Peta overboard into the deep waters of the Caribbean, he thought no one would miss them or go to the trouble of tracking down their killer. In judging others by his own grotesque character traits, he was wrong: they were two much-loved people who, even to this day, are sorely missed. What their story shows in abundance is that love never dies... even after 40 years. One man's breathtaking act of inhumanity and evil can snuff out life and cause an unimaginable, wanton trail of destruction but it cannot extinguish love. In that, Boston miscalculated.

In a world where dreadful acts of terrorism hit our headlines weekly, if not daily, it is all too easy to become inured to man's inhumanity to man but Boston's actions were not driven by religious belief or political fervour, nor a hot-headed moment of madness, committed on the spur of the moment: they were premeditated. He had at least thirty-six hours to think through the consequences. His response to the human kindness shown by Chris and Peta was pure, cold-blooded evil.

Sometimes there is no meaning to what happens to us or those we love. It's pointless asking 'Why did it happen to my family?' because 'Why not my family?' Life isn't fair and never will be. You have to accept that death is part of life and that life moves on, as indeed it should. But what shouldn't be accepted are injustice and the triumph of evil.

Walking a small section of the Camino de Santiago pilgrims' way in Spain in June 2017, I visited the awe-inspiring medieval Santiago de Compostela Cathedral. In its precincts, the rhythm of life goes on unabated, but in its magnificent, hallowed interior, time stands still. The solidity of the building contrasts with the ephemeral nature of life and it made me think of Chris and Peta's butterfly lives. In one of the small dark side chapels, I lit two candles for them. As I watched them brightly flicker but then quickly burn down and die together, it felt a fitting end to what has been a long goodbye. Now felt the right time to let go. Closure had brought acceptance.

To me, Chris was special. In death, as much as in life, he changed my heart and mind for ever. He is not forgotten

.

EPILOGUE

FAIR WINDS AND FOLLOWING SEAS – THE MOTHER'S STORY

E very mother's wish is for their newborn to be healthy and blessed with a long, fulfilled, well-lived life. In my experience, there is nothing more devastating than the loss of a beloved child, and it is especially painful when that child happens to be embarking on a meaningful career as a doctor of medicine. Chris had so much to achieve and to give, which made his death even harder to accept. With all our hopes and ambitions for him just starting to be fulfilled, it was a very bitter pill to swallow. As his mother, a part of me died with him.

Going to Chris's degree ceremony in Birmingham in July 1976, I recall how proud my husband Charles and I were to see him in his cap and gown when he was presented with his Bachelor of Medicine certificate. It had been a rain-soaked morning but the sun emerged as we came out of the graduation hall and seemed to underline the happiness of the day. Life felt good. Thankfully, we had no sense of what was to come.

Chris's mantra was to live life to the full and seize each day. He had a zest and passion for living and not just existing and no one could clip his wings.

Christmas Eve 1978, when Chris and Peta had been missing for some six months, I was looking out of the large picture window at home in Cheshire, wishing, begging and praying for some sign; some tiny signal to tell me that they were alive or dead – anything to be relieved of the soul-destroying uncertainty of not knowing where they were. The bright moonlight rained down as if to shine a spotlight on my solitude, and I looked at all the twinkling stars and infinite darkness. The stars blinked back, uncompromisingly... nothing, nothing, nothing.

In a moment of total black despair, I wrote to Boston, pleading for any information he might have on Chris and Peta, but, of course, he never replied. I found some solace in writing letters to Chris that I kept to myself. Paradoxically, when some months after his death, mail arrived bearing his name, it twisted my heart to see 'Christopher Farmer' in black and white but paradoxically, it gave me comfort because, for a split second, it brought the illusion that he was still alive.

As long as I live, I will never forget the sense of utter desolation on hearing the news from the Foreign Office, in February 1979, that two tortured bodies had been found floating in the sea off the Guatemalan coast and we were to prepare ourselves for them being our missing two but literally nothing can prepare you for that. If I close my eyes and take myself back to that afternoon, I can still taste the shock. It was the sheer, agonising disbelief that this could happen to my dear, dear son. I remember driving home from work with the burning tears coursing down my face and I screamed to the empty car: 'My son has been murdered!'

The sea, which had for so long been such a source of great joy on our family holidays in Anglesey, began to hold a poignancy for me, as indeed it still does to this day. I can never ever look at it without thinking of them. Chris, so full of life, loved the sea, but who would have ever guessed he would have died from drowning? We were on holiday in the Algarve when we received the news of their positive identification. When I looked out from the hotel bedroom window to the vast expanse of Atlantic Ocean, all I could see was the image of their bound, tortured bodies floating just beneath the surface of the water, out at sea. I often wonder what Chris's last thoughts were when he was drowning. Did he think of us? Did his brief life flash before him as they claim it does when you're drowning? Did he know how much he was loved? My imagination played havoc with me, and my mind constantly questioned why and how they could have met such a gruesome, macabre end.

There is not a single day since that I haven't thought of him and in so many ways it is an unending tragedy but time has blunted the initial heart-stopping shock. Over the years, the unending days and nights of opaque black despair slowly gave way to grey days of aching emptiness until eventually some kind of normality was restored, interspersed with occasional rays of warm sunshine. But his death is seared on my mind for ever. The grief has woven its tentacles into so many different facets of mine and my family's life. The sheer, wicked gratuitous waste of life is what never ceases to appal me. Anything more callous than Boston's actions is hard to imagine.

I remember in the aftermath going to our doctor and asking for sleeping pills to help me sleep, and she said there is no medication for grief and I must just work through it. And she was right: no one and nothing can mitigate the shock, the horror; the sheer hideousness of it all.

DEAD IN THE WATER

When it first happened, I felt so sorry for people who felt awkward in my company because they didn't know how to handle me or the subject. God knows, I didn't know myself! I remember when they asked how I was, I would reply: 'Oh, OK,' but inside my heart was breaking.

Everyone has different ways of coping with grief and in Charles's and my case, being very pragmatic people, we chose the only way we knew and that was to throw ourselves into finding out what and why it had happened. It has always been our belief that Boston's sons held the key to this senseless crime, and so it has proved to be the case. Coupled with losing their mother, it must have been an intolerable strain for them to witness such a depraved act and one can only imagine the distress and feelings of horror that they must have held for so long. Are they able to blot it out or have they been constantly drawn back to the events on the boat?

I find it comforting to keep Chris's memory alive by talking about him. The recent events have been a gift to me because they have reawakened memory and in a sense, brought him home. Revisiting their story has naturally reopened old wounds but I can only be thankful that I now know what happened and that Boston was arrested, charged and awaiting trial in custody.

I am supremely grateful to Greater Manchester Police, Interpol, the U.S. District Attorney's Office, the FBI and the Sacramento Police Department for all their hard work. It has been a long, painful journey indeed, almost half of my life. I have looked inside myself, faced the black dog of despair and, at times, had to dig deep for the strength that I knew could only come from within. Now, I feel at peace. I am not looking for answers anymore. It has been a balm to heal some of the very deep wounds of the past.

EPILOGUE: FAIR WINDS AND FOLLOWING SEAS

I find it sad that Charles, who gathered so much of the crucial evidence, died never knowing the circumstances of Chris's murder. He would never have believed all that has happened since his death in 2013.

With the benefit of modern-day communications, Penny picked up where Charles and I had hit a brick wall and, along with a panoply of agencies, gave us answers. I think it is truly astonishing that we have now learnt so much about what happened when in 1978 and the aftermath, we knew scarcely anything. Penny has been a wonderful ambassador for our family and I am immensely proud of her, as I am of all my three children.

For anyone who ever considers taking life, let there be no doubt of its far-reaching consequences – it shatters far more than the life of the murdered. There are still large pieces of shrapnel from the bomb that hit my family four decades ago. They are evidenced at every anniversary and family milestone and for me, each and every day. When Chris left for Australia, we put a bottle of champagne in the fridge for his planned return, one year later. It has become a tradition that we make a toast to Chris and Peta at Christmas and on Chris's birthday. It is a hollow celebration without the chief participants and yet I know he would approve of the sentiment behind it.

Their story is riddled with twists, turns, coincidences, misfortune and serendipity and in amongst them all is a quite astonishing fact that we only discovered during the writing of this book. From Russell's testimony, we now know that Chris and Peta died early on the morning of 4 July 1978... ironically, American Independence Day.

Winding the clock back 22 years to 4 July 1956 [a date that is seared in my mind], Chris, aged three, was early that morning

273

playing in his bedroom. I was tending to my eldest son Nigel, who was in bed with tonsillitis. Ever the adventurer, Chris climbed on to the windowsill. Unbeknownst to me, the window cleaner had the previous day accidentally left the window ajar. Leaning against the window, Chris fell from the first floor on to the concrete paving slabs below. Hearing the scream, I entered the room and ran to the open window. My pounding heart was in my mouth as I looked down to see his small crumpled body lying on the ground below. That image will never leave me. My blood froze as my first thought was he was dead.

I ran downstairs faster than I have ever run in my life. By nothing short of a miracle, he was alive! Rushed to hospital in an ambulance, I helped to nurse him, desperately trying to make him stay awake, telling him over and over again the story of *Goldilocks and The Three Bears* in order to stop concussion setting in. The doctors told us he was unbelievably lucky not to have died. The odds were very much stacked against him not suffering brain damage. By some massive good fortune, he made a remarkable full recovery and within a week, he was out of hospital.

Not only is the symmetry of dates and time of day quite bizarre, but what makes it even more extraordinary is the fact that the first injury that Chris sustained from Boston's brutal attack was a fractured skull – the exact same injury that he suffered when he fell out of the window.

Given his almost inexplicable escape from death at such a tender age and his subsequent great lust for life, Charles and I often felt that Chris was living on borrowed time and tragically, this proved to be the case.

I feel enormously privileged to have been his mother and to have known him for 25 precious years. My heart bursts with love and pride for Chris and will remain so till the day I die.

APPENDIX 1

THE ANGLO-AMERICAN 'A' TEAM

My family gives thanks for the outstanding collaborative work of the Greater Manchester Police Cold Case Review Unit, the US Department of Justice for the Eastern District of California, the Federal Bureau of Investigation (Sacramento Field Office), the Sacramento Police Department and Interpol. Without their exemplary work and unstinting dedication, the case would never have been solved.

Collectively, the following individuals brought us closure:

Greater Manchester Police

Force Review Officer Martin Bottomley
Detective Constable Michaela Clinch
Detective Constable Julie Adams

U.S. Department of Justice, U.S. Attorney's Office for the Eastern District of California

Assistant United States Attorney (AUSA) Matthew D. Segal

Chief, Special Prosecutions Unit

AUSA Heiko P. Coppola

AUSA Jeremy J. Kelley

Supervisory Legal Administrator Donna Castruita

Lead Legal Assistant Jamielynne Harrison

Victim Witness Assistant Senta Parker

Higher-up supervisors: U.S. Attorney Philip A. Talbert, First Assistant U.S. Attorney Philip A. Ferrari, AUSA John K. Vincent (Chief, Criminal Division)

Federal Bureau of Investigation, Sacramento Field Office

Special Agent David J. Sesma

Special Agent Marcus W. Knutson

Victim Specialist Carol Watson

Plus, other FBI Special Agents in New York and Guatemala

Sacramento Police Department

Detective Amy Crosby

Detective Janine LeRose

Police Clerk Mary Ann Johnson

Lieutenant Robert McCloskey

APPENDIX 2
THOUGHTS ON THE CASE

What the British and American detectives, prosecuting attorney and the FBI said about the case:

Martin Bottomley, Force Review Officer, Greater Manchester Police

I have always felt a personal connection to this case, not just as an investigator, appreciating the horror and brutality of these murders, the physical suffering they endured, the perpetual mental torment of their loved ones, but also, a deep empathy as a contemporary of the victims. I attended the same school as Chris and joined Greater Manchester Police (GMP) as a young graduate only a month after Chris and Peta were last seen alive.

The very purpose of GMP's Cold Case Review Unit is to continually review unsolved crimes, to trace new or previously reluctant witnesses, and consider advances in scientific techniques to see if any such developments may lead to new lines of enquiry. In this 38-year-old cold case it was the internet which acted as the catalyst for ultimately solving the most senseless and cold-blooded of crimes. In my 39-year career with GMP, this case has been one of the most fascinating and tragic that I have worked on.

All murders have an enduring impact on loved ones, but I have never before witnessed the gracious stoicism of a lady at the age of ninety-two, who has for almost four decades, at the same time grieved and been living in limbo, never knowing what really happened to her son. When we discovered the truth and the full horror of what happened on the boat, I was dreading narrating the events to Chris's mum. However, I should not have been surprised at her bravery and her desire to know every last detail, no matter how hurtful. I felt privileged to be in her presence.

Detective Sergeant Julie Adams, Greater Manchester Police

I still laugh when I remember hearing Chris's voice on the last cassette tape recording that he sent home, and which I transcribed. He spoke so animatedly of their travels and, in particular, when signing off, telling you what you could do with the books he had left for you to read, he seemed such a funny and entertaining character. Hearing his voice at a time which turned out to be so close to his death was particularly upsetting, as we now know what was to come. It made the listening all the more difficult and poignant.

Ambivalence sums up my feelings for this fascinating but very sad case, and Peta's last written words are the definition of tragic irony. The fact that I got to meet Chris's wonderful family was a privilege.

I am so sorry that you haven't achieved the closure that we had all hoped for. I can't imagine how as a family you have carried this with you all this time, and to have got so close to justice. At least we can say that Boston died in custody, safe in the knowledge that his time was indeed up.

Detective Constable Michaela Clinch, Greater Manchester Police

When I got the call from Penny on 5 October 2015 about the murders of Chris and Peta, I was really pleased to have been the member of the Unit to pick up the telephone. There were two reasons – first, it was a fascinating case for me in that they were British people travelling in Central America, apparently killed for no reason whatsoever, and dating back to 1978, which was long before GMP recorded anything on computer. Second, because my heart went out to Penny and her family, trying to get answers after almost 40 years. And then, when they gave me the family's file of what had taken place in 1978, and I started to read just how much Audrey and Charles had actually done to try and find Chris and Peta themselves, it made me think about when I was travelling and living abroad. Like Chris and Peta, I was in my twenties, and had I disappeared, that is exactly what my parents would have done: it made it more personal.

It was so glaringly obvious that Boston was guilty and he just had to be brought to justice. I was bitterly disappointed when it became apparent that we in the UK did not have jurisdiction in the case, but thank goodness, we got the team in America that we did!

Assistant United States Attorney (AUSA) Matthew D. Segal, Chief Prosecutions Unit

It took decades for this case to break, but then almost every unlikely thing that happened promoted justice. The Sacramento

Police Department obtained eyewitness testimony from the sons. The Greater Manchester Police recovered, from a retiree's garden shed, photocopies of the case's most important documents. The Federal Bureau of Investigation identified Americans and Guatemalans who had worked on the case in the 1970s and 1980s and found those witnesses alive and with good recollection.

What frustrated justice in this case was its least unlikely occurrence: an elderly man succumbed to disease after decades of hard living. But Boston died having received full disclosure under the Federal Rules of Criminal Procedure. From that, I infer that the defendant believed what the prosecuting attorneys, Heiko Coppola, Jeremy Kelley and I believed: the investigators had done outstanding work, and, at trial, the government was ready to prove to a jury beyond a reasonable doubt that Silas Duane Boston, within the special maritime jurisdiction of the United States, cold-bloodedly murdered Dr Christopher Farmer and Peta Frampton.

I regret that we could not bring this 1978 Caribbean murder case to a conclusion, but I am also grateful that the Manchester and Sacramento teams together were able to take it as far as we did for the victims, their survivors, and the truth.

Coming of age in the 1980s and 1990s in San Francisco and New York, I heard a lot of music from Manchester. I evaluated this case only on its merits, but whenever Greater Manchester Police called me from the city of New Order and The Smiths, my younger self was excited to be a good partner in the Anglo-American Special Relationship.

[A]Detective Amy Crosby, Sacramento Police Department

This was, by far, the most interesting and complex case of my career. The innumerable twists and turns, moments of excitement, waves of disappointment and overall intrigue often proved at times as if a continual crescendo was building and the result would be deafening.

Silas Duane Boston was a fascinating, yet horrifying person, who led a life of death, destruction and doom. How the pieces of this beyond-mysterious puzzle fit together was amazing. Each piece was literally an integral component of the archetypal mystery that would baffle even the most seasoned of detectives. The nexus of ties, and how each came to fruition, simply astounded me! Case in point: the Farmer family reached out to Greater Manchester Police at the same time I was assigned the case and reached out to Vince Boston. Greater Manchester Police reached out to Interpol at virtually the same time that I did and two agencies, half a world apart, were brought together. The disappointment of Greater Manchester Police advising me they did not have jurisdiction was followed by the excitement of the U.S. Attorney's Office saying they could prosecute this case. Again, as during so many other moments of this case, the sheer ebb and flow of progression and regression astounded me. But persevere we must and we did!

The collaboration between prosecutors and investigators that spread across three continents was incredible. The case could not have proceeded without evidence that had been gathered almost forty years ago. The disappointment of Boston dying was followed by the respectful elation of finally getting to meet the Farmer family.

It has been a true privilege working with such an amazing team of professionals and I say, with heartfelt feeling, that this investigative journey, with all its peaks and valleys, has been an odyssey and I am most grateful for having been a piece of the puzzle.

DEAD IN THE WATER

[A]FBI Special Agent David J. Sesma

I was asked by the U.S. Attorney's Office to investigate Silas Duane Boston and immediately recruited FBI Special Agent Marcus Knutson out of our Sacramento office, who is an expert in cold cases and complex criminal matters. SA Knutson and I worked with Sacramento Police Department Detective Amy Crosby and were able to use the expansive and wide reach of our FBI assets and partners around the globe to track down leads to help bring Mr Boston to justice.

Whilst Mr Boston passed away before he could face a jury of his peers, the Farmer and Frampton families were delivered some solace after Mr Boston was arrested. I will not forget the graciousness of the families who thanked us in person for helping them hold Mr Boston accountable for his alleged crimes.

[A]Retired Chief Inspector David Sacks, Greater Manchester Police (who worked on the case from November 1978 to 1980)

It was one of my most memorable cases. I have dealt with a lot of horrible things during my police career but this case stuck out for me because it was two young people with everything to live for who literally, by pure chance and ill fate, happened to meet a total psychopath.

It was very frustrating because we weren't allowed to deal directly with Sacramento – the protocol was such that everything had to go through Interpol, which acted like a filter. The murder rate over in Guatemala was terrible – as it still is today – but it's incredible that it wasn't investigated. All that evidence – for example, the weights and ropes were disposed of, with no forethought or consultation with the Guatemalan police.

The case was very poorly handled in Sacramento. When Sacramento PD did eventually get Boston in for questioning in

APPENDIX 2: THOUGHTS ON THE CASE

1981, he was questioned as a witness rather than the hot suspect that he was. It was lack of supervision in Sacramento PD that caused the case to flounder and let Boston get off scot-free.

I wanted to look Boston in the eye and give him an imperceptible nod to say: 'We got you'. I was denied that. Although he wasn't convicted, the truth had at last come out. He was caught and arrested and he died in custody and with such overwhelming evidence, the outcome would have been a foregone conclusion.

CHRIS'S MUSIC

Chris was passionate about his music and rarely went anywhere without his boombox. Here are some of the soundtracks of his life:

Bob Dylan – *John Wesley Harding*; *Desire*
Burning Spear – *Marcus Garvey*
Captain Beefheart & His Magic Band – *Safe as Milk*;
    Bluejeans & Moonbeams
Cat Stevens – *Catch Bull at Four*; *Tea for the Tillerman*
Country Joe & The Fish – *CJ Fish*
Crosby Stills Nash & Young – *Déjà Vu*
Curved Air – *Air Conditioning*
David Bowie – *The Rise and Fall of Ziggy Stardust*;
    Hunky Dory
Duster Bennett – *Smiling Like I'm Happy*
Eagles – *Desperado*
Eric Clapton – *461 Ocean Boulevard*
Frank Zappa – *Zoot Allures*; *One Size Fits All*

DEAD IN THE WATER

Genesis – *A Trick of the Tail*; *The Lamb Lies Down on Broadway*

Geno Washington & The Ram Jam Band – *Sifters, Shifters, Finger Clicking Mamas*

Ginger Bake – *Ginger Baker's Air Force 11*

Hawkwind – *X In Search of Space*

It's a Beautiful Day – *White Bird*

JJ Cale – *Naturally*; *Okie*; *Troubadour*

Jackie Lomax – *Home Is In My Head*

Jeff Beck – *Blow By Blow*

Jefferson Airplane – *Bless Its Pointed Little Head*; *After Bathing at Baxter's*; *Somebody to Love*

Jefferson Starship – *Miracles*

Jerry Garcia – *Garcia (Compliments)*

Jim Morrison and The Doors – *An American Prayer*

Jimi Hendrix – *Axis: Bold As Love*; *Rainbow Bridge*

Journey – *Journey*; *Look Into The Future*; *Next*

Judee Sill – *Judee Sill*

Judy Collins – *Who knows Where the Time Goes*

King Crimson – *In The Court of the Crimson King*

Kokomo – *Kokomo*

Led Zeppelin – *Stairway to Heaven*

Leonard Cohen – *Songs of Leonard Cohen*; *Songs from a Room*

Little Feat – *The Last Record Album*

Loudon Wainwright III – *Album II*

Love – *Forever Changes*

Melanie – *Garden In the City*; *Candles in the Rain*

Mike Oldfield – *Tubular Bells*

Neil Young – *After The Gold Rush*; *Harvest*

Nick Drake – *Five Leaves Left*

CHRIS'S MUSIC

Paul and Linda McCartney – *Ram*

Paul Horn – *Inside*

Paul Kantner and Jefferson Starship – *Blows Against the Empire*

Paul Kantner and Grace Slick – *Sunfighter*

Peter Gabriel – *Car*

Pink Floyd – *A Nice Pair*; *The Piper at the Gates of Dawn*; *A Saucerful of Secrets*; *Relics*; *Wish You Were Here*; *Animals*

Roy Harper – *Valentine*; *Stormcock*

Santana – *Welcome*; *Caravanserai*

Supertramp – *Crime of the Century*

Tangerine Dream – *Phaedra*

Terry Riley – *A Rainbow In Curved Air*

The Allman Brothers Band – *Brothers and Sisters*

The Doors – *13*

The Grateful Dead – *Live/Dead*; *Blues for Allah*; *From the Mars Hotel*

The Mighty Groundhogs – *Who Will Save the World?*

The Mothers of Invention – *Freak Out!*

Various – *A Clockwork Orange* (soundtrack)

Various – *Buddha In Mi*

Various – *The Harder They Come* (soundtrack)

Various – *The Nonesuch Explorer*

Various – *The Rock Machine Turns You On*

Yes – *Going for the One*; *Close to the Edge*